THE DEVIL'S CINEMA

THE DEVIL'S CINEMA

The Untold Story Behind
Mark Twitchell's Kill Room

STEVE LILLEBUEN

McClelland & Stewart

Library and Archives Canada Cataloguing in Publication

Lillebuen, Steve
The devil's cinema : the untold story behind
Mark Twitchell's kill room / Steve Lillebuen.

ISBN 978-0-7710-5033-6

1. Twitchell, Mark, 1979–. 2. Murderers – Alberta – Edmonton – Biography.
3. Murder victims – Alberta – Edmonton. 4. Murder – Investigation – Alberta – Edmonton.
5. Trials (Murder) – Alberta – Edmonton. I. Title.

HV6248.T95L55 2012   364.152'3092   C2011-904266-5

Published simultaneously in the United States of America by McClelland & Stewart Ltd.,
P.O. Box 1030, Plattsburgh, New York 12901

Library of Congress Control Number: 2011931119

We acknowledge the financial support of the Government of Canada through the Book Publishing Industry Development Program and that of the Government of Ontario through the Ontario Media Development Corporation's Ontario Book Initiative. We further acknowledge the support of the Canada Council for the Arts and the Ontario Arts Council for our publishing program.

The Dexter Morgan quotations on p. xiii and p. 102 are from *Darkly Dreaming Dexter* by Jeff Lindsay, published by Vintage Books, a division of Random House, Inc.

Typeset in Dante by M&S, Toronto
Printed and bound in Canada

ANCIENT FOREST
FRIENDLY

McClelland & Stewart Ltd.
75 Sherbourne Street
Toronto, Ontario
M5A 2P9
www.mcclelland.com

1 2 3 4 5   16 15 14 13 12

For Sarah,
with my love and gratitude

CONTENTS

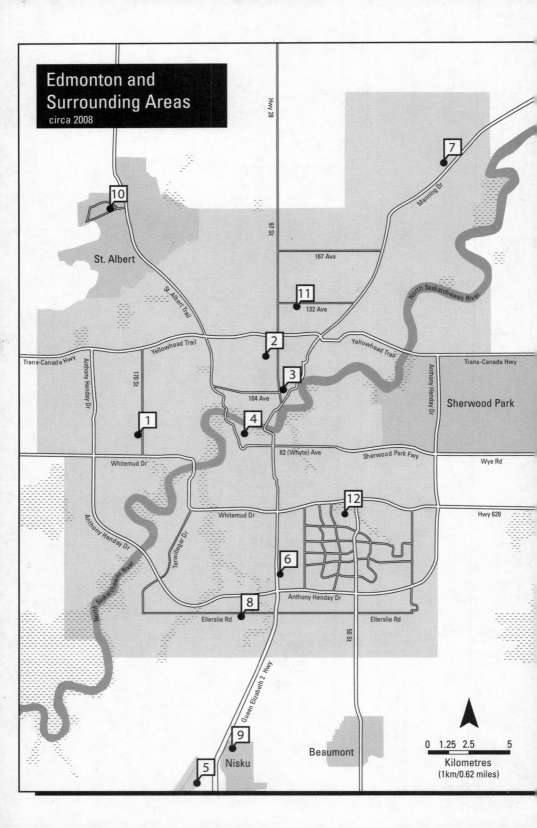

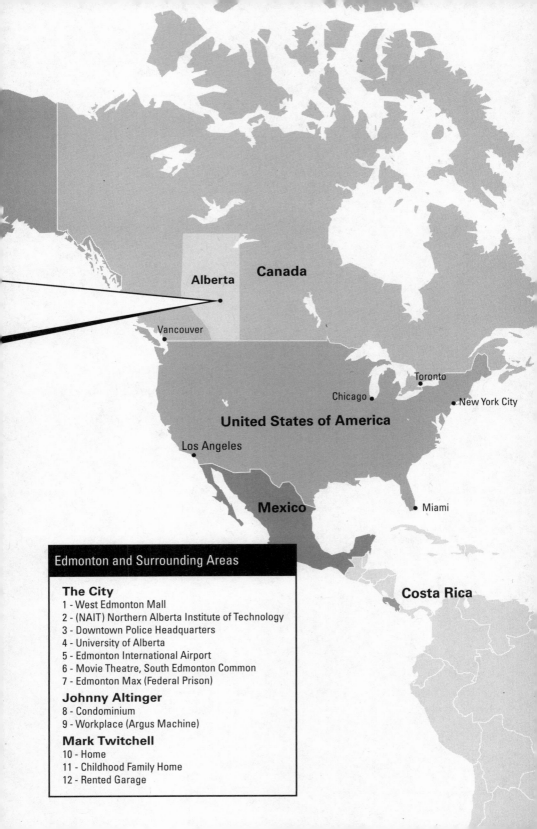

Alberta

Canada

Vancouver

Toronto

Chicago

New York City

United States of America

Los Angeles

Mexico

Miami

Costa Rica

Edmonton and Surrounding Areas

The City
1 - West Edmonton Mall
2 - (NAIT) Northern Alberta Institute of Technology
3 - Downtown Police Headquarters
4 - University of Alberta
5 - Edmonton International Airport
6 - Movie Theatre, South Edmonton Common
7 - Edmonton Max (Federal Prison)

Johnny Altinger
8 - Condominium
9 - Workplace (Argus Machine)

Mark Twitchell
10 - Home
11 - Childhood Family Home
12 - Rented Garage

A NOTE TO READERS

In a city of oilmen, an aspiring filmmaker imagined he could be something better than working class, more fantastic, grand even – take a chance at Hollywood fame. Hardened financial investors were already opening padded wallets to support the young man's outlandish concepts. Friends adored him, viewed him as a ticket to riches. And actors were flying into the prairie capital of Edmonton, Canada, for their chance to work with him.

The man they trusted, however, had been guarding an appalling secret. One of his strange new plans would soon consume him, blurring the lines between fiction and reality, sending studio executives into hiding at the horror they were accused of inspiring: a murder in the most incomprehensible, post-modern way.

In the following pages I tell a story of love, death, and the World Wide Web. It is a book of determined friendship and determined madness, of veteran detectives left to question long-held understandings of their usual suspects.

But no matter how unlikely these events may appear, this remains a work of non-fiction. In fact, this true-crime narrative has been drawn from years of journalistic research.

Anything in quotation marks is taken from a written document, court testimony, or interview. Detectives and witnesses shared their experiences over hundreds of hours. Last of all, the killer himself granted unparalleled access into his life, revealing the foundations for his startling ideas through extensive interviews and more than three hundred pages of personal writings. But even then, parts of this story rely heavily on sworn evidence presented in court. It was a trial I witnessed first-hand, a month-long criminal proceeding that finally revealed the unimaginable details of what had really transpired within the darkest of minds.

STEVE LILLEBUEN

"I was a near perfect hologram. . . .
A neat and polite monster, the boy next door."
– DEXTER MORGAN, fictional serial killer

———

"Anyone can turn out to be a psycho
without being overtly obvious about it."
– MARK TWITCHELL, real-life filmmaker

PART ONE

DOWN THE RABBIT HOLE

THE EDGE OF THE WORLD

WELCOME TO DEADMONTON:

Standing atop the rolling prairies of western Canada, the city is the last major stop heading north before the uninhabited, the unfamiliar, the unknown. Its real name is Edmonton, but nobody calls it that. Within the sprawling city streets, the civic slur surfaces and flows from home to home, mouth to ear, like a morbid whisper. And no one really knows how it all started.

Historians joke that the epithet likely began more than one hundred years ago, when European fur traders built the first fort above the steep banks of the North Saskatchewan River. Whether explorer or modern tourist, there's never been much of a reason to visit the place since. Even elected officials have accepted this region's lacklustre image with their own brand of dark humour. "Edmonton is not the end of the world – it's just easier to see it from there," once quipped Ralph Klein, a colourful and well-known politician. Many have adopted a similar self-deprecating attitude, wielding such an ethos like an invaluable tool while residing in the northernmost major city of North America.

Edmonton has a certain charm despite its remoteness – an atmosphere of progressive conservative values that is neither pretentious nor condescending. As the capital of the western, landlocked province of Alberta, Edmonton has plenty of government jobs available, offering benefits, nine-to-five working hours, and weekends off. But the non-stop buzz of big-city living certainly lies elsewhere. The downtown core still shuts down on the weekends, and most stores close when the office drones head home. The rat race runs in a lower gear in Edmonton, which is polite and kind, like a country town but nearing a million residents. Everybody seems to know everybody.

Snowy winters this far north can blanket half the year. Indoor activities tend to thrive in these cases, whether citizens huddle under the comfort of shopping malls, restaurants, or movie theatres. It is no surprise then that the city is home to one of the world's largest shopping centres. West Edmonton Mall often overflows with frantic shoppers, scurrying its vast corridors and eight hundred stores like ants in a colony disturbed by the curious prodding of a destructive child.

In contrast to the bleakness of winter, the remaining seasons can be quite glorious. Festivals emerge from the spring thaw. Long summer evenings transform the river valley into a lush forest. Historical inner-city neighbourhoods that date back to the Klondike Gold Rush are crammed with people, each pub dusting off its patio for a round of cold Canadian beers. But when autumn returns, everyone heads back indoors to hibernate. The hockey season entertains. Town pride has been hinged on the long-past success of the Edmonton Oilers, once an NHL sporting dynasty and home to the greatest player of all time, Wayne Gretzky. Edmonton began calling itself the "City of Champions."

There's plenty of cash to go around – almost too much at times. For when oil booms, the town explodes. In 1947, drillers struck oil at Leduc Number One, sparking the region's first black gold rush. As oil prices boomed again in the 2000s, an oil sands deposit with more recoverable oil than Saudi Arabia became feasible for extraction on a massive scale. Such potential attracted thousands of young men craving a quick job, a fast buck, and a dirty weekend. The city's nickname therefore took on deeper meanings through the years as successive oil booms fuelled immigration, untold wealth, and surges in violent crime.

This landscape and culture can appear strange to outsiders. The city is often misunderstood and criticized. It is a community on the edge, a "boiler room" to the *New York Times*, and a "visually unappealing corner of Canada" to London's *Daily Telegraph*. The city has fought back against such insults, but a prolonged defence has had little impact. No matter what the city does, no matter what its people say, no matter how things may change here for the better through the years, Edmonton has always been treated as a dull, boring place to ever call home.

Truth be told, the city is isolated. A road trip to Jasper and its world-class skiing resorts in the heart of the Rockies is a four-hour drive straight west. A visit to the southern big-sister city of Calgary takes more than three hours, even when speeding past the late-summer burst of yellow canola on a near-straight-shot highway. And the money pump of modern oil revenue linked to the city's prosperity is a gruelling, six-hour drive up north to Fort McMurray along a road dubbed "Death Highway" for its staggering fatality rate. Young oil workers are killed every year, flipping their pickup trucks into ditches, striking others head on, causing crushing, gruesome injuries. They are often speeding, drinking and driving recklessly in some cases, trying to cut that long, boring drive into something more manageable. Instead, their blood is spilled over a highway they thought was paved with gold.

BY 2005, THE OIL money was flowing again and so were the drugs. Crime levels reached new heights as old records were broken, one by one. People were killed in homes, outside bars, and at parties. The bodies of prostitutes were being strewn like garbage on the city's eastern outskirts. Three people were stabbed at a wedding, and two pregnant women were slain. A girl's eighteenth birthday party was shattered when a passing driver pulled out a gun and began firing from his car. The mall proved dangerous too. A thirteen-year-old girl who liked to hang out in the food court was lured from West Edmonton Mall and found on the fourth fairway of an out-of-town golf course. She had been raped and beaten to death so viciously it took days to identify her body. Even those in custody and watched by prison guards weren't safe. An inmate awaiting his dangerous driving trial was beaten to death over a minor debt. His bruises looked like footprints. It was the first homicide at the city's remand centre, and while the police had every suspect behind bars, they could never prove which one did it.

Edmonton was in the middle of a crime wave. Many were terrified. Politicians were asked repeatedly how crime rates could be brought back under control. Detectives were working double shifts to keep up with the rising body count and even then they fell behind.

The year ended with a record thirty-nine homicides. There were eleven more murders than the previous year, which had set its own record. While some North American cities routinely witness far more murders each year, Edmonton's small population meant the prairie community had been elevated to an unwanted status: the most violent city across the nation. On a per capita basis, no other city in the country had suffered more homicides. At least seventeen gangs were active, with roughly eight hundred members. Drugs were everywhere.

"Deadmonton" had become a startling reality.

Few outside the city knew or cared that this sordid tale was unfolding. In fact, few even thought of Edmonton at all. For these ill fortunes were not unlike those of any other major city, and life moved on. But what no one noticed at the time, especially those who were closely watching the city's highs and lows, was that something strange, an oddity, had taken root in the shadows of this bloodbath.

A young salesman who had spent years living in the American Midwest ultimately decided this was the year to do the opposite of what so many of his Edmonton-born peers had been doing: he was moving back to the city, by choice, to launch his new career.

He was going to become a film director. Charismatic and cheerful, he believed his birthplace was well suited to help him begin this astonishing journey. While he didn't fit in with the masses – he hated hockey, didn't drink beer – he envisioned likeminded sci-fi geeks and film fans would come out of the woodwork and help him craft his grand plans until they came to fruition.

So he packed up his vehicle that summer of 2005 and hit the highway, driving northwest across America as he headed back to the Canadian prairie city he had once called home.

He would find friends quickly, get married for a second time, and cherish this new life. And in just over three years, by the later months of 2008, he would finally achieve the recognition he was so desperately seeking, but perhaps not in the way he had first intended: ABC, NBC, CBS, CNN – even Hollywood. They all wanted a piece of him.

Before he was finished, everyone would know his face, everyone would know his car, the world would know of his work.

He believed his ideas were some of the greatest of all time.

MISSING THE ACTION

REMOTE IN HAND, BILL Clark turned up the volume on his television as the NFL pre-game show rolled on. It was nearing two o'clock on a Sunday in October and while the sun had chewed away the morning chill, it was still slightly below freezing. Clark was happy to be inside and sitting on his couch, heat drifting out of the furnace, as he settled in for the afternoon game.

Veteran homicide detectives like Clark were well into the home stretch of the year. There were twenty-two homicides so far in 2008, and while it wasn't looking like another record-breaking year, many of the cases remained unsolved. It was the same old story: lack of evidence, uncooperative witnesses, guys who didn't see nothin' or hear nothin', and triggermen who lied or blamed others. All too often murder victims were about to pull themselves up and out of a "high-risk lifestyle" when multiple gunshots rang out in the night. Edmonton's homicide cops treated the trend like a sick joke. When the body of another gangbanger was found dumped in a park, someone in the office would inevitably ask, "Hey, was he turning his life around? Don't ever turn your life around or you'll end up dead." Laughter would ensue. It was a way of dealing with the relentless trauma of a high-stress job few people outside of the police force would ever understand. But on this Sunday, in front of the TV, Clark could hopefully put all of that job stress behind him. His biggest problem at the moment was deciding what type of snacks to eat while his wife left him alone with his beloved NFL season.

The first play was about to begin when Clark's cell phone started vibrating. He cringed. He was on call and it didn't look good. On the line was his buddy Mark Anstey, another homicide detective working in their office at downtown police headquarters.

"Sorry, Bill. We gotta go out," Anstey said. He was on call too, having just been pulled away from a Sunday buffet with his family. He had got a call from their boss, who relayed how officers at southwest division station had a file, but they wanted it escalated to the homicide unit. "It's a missing person and they suspect foul play."

Clark rolled his eyes and threw his head back in the air. "And *why* do they suspect foul play?" He thought the officers who were trying to pass on the file better have something more than just a missing person. It wasn't the homicide unit's mandate to take on such cases.

The city had been divided like a grid into five police divisions, with each division station given its own batch of criminal detectives. But whenever a case appeared to be more serious, something that might involve a possible suspicious death, the files were often handed to homicide cops at downtown headquarters. Clark and Anstey were detectives in the unit on a rotation of more than a dozen other veterans of the same rank. Each had competed for years to earn a coveted spot on the roster and a desk in the unit's third-floor office. Seemingly pointless cases were now supposed to be behind them.

Clark knew there were thousands of these types of files every year. He had to screen these calls or they'd be bombarded with investigations. In his experience, nearly all missing persons were found quickly, with nothing criminal to blame anyway. They were sometimes runaways or suicides, their bodies found floating down the city's river, another jumper off the High Level Bridge. Clark pleaded with Anstey on the phone: "Tell me something more."

"There's some funny stuff," Anstey explained. The missing man's friends had been looking for him for a week. They had emails from him saying he was away, but they didn't believe it. Their boss wanted the two of them to go out, just take a look and decide whether homicide even had to be involved. If they did, they'd call in the whole team.

Clark sighed. He shut off his television, put on a coat, jumped in his car, and was down on the south side within forty-five minutes. Football would have to wait.

In the station, Clark spotted Anstey. Both were seasoned cops, bald, and sporting police moustaches dusted with grey. Clark was heavy-set while Anstey was tall and thin. They were fathers with teenaged sons and daughters. Clark was known as the bulldog in the office, sounding bad-tempered when needed, his piercing blue eyes dissecting his suspects. But he had a soft side too. He had saved an infant during Edmonton's 1987 "Black Friday" tornado that killed twenty-seven people and taken the time to reconnect at the twentieth anniversary of the disaster with the "miracle baby," now a young woman, who was eager to thank him. Anstey was far more restrained than Clark. He was a cop who loved to chase leads, not interrogate suspects. His reading glasses dangled on the tip of his nose as he scanned police reports and evidence. He had even won a policing award for solving the slaying of an elderly woman in her own home; the killer, a prostitute on the run from the botched robbery, was tracked down far away on the West Coast.

The two of them had yet to discuss who would be the lead detective, or primary investigator, as everyone gathered in one central room. Clark recognized a southwest division detective as someone he was in police training with decades ago. There was another detective and a group of young constables and other officers he didn't know.

A staff sergeant chaired the briefing as they were brought up to speed on police file 08-137180. The missing man was Johnny Brian Altinger. He was thirty-eight and single, lived alone in a condo on the south side, and worked as an oilfield pipe inspector at Argus Machine, just outside city limits. He had gone on a date on the night of Friday, October 10, 2008, with a woman he had met on the online dating website plentyoffish.com. They must have hit it off like fireworks since Johnny had started writing emails and updates on his Facebook page about the amazing catch he had hooked. She was filthy rich and willing to share. In one email sent out to many of his friends, he bragged about finally finding romance and being out of the country for a couple of months. His friends passed that email on to police:

> Hey there,
>
> I've met an extraordinary woman named Jen who has offered to take me on a nice long tropical vacation. We'll be staying in her winter home in Costa Rica, phone number to follow soon. I won't be back in town until December 10th but I will be checking my email periodically.
>
> See you around the holidays,
> Johnny

The email had been sent on Monday morning – October 13, 2008 – three days after Johnny's date. Most of Johnny's friends saw it as a bit impulsive but didn't think too much about it. But his closest friend, Dale Smith, was worried. It didn't seem like something Johnny would do, no matter how beautiful or wealthy this girl could be. Dale couldn't get his friend on the phone, and when he went to his condo, he noticed that Johnny's car, a sporty cherry-red Mazda 3 hatchback that was only three years old, was missing from his parking spot. Johnny hadn't covered his two motorcycles with a tarp either, which he always did when he left for a vacation. Even if he had left in a rush, it still would have been out of character. Dale spent days calling the police before officers finally took the disappearance seriously, realizing a few things weren't adding up. On the late evening of Friday, October 17, a week after Johnny's date, police finally became involved and agreed to take on the missing persons report. Clark and Anstey had been called in two days later as the search so far had failed to locate him.

Clark was listening in to this briefing, seeing that things were a little odd, but he wasn't writing down a lot of notes in his binder. His pen dangled above his page and skipped over a lot of the detail. He wasn't really feeling this one just yet. He looked over and saw Anstey was scribbling quite a bit, taking extensive notes.

They were told that patrol officers had already visited Johnny's condo and taken his desktop computer. A quick peek around on the hard drive revealed a phone list with a whole pile of names.

Clark and Anstey wanted to cover off each angle. After all, if the missing man really was dead, it would end up on their desk anyway. It was better if such legwork was done at this stage than days later, when the homicide team would be forced to play catch-up on simple tasks.

"We need to call everyone on this phone list," Clark announced to the room of officers. "What if he's just at someone's house?" He turned to Anstey. "If he is, Mark and I can go home. That will be end of it."

Officers started divvying up the phone list in the room as the formal briefing ended.

Clark elbowed Anstey. "Listen, do you want me to take this? We need to figure this out right now." Someone had to be the primary. "If I'm taking it, I gotta be writing a lot more than I'm writing now. I'm just listening."

In a normal police investigation, becoming the primary investigator on a case is a mountain of paperwork. Everything has to be written down. Every detail. Every decision. If the investigation proceeds to a court case, detectives have to take the witness stand and explain the entire direction of their case under harsh cross-examination. It results in binders of information, hundreds of pages for even a simple and small file. The primary is the boss man, directing the speed and flow of information, making the major decisions, delegating tasks to other officers. It is endless work at the best of times.

But Anstey reassured him. "No, no, I'll take it." Anstey didn't mind the job at all. He found it was "tailor made" for his skills and interest in investigative work. He had been a primary with Clark, helping him a few times before, and knew they worked together well. But he didn't realize at the time that by volunteering for such a task, he had just agreed to be responsible for the biggest homicide file he had ever seen. His investigation would soon be winding through a strange avenue of characters and motives he never imagined possible. And this police chase would see him unexpectedly choose to retire from the force early, making it his last.

THE STATION WAS ELECTRIC. Phones rang and people shouted. Clark and Anstey found spare desks and were working the phones near southwest detectives. The buzz of a busy office bounced off the walls. Officers were constantly moving in and out of the station, starting up conversations, blurting out information as detectives asked questions. The investigation was in full swing.

Clark scanned the names on his copy of Johnny's phone list. The detective had grown up in the blue-collar community of Beverly, an area northeast of downtown Edmonton that became part of the big city as urban sprawl surrounded it. He became a cop and had worked patrol for years, then spent a great deal of his career as a detective in liaison with the city's maximum security prison, charging inmates for drugs and assaults, before he was moved up to the homicide unit in police headquarters. To his surprise, as he looked over Johnny's phone list, he recognized the name of a guard at the Edmonton Max, the federal prison, his old turf. Clark dialled the number.

The guard picked up and said he had met Johnny through a friend, another guard at the Max, because Johnny fixed computers in his spare time. But he hadn't seen him in months. "He's a super nice guy," the guard told Clark over the phone. "He's a bit of an odd fella, a little bit different, but he has a personality to please people." Clark asked if he thought someone could have taken advantage of Johnny. The guard thought he'd be an easy mark. "He's not a ladies' man. He's more of a nerd and a loner." Johnny had come into a lot of money recently, he said. He had bought a home before the last oil boom and sold it during the peak, making a tidy profit off exploding house prices that allowed him to purchase a new condo.

Clark then called the other guard that his former colleague had mentioned, but the man only rehashed a lot of the detail Clark already knew. He also told Clark that Johnny was no stranger to online dating. He had been meeting girls on dating websites for years. As far as family members who might know where he is, the guard said Johnny's mom was a real estate agent on the West Coast, where she lived with her partner. Johnny's dad had died years ago, and he had a brother with a couple of kids. Clark said thanks and hung up the phone.

Anstey had finished his call too. They started running ideas off of each other. Clark loved it because with every idea he came up with, Anstey had to write it down. He was keeping him busy.

One of the constables broke up their conversation and pulled Anstey aside. Christopher Maxwell had been working on the file since the very beginning. "There's something really wrong here," he told Anstey. "I don't know. What are *your* thoughts on this?"

Anstey was honest. "Well, my thoughts are he's probably with some girlfriend in Two Hills." He shrugged, just picking a name of a random town a few hours out of the city. "I mean, I don't believe the Costa Rica thing for a second, but it's gotta be something like that." He figured homicide would be off the case in a few hours.

But Maxwell wasn't convinced. "No, there's something really wrong here," he said. "I've got a bad feeling about this."

Anstey thanked him for his insight as Clark started shouting out questions to the officers gathered nearby. "Hey, have you guys checked the airport parkades?"

They told him yes, a few times actually. But Anstey wanted the search expanded. Every nearby hotel, all the roads near Johnny's place. He wanted officers to start searching parking lots.

"What about the airlines?"

The officers said some had been called but not all. The computer system used at the airport was archaic. A detective couldn't just call up and ask if Johnny had boarded any flights this month. They had to check with every airline, one by one, for each day separately. It would take hours. And since it was a Sunday afternoon, the ticket booths were unstaffed. It would have to be a task put off until Monday, when they could also check with customs and officials in Costa Rica to see whether Johnny had left the country at any time since his last known sighting on Friday, October 10.

Clark got a call from Johnny's friend Dale and peeled off a few more details from him, including email addresses for Johnny's mom and brother. He wrote them an email, saying the police had concerns about Johnny and needed his family to call them. He tried to be careful with his words. No need to alarm them. But Johnny's mom was in Mexico and the news that her son was missing would jolt her away from the soft, sandy beaches of her early winter vacation.

It was time to broaden the search and call in more help. Clark phoned the forensics office to assemble a team to visit Johnny's condo. Maybe they could rule out anything suspicious.

Six o'clock approached and the phone list had been exhausted with no sign of Johnny. Clark was thinking about what else they could be doing. "Okay, where exactly did this guy go missing?" He turned to whoever in the room was listening. "Where was this woman's house?"

A constable walked over and told him that was the strange part about this whole case. Johnny had emailed the directions his date had given him to one of his friends right before he left his condo. Patrol had followed the directions, which didn't lead to a house at all. Instead, they led down an alley to a detached garage.

Clark looked at the constable like he was crazy. "Well, have we looked inside the garage yet?"

"Only briefly, not a good hard look," the officer said.

The garage was rented separately from the house. The tenant who was renting the garage was a man named Mark Andrew Twitchell. He had come down to the garage one night and shown a few officers what was inside. It was being used as a movie set. The guy was a local filmmaker.

"Who else has keys?"

"Two of his friends who are in his production crew."

Their names were Mike Young and Jay Howatson.

Anstey assigned a southwest detective to start typing up a search warrant to access the garage. It would take a few hours to write and then it had to be walked downtown to be signed by a judge. Patrol officers were then asked to go door to door and inquire whether neighbours had seen Johnny's red car or anything else that might have been suspicious.

Clark thought their next steps seemed simple enough: three men had access to the garage where Johnny was last known to be headed, so one of them might know something. They all had to be interviewed.

He didn't realize, however, that southwest detectives were one step ahead of him, having been working on the file since Friday. Mark Twitchell had already come down to the station the previous night and been interviewed by a detective on night shift. He had made a video recording of the interview.

Everyone shuffled into a cramped room to watch the video. The camera had been mounted near the ceiling of the interview room. In the footage, a tall detective with a baritone voice sat at a table. Across from him sat Mark Twitchell, relaxed and wearing a black T-shirt and jeans. He was in his late twenties, an energetic guy, clean-shaven, with a baby face, short black hair parted to the side like a schoolboy. He was really chatty. Every question the detective asked was answered. The cop had covered off what they knew so far, and Twitchell looked as stumped as the police. He didn't know anyone named Jen and certainly never met a man named Johnny Altinger. He was a filmmaker who had been renting the garage for studio space. He was behind a *Star Wars* fan film, but the detective in the video hadn't heard of it. He told the cop that the last project filmed in the garage was a psychological thriller, for which his crew had shot a few horror scenes involving a samurai sword and fake blood. The film had been completed a few weeks ago and was now in post-production.

Clark watched the video closely and jotted down his observations. *Very open and forthcoming in the interview.* He kept scribbling down his thoughts on this Twitchell character, which were all positive. He summed up the filmmaker in one clear sentence: *Does not come across as deceptive.* Later, it occurred to Clark that if the guy was so cooperative, maybe he'd be willing to let them see inside his garage one more time.

A STEAL OF A DEAL

JOHNNY ALTINGER'S PLACE WAS on the outskirts of the city, just below the southern leg of the ring road. It was here where three officers from the forensic identification team, or Ident, gathered on the evening of Sunday, October 19, to begin a search for clues to Johnny's whereabouts.

Sergeant Randy Topp, Constable Nancy Allen, and Constable Gary Short had been on the third watch of the forensic unit's police roster when Detective Clark had given them a call. Carrying a video camera, still camera, and a bunch of other gear, the team arrived at 11445 Ellerslie Road and opened the door to suite 103. The constable who had approached Detective Anstey with his concerns came down with a key provided by Johnny's friends.

It was their job to record and document each location just as it had been left and to gather any evidence connected to a crime. Their work was often the backbone of an investigation, with forensic team photos, video, and exhibits used as evidence in a court of law.

Topp entered first and filmed each room of the condo. Short followed and snapped photos.

The condo was small. A white motorcycle helmet sat on the kitchen counter, next to an empty bottle of Mike's Hard Lemonade and a couple of dirty plates. Beside the kitchen island were two director's chairs made of red fabric and varnished wood.

It was a typical single man's lair. The living room had a long white leather couch and a huge flat-screen television. The walls were bare. In the bedroom, Johnny's suit jacket lay crumpled on the bed, as if thrown off his body at the last moment, discarded as a step too far to impress his awaiting date.

There wasn't much for Allen to do. She was an exhibit handler, but there was nothing that looked like evidence of a crime to collect. She grabbed three pairs of underwear, a baseball cap from the bedroom closet, an electric razor, a deodorant stick, and a bathrobe. She'd send the articles off to the crime lab so they'd have a DNA profile for Johnny on file, if the case ever turned into anything more serious.

But on first blush, there was nothing in the condo to suggest a crime had been committed. There were no signs of forced entry and no bloodstains. The only odd thing was Johnny's computer desk. An officer had already removed the computer a few days earlier to get Johnny's phone list. But an empty spot on the desk remained where a printer would normally be located. It was missing.

———

BILL CLARK TOOK HIS foot off the gas as his car descended into the parkade beneath downtown police headquarters. After spending most of his Sunday on the city's south side, he was finally heading back to the comfort of his own office. The building lay on the forgotten east side of downtown, next to a muddy, gravel parking lot that filled and emptied every weekday with commuters who lived nearly an hour away in the suburbs and refused to take a bus. The lot was the neutral zone between luxury bankers and lawyers and the gritty peep shows and prostitutes who still mingled three blocks away, near the scummiest bars in the city. The police building itself was drab: giant slabs of unpainted concrete, sparse windows, maroon tile floors, fake plants. Outside, three navy-blue flagpoles flew the colours of the Edmonton Police Service and Canada's Maple Leaf. Across the street was the York Hotel, where one man was famously stabbed in a bar fight but waved off a paramedic so he could sit down and finish his beer. It was that kind of neighbourhood.

Clark rode up the elevator to the third floor, shuffling over to his crowded desk in the corner of the homicide unit. It was still early Sunday evening and he thought there was plenty of time left in the day when he learned the search warrant request had been denied. The police couldn't provide enough evidence that a crime had been committed. Clark tried to brush it off. A patrol car had been sent to secure the garage so no potential evidence could be removed while they dug up more information for a warrant. But Clark wanted to speed up the process. He fell back on the plan to do a consensual search. He had already left messages for Twitchell's two film production assistants to no avail. It was finally time to call the filmmaker himself.

A deep voice answered the phone as Clark nudged his belly into his desk, phone clasped in hand. The man was polite as Clark pitched a request to search the rental property. "Will you be willing to give us access to the garage?" Clark asked with a big smile, as if the man could see it through the phone. "We just want to take a look around, just cover it off."

"Absolutely," said the filmmaker. "No problem."

"Great. Can you meet us there? Or what works for you? We don't want to inconvenience you. Do you want to meet us at the garage?"

"Yeah, I'll meet you there."

"How long?"

"Give me about forty-five minutes."

"Oh. Where are you?"

"I'm in St. Albert."

Clark realized it was a big ask. The man was in a bedroom community near the far northwestern outskirts of the city. "Why don't you just give us the keys? I can send someone out to meet you."

"Tell you what, I'm actually going to my parents' place anyway so we could meet around there?"

"All we need is your consent, there'd be a form for you to sign. We just want to have our guys go in and have a quick look."

"That will be fine."

Clark arranged for the filmmaker to meet an officer at a convenience store not far from where he was heading in northern Edmonton. He hung up the phone, picked it back up, and dialled the southwest station. This Twitchell guy sounded easy to talk to, and Clark figured he could just grab someone in the office to drive down and pick up a key. After all, what could possibly happen on such a straightforward mission?

DETECTIVE BRIAN MURPHY KEPT the engine running in his unmarked police car as he waited in a 7-Eleven parking lot, scanning vehicles under the glow of streetlights. He spotted a man sitting in a maroon Pontiac Grand Am and figured it must be the guy he was supposed to meet: Mark Twitchell.

Although drowsy from a fifteen-hour-long Sunday shift, he dialled Twitchell's number and the man in the car answered. "I'm sitting right here," Murphy said. "Look behind you." He gave a little wave.

The man crawled out of his car and jumped into Murphy's. He shook the cop's hand as he settled into the passenger seat. Murphy, who had a soft and polite voice he had trouble raising under his black moustache, found the man friendly, perhaps boisterous. The two of them talked for a few minutes.

Twitchell's face had relaxed. "Listen," he said, looking at Murphy in the car. "I have some things that have been happening to me recently that I want to make you aware of."

"Okay."

He told Murphy that his car had been broken into about eleven days ago, back on October 8. Two rental receipts for the garage in Mill Woods, a cheque, sunglasses, and some change had all been taken. A few days later, on October 12, he discovered his front door was unlocked when he came home. And his wife, who was "like OCD, like Jack Nicholson," would never have forgotten to lock it. It worried him, but there didn't appear to be anything amiss.

Murphy pulled out his notepad. He had spent most of the day phoning Johnny's friends and really knew nothing about the file. "This is all new information so I should be writing it all down."

"Okay," Twitchell continued. "On October 15, I went to Home Depot to pick up some cleaning supplies to take down to the garage." He paused as if he was remembering details. "But as I was driving, I decided I wanted to pull into the side and get some gas. In the parking lot, a man came up to the passenger side of my car. He knocked on the window. I looked over." Twitchell said the man was making circles in the air with his finger, telling him to roll down the window. "I rolled it down and the fellow leaned in."

Murphy was taking it all down.

"He said he had just met this girl. She's very wealthy and she's going to take him away on a vacation for three months. She told him that he should get rid of his car because when they get back from vacation she was going to buy him a new car. So he asks me: 'Do you wanna buy my car?'" Twitchell seemed to enjoy telling the story. "I told him, 'I don't have enough money to buy a car.' The guy looks at me and points and says,

'Well, how much money do you have in your wallet?' So I pulled out my wallet and I say, 'I've got forty dollars.'" Twitchell turned to Murphy and exclaimed, "The guy said, 'Sold!'" It was a done deal.

Twitchell said the man drove the car to his rented garage a couple of blocks away. They talked about the car, Twitchell expressed some concerns about the registration and insurance but coughed up the forty dollars and was handed the keys. By coincidence, the man told him his name was also Mark. He said he didn't get a last name.

Twitchell said he could tell the guy was agitated and apprehensive. "The last I saw of the guy, he was walking down the alley."

Murphy jumped in after a moment, his pen a few steps behind Twitchell's telling of the story. "Well, can you give me a description of this fellow?"

Twitchell offered a very detailed answer: male, Caucasian, six-foot-two, medium build, late twenties or early thirties, black hair, and he had a tattoo of a Celtic knot on the right side of his neck.

"What's a Celtic knot?"

Twitchell tried to describe it. Murphy handed him his notepad and Twitchell scribbled down a drawing of the tattoo. "He had a green wind-breaker, jeans, black runners, and a white T-shirt."

The car was a 2005 red Mazda hatchback.

"So I was walking around the vehicle," Twitchell said. "And I noticed that it has a stick. And I can't drive a stick." But his friend Joss Hnatiuk could drive one, he explained. Joss came down and parked it at his parents' house a few blocks away. Twitchell didn't explain why he wanted the car moved.

Murphy thought it bizarre. "Listen, the other investigators will have to know about this."

Twitchell nodded.

"We're probably going to want you to give a statement in relation to this new information and possibly do a photo lineup to try to identity this fellow. I'm going to phone the detectives, fill them in on the information, and see what they want to do."

Murphy checked the clock. It was 10:33 p.m.

BILL CLARK WAS SITTING at his desk when the flow of information stalled. The forensics team had moved on from Johnny's place, having found nothing, and were waiting at the garage for the key. Both of Twitchell's film production assistants, Mike and Jay, had called Clark back and agreed to give a statement the next evening.

As he sat there, hands clasped behind his head, Clark heard Mark Anstey raise his voice from his desk across the room. He looked over and saw Anstey was on the phone with a strange expression on his face. He put the phone to his chest and turned to Clark with disbelief in his voice. "Twitchell just told Murphy that he bought a red car off a guy on October 15 for forty dollars."

Clark stopped. "What?" His mouth hung open. This was no longer a standard missing persons case. He blurted out his thoughts in an unedited stream as they came to him. "Holy fuck! He killed the guy!" He spun around in his chair. "Okay, okay, maybe he didn't kill him." He shot a confused look at Anstey. "But who the fuck buys a car off a guy for forty dollars? . . . How much is this car worth?"

"I dunno," said Anstey. By one early estimate, it was probably worth at least $6,000, maybe $10,000, certainly not $40.

"Oh man, this guy is involved." Clark rubbed his head, his eyes wide in disbelief. "He's involved in something."

The case had gone from first to top gear in an instant, but Anstey and Clark had only seconds to decide on their next move.

Clark talked fast. "Mark, we gotta bring him in. We gotta. . . . But we've got nothing on him. So what do we do?"

BRIAN MURPHY HELD HIS cell phone close to his ear as the detectives at the other end of the line tossed around ideas. Twitchell sat beside him, oblivious to the chaos his little story had created. The decision was made to send a patrol car to take Twitchell to headquarters voluntarily. "Okay," Murphy said, turning to Twitchell to ask if he was willing to give a second statement, which he was. "Why don't you lock your car?" Murphy pointed at the maroon Grand Am parked on the south side of the 7-Eleven. "If you've gotta go to headquarters, you better lock your car."

Twitchell jumped out, locked his car, and returned to wait with Murphy for the patrol car to show up. When it arrived, he climbed in the back.

Murphy stayed on the phone in his car and heard a buzzing in his ear again. He rolled down his window and shouted out at the patrol car. "Mark, they've changed their minds. They'd like you to drive your own car down to headquarters."

Twitchell nodded from the backseat. "But I don't know where headquarters is."

"Well, you can follow me," Murphy offered in a chuckle.

The two cars made their way downtown.

Murphy knew Twitchell was key to the investigation, but it also meant his fifteen-hour shift was going to get a lot longer. And the police would also soon discover how incredibly fortunate they were to have Twitchell's car parked at headquarters. It would change everything.

───────────

IN THE SOUTHEASTERN SUBURBS, on a quaint corner lot surrounded by spruce and cedar, stood a tall white house with emerald green trim. To anyone driving by it was just another suburban address, but for Joss Hnatiuk, it was home. At twenty-five, Joss, a big, tall man who sported a head full of short and curly brown hair, had a quiet disposition and still lived with his parents. He was trying to get a multimedia company off the ground as he installed security systems to pay the bills. Twitchell was helping him, and they envisioned a rich future together.

But tonight, in the stillness of the late Sunday evening, an unexpected ring of the doorbell broke the silence as midnight neared. Joss had just returned from a premiere screening of a feature film in which a friend had been cast in a small role. He opened the door, and to his surprise, he found a gathering of police officers.

Outside on the driveway, boxed in on two sides, was a red Mazda 3. The licence plate had been removed.

Joss looked at the detective standing in front of him. Another officer was busy writing down the vehicle's identification number. Joss reached his own conclusions. "I take it that the car is stolen?"

FACING FACTS

Mark Twitchell sat in police headquarters, his arm draped across the back of a little couch in a tiny room on the third floor. Late Sunday night was slowly turning over into Monday. A copy of the Bible lay on a coffee table nearby.

Detectives Bill Clark and Brian Murphy were chatting in the monitor room three doors down. They could see Twitchell through a bank of televisions and cameras hooked up to each room. Clark had left Twitchell alone in one of the "soft" rooms, designed to make someone feel comfortable. The one where Twitchell was cooling his heels featured an oil painting of a barn in a snowstorm.

Clark's head was spinning. The last thing he wanted was the guy to call a lawyer. At the same time, Clark wanted to keep an open mind. Twitchell's story was certainly bizarre, but it didn't mean he was guilty of anything. Not yet. For all he knew this guy could turn out to be just a weird filmmaker who really did get lucky and buy a car for forty dollars.

The forensics team arrived at Joss Hnatiuk's house, having been pulled off the garage to focus on the recovered Mazda. Constable Gary Short grabbed his camera and started taking pictures just as Joss and a detective drove off to the southwest division station.

The remaining constable ran the Mazda's serial number, and sure enough, it was Johnny's missing vehicle. A tow truck was called. The vehicle was headed for the police lot for a detailed examination.

Eyes dry and feeling tired, Clark looked over Twitchell's new statement, scanning the eight pages it had taken him more than two hours to write. Two o'clock in the morning approached. The statement included the October 15 car sale story and new information. There were more names listed for the crew behind Twitchell's films – David Puff, Scott Cooke, actors Chris Heward and Robert Barnsley – and a revelation that he had sent an email a few hours ago to the southwest detective who had interviewed him the previous night, which would detail the car story too. Clark kept reading. Twitchell claimed he noticed the padlock on the back door to his garage had been changed when he met a constable there hours before his first police interview. Inside, Twitchell said his duct tape, garbage bags, and paper towels had been used while it looked like something had been burned in an oil drum. Twitchell's statement continued:

> It seems that whoever broke into my car on the 8th used all of the information they stole to use my location and personal property for who knows what. . . . I am alarmed that unknown persons know where I live and may be entering premises I'm supposed to be in control of. I don't know if the person who sold me the car is involved but looking back it certainly feels that way and I have to wonder if I'm being targeted or if it's a nasty coincidence.

Clark flipped through the pages a few more times. He yawned. The story sounded like bullshit. In policing circles, Twitchell was offering what's known as an "alternative suspect" theory. Clearly the guy was worried they were on to him so he was already shifting the blame. In his statement, Twitchell had added a new detail: he now described a phone call as the motivation for pulling over, which led to the meeting with the mystery car seller. Perhaps he realized after telling the story to Murphy that there wasn't actually a gas station in the area where he had claimed to meet the man.

IN A POLICE INTERVIEW room on the other side of town, Joss was hesitant to open up about his dealings with Twitchell. Sitting beside a detective at southwest division, Joss slowly revealed that he had helped the filmmaker, a good friend, with a short film production in the garage at the end of September.

Twitchell's script had featured a serial killer who was targeting unfaithful husbands. These men were tortured and then stabbed. Joss remembered how the death scene used "lots of blood." In the corner of the garage they also had an oil drum. While it wasn't used during the film shoot, Joss understood it was a "burn barrel" that the killer would use to dispose of the remains of his victims.

CLARK KNEW THE GAME was about to begin, but the problem was he had very little evidence. If the case was going to move ahead tonight he would likely need Twitchell to confess – but to what? Clark talked it over with Anstey, and they figured he needed to start positive. If Twitchell began saying anything that implicated him further, Clark would have to stop the interview and read him his rights. Until then, he'd play the role of bumbling idiot cop. Big smiles, lots of nodding.

Clark strolled into the interview room and Twitchell stirred awake. "Hey, Mark, thanks for waiting." Clark took a seat in a chair across from him.

The two of them talked for an hour and a half.

Twitchell needed little prodding. He was soon telling Clark all about his life and the strange things that had transpired in the past few weeks: Twitchell was a married man and a young father. His wife, Jess, was on maternity leave from the Workers' Compensation Board. Their baby, Chloe, was now eight months old, and she had been sleeping through the night after the first few weeks.

Twitchell loved *Star Wars* and had directed a fan film based on the sci-fi series. That's where he had met Joss and became friends with Mike and Jay, his current production assistants. He said one of his email addresses had the name "Kit Fisto" within it, a reference to a Jedi knight in *Star Wars: Attack of the Clones*. Clark shrugged it off, having no idea what Twitchell was talking about when he described the "green dude who smiles a lot" with a lightsaber.

Twitchell said his film career had been developed with a laptop while sitting in coffee shops. His income came from a combination of money raised from film investors and revenue from selling handmade *Star Wars* props on eBay. He had just shipped a codpiece, which covers the crotch, for a Darth Vader costume, the day he dropped off the cleaning supplies at his garage.

He had two cell phones. The call he had taken before buying the forty-dollar car was from a Los Angeles producer who was helping Twitchell find investors for a planned comedy feature called *Day Players*. Twitchell could go on for hours, even though it was the middle of the night.

Clark made notes, slowly directing Twitchell to topics relevant to the investigation. Murphy listened in the monitor room, taking his own.

The oil drum in the garage had been purchased online, like most of Twitchell's possessions. He had filmed his horror movie at the end of September and then gone back to the garage in the late afternoon of October 10, the day of Johnny's disappearance. He was cleaning up the film set between 3:00 p.m. and 5:30 p.m. Twitchell said he was concerned about the fake blood mix they had used – a mixture of corn syrup and red food colouring – because it could start "attracting bugs."

Clark had Twitchell tell the car story twice, then he had him tell it backwards. The same odd details emerged: a mystery man with a Celtic knot tattoo and a sugar momma who was taking him on a vacation. His willingness to unload the car for forty dollars, no bill of sale. Twitchell taking the licence plate, keys, and leaving them in his own car. The basic story, however, had changed multiple times, sometimes with added detail, other times with the order of events changed around. In the version told to Clark, Twitchell had gone to the gas station to fill up a jerry can in his trunk – good for emergencies, he said, and for a lawn mower he was going to buy some day. "I think I might've forgotten to put that in the eight-page version of the statement," said Twitchell. "But anyway . . ."

By the time Clark left the room, it was nearly 4:00 a.m.

IN THE DARKNESS, NEIGHBOURS living near the garage had been awakened by police knocking on their front doors. Officers were asking questions. Next door to the garage, and nearing retirement age, Mike and Lynda Warren clearly remembered seeing a group of young men making a movie. They had placed black plastic over all the windows. One man they saw often. He drove a Pontiac Grand Am and had short black hair. The last time they saw him was on the weekend. Peering through their fence, as neighbours sometimes do, they spotted him changing the padlock on the garage door.

Farther down the road, another couple was startled awake by police officers. They remembered seeing a red car, definitely something sporty like a Mazda, parked outside that same garage on October 14. It was the day of the federal election and they had walked right past it on their way to the polls.

—

"Boy, is that guy lying!" Clark exhaled a long sigh as he staggered into the monitor room, rubbing his bald head and giving Murphy a look through his fatigue.

"Oh, yeah!" Murphy nodded.

"Is there anything more, anything I can go over with this guy?"

Anstey walked in and the three of them talked, realizing there was nothing else.

Clark had heard enough. He was exhausted. He had been up for twenty hours. It was time to press the issue. "I'm going to confront him. If we don't get a confession he's walking out of here anyway, so let's see what he says."

Anstey and Murphy agreed.

Clark tried to find the energy. He didn't drink coffee so it was proving difficult to stay sharp. At least he knew Twitchell's reaction would tell him everything. When confronted, an innocent man always loses his composure and denies everything. Clark would know something terrible had happened to Johnny if Twitchell's reaction was anything different.

Joss didn't want to spill the story on Twitchell. After all, he believed the man would make him millions and their film ideas were going to be hits. Already investors were handing over thousands to finance *Day Players*. Joss and his family had even put up $30,000 of their own money for the film. But the detective pressed on and Joss finally complied: he told the detective he had removed the Mazda's licence plate and cleaned the car "a little," but then he left it alone, parked in the driveway of his parents' house. Twitchell had the key. Joss remembered the day Twitchell had called him to help move the Mazda quite clearly. He had been at work on the afternoon of Friday, October 17.

Another detail then came back to Joss that he thought the police may want to know about. His grandfather was a retired cop so Joss respected the law. About a month ago, he said, Twitchell had asked him to be a reference on a new purchase that required a bit of paperwork. And Joss didn't mind.

Twitchell, for an unknown reason, had suddenly expressed interest in buying a gun.

—

THE METAL DOOR TO the soft room clinked open. Twitchell, appearing tired, turned to see Clark shuffle back inside the interview room, legal pad in hand.

"Mark, you remember what I mentioned to you earlier?" Clark pushed the door shut behind him, making sure the latch had closed. "About, uh, contacting a lawyer?"

"Uh-huh."

"That still holds true, okay? Just so you're aware. If at any time we're talking and you wanna contact a lawyer, you can do so. I'll take you to a phone." Clark sneaked a quick downward glace at his notepad. "There's something else I wanna tell you . . . Mark."

Twitchell was hunched over, holding his chin up with one hand.

Clark dropped his papers on the table and turned to face him. He took a quick breath, then launched in. "There's absolutely no doubt in my mind that you're involved in the disappearance of John Altinger." He chopped each word with his hands like he was lecturing Twitchell, towering over top of him.

Twitchell blinked rapidly, looking up at Clark in sudden shock. His eyes flared as he locked on to Clark's gaze.

Thirteen seconds passed in silence as they stared at each other.

Twitchell slowly leaned back into the couch, his fleece jacket rustling against it. He dropped his hands between his knees and tried to regain his composure.

Clark raised his voice again. "No doubt in my mind at all, Mark." He was nearly shouting.

Twitchell looked stunned. He opened up his hands to Clark like he was pleading for scraps of food before finally responding. "Uh, wha, why?"

Clark shuffled backwards to take a seat, ignoring the question, realizing he was now in for a marathon. Twitchell had become a prime suspect. He dropped down on the edge of the chair, his elbows resting on his thighs, opening up his body language. "As I said, Mark . . ." He shook his head, lowering his voice. "There's no doubt in my mind that you're involved in this disappearance."

Twitchell exhaled in a heavy sigh that seemed to empty his lungs. His body deflated. He collapsed and buried his face in his hands, gasping for a breath. Rubbing his forehead hard, he stared down at the office carpet, avoiding the detective's probing stare.

But Clark kept hammering away. "I just wanna get to the bottom of this because this is *not* gonna go away. It's not gonna *leave* you, Mark."

Twitchell drummed his forehead with his fingers, hiding half his face. "I, I don't understand."

"I'm gonna explain some of the reasons to you," Clark said, pausing for effect. "But you *do* understand."

Twitchell sat up straight, squinted, and clasped his hands together again. He listened closely, expressionless.

"You're involved in this and unfortunately . . ." Clark shrugged his shoulders. "Something got carried away. Something got carried away with this guy." He kept nodding as he changed his tone to that of a father-confessor. "I mean, talking to you here tonight, you seem like a decent guy. And I think that something happened that night that maybe you just didn't have total control of. And I'm here to get to the bottom of it. Because it's not gonna go away. This is gonna stay with you . . ."

Twitchell shook his head, staring at his palms as he sighed yet again.

"We need to clear this up here and now. We need to clear this up tonight."

Twitchell shook his head in defiance.

"You need to tell me the truth about what's going on," Clark stressed. "What happened . . . with this fella?"

But the room was silent. The low hum of fluorescent lights droned on as the clock ticked past five in the morning. Twitchell did not respond. Clark, speaking slowly as his fatigue settled in, reached for an explanation. "I mean, did this happen because of the movie thing? . . . Something that went too far?"

Twitchell fell back into the couch and threw his hands up in the air. "I have no idea what the *hell* is going on," he said, his voice quivering.

But Clark was relentless. "You *do* have an idea," he said, staring him down. "You have a very good idea, Mark, about what's going on. You know *exactly* what happened there that night."

Twitchell clutched his forehead again, sighed, and dropped his head into his hands. He refused to open up.

Clark pressed on, scolding the filmmaker for more than an hour. He probed for a weak spot, circling back repeatedly to Twitchell's wife, Jess, and his baby, Chloe. *Think of your family.* Clark repeated it. *What are they going to do? What are you going to tell your wife?* He laid on the guilt, then built him up with praise. *You're a smart guy. Decent guy. Have a conscience.* He seized on anything that might get Twitchell to talk, anything to pry him open and unburden himself, get him to spill the story.

Twitchell looked rattled. "This can't be," he peeped. "I don't –" His whole body language had changed. Clark saw his posture close in on him like he had become a shamed man, lost, powerless, and under attack. "I just don't understand," Twitchell whimpered.

Clark reached for his notes. The case wasn't too difficult, he explained: a guy was missing, the police knew he had gone to Twitchell's garage, and he had already admitted in the interview that the missing man's licence plate and keys were in his own car. On top of that, here he was with a ludicrous story that he had bought the missing man's vehicle for only forty dollars with no bill of sale from a mystery man with a Celtic knot tattoo. Twitchell had said repeatedly that he bought the car on October 15. But having checked in on the rest of the police team during the break earlier in the night, Clark knew Joss had already revealed how Twitchell had called him to move the car on October 17, while a neighbour had spotted the Mazda parked at the garage on October 14. And Twitchell's version of events had changed repeatedly. It had changed from the previous night's interview, changed from his written statement, and continued to change even while he was talking with Clark. The detective knew Twitchell was lying about the padlock and was suspicious about the barrel. The jerry can in his trunk made no sense either. Who buys a can of gas for a lawn mower they don't own? Nothing was adding up. It was time to fess up.

"You've changed your whole story. Told all kinds of different lies."

As Clark picked off the list of inconsistencies, Twitchell hid his face with his hands and avoided looking at him. He stroked the bridge of his nose with his index finger, sighing repeatedly.

"What happened to John, Mark? What did you do to him?"

"I'm done," Twitchell said. Clenching his first, he pressed his knuckles against his temples. He wanted out. "I'm just not talkin' anymore. . . . This is ridiculous."

Clark didn't budge. "Well, what is your explanation? You haven't answered any of the questions! If you didn't do anything wrong, why wouldn't you answer those questions?"

He stopped the interrogation briefly and tried to engage Twitchell as a friend.

"What drove you to this? Obviously there's something going on behind the scenes that I don't know about. You seem like a decent guy that, hell, I'd even go have a beer with."

Twitchell looked up for a second and then furrowed his brow, deep in concentration.

"That's the type of guy you come across as being," Clark added, smiling. "Yet, you're involved over your head in this."

Twitchell had seen this good cop, bad cop routine before and called Clark out on it: "Is anything that you're saying genuine or is this some sort of tactic?"

"You gotta get away from the acting part, Mark, and listen to what I'm saying." Clark turned aggressive. "You have told me *nothing* but lies. An innocent man does not come in here and tell lies. That's *genuine*, Mark. . . . Everything I'm telling you in here is genuine." He stopped for a second to let it sink in. "So get outta your film producer mode and the facade of thinking that everyone's an actor."

Twitchell made a face and adjusted his feet.

"This is real life, all right? Real life. If you were telling me the truth, you would have one story. One story that would flow from beginning to end." Clark waved his hand from right to left. "And you could repeat that story one hundred times with no changes." He snapped his fingers. "Yours is soooo bad."

Twitchell remained silent, thinking, before finally responding. "I, I just . . . I know we're not sitting in a movie, but it's the cop thing."

"This is real-life stuff," Clark said. "You gotta get away from the movies."

"Yeah, I know." He sighed.

"That's the problem here." Clark pushed one last time. "You're not gonna be able to live with yourself, with this, for the rest of your life."

Twitchell crossed his legs, tucked his head into his shoulder, and spoke softly: "You'd be surprised with what I can live with."

Clark thought he had hit on something. He wanted a confession and moved in. "It's gonna eat at you and eat at you. It's gonna affect your family because it's affecting you. So let's get to the truth and then we can end this. The problem is you don't wanna tell me the truth." He hit him with a rapid series of questions. "Why don't you wanna tell me the truth? Can you answer that question, Mark?"

Twitchell's armour split open. "Because I'm scared," he stammered. "I always have this instinct to wanna be able to try to hold on to . . ." He let it trail off. "I don't even know what."

Clark tried to reassure him, comfort him, get him to keep talking. "That's a perfectly natural feeling at this time. What's going through your mind right now, Mark?"

Twitchell was frowning. "Almost nothing. Anything I try to push out is like . . . What's it like? . . . It's like skating uphill." He gave up. He reached for a tissue off the side table and blew his nose. "I'm too tired to formulate thought anymore."

"I don't think you need to formulate thought. What I think you need to formulate is the truth. There's two sides to every story."

"Yeah, but stories come with questions." Twitchell grabbed another tissue. "And more answers and more stories . . ." He was shutting down again.

Clark was losing him. It was after six now. Twitchell was rubbing his eyes. "Life goes on," Clark offered gently, "and we deal with those mistakes."

"Well . . ." Twitchell looked miserable. "I guess my marriage is over now so I don't really have to worry about protecting her anymore." He was ripping tiny pieces off the corner of the tissue.

"Your daughter will be taken care of."

"Yeah."

"Your wife's here, your mother and father. Your parents are in Edmonton, are they not?"

Twitchell mumbled yes, biting his lip.

"I can see this is eating you up." Clark stopped and tried again. "What happened between you and John, Mark?"

Twitchell was silent. He looked down at the tissue and started twirling it in his fingers. "Ahhhh," he groaned. "I can't even get there right now."

He turned to Clark to offer him a solution. "I wanna get to the finish line, but at the same time I think consulting with a lawyer is gonna be really important."

"You can do that at any time you want. I told you that right from the start."

Twitchell stretched out his arm across the back of the couch and seemed to open up again. "Do you have any idea what it's like living with constant apprehension?"

"Can't say that I do."

"I'd like to not feel that anymore," he muttered, then exhaled.

"Well, this is your chance to get rid of that feeling."

"Oh, but it brings on a whole new type." He shot back to life with a sudden burst of energy and pulled a pen and paper off the couch cushion beside him. He slapped the paper down on a binder and placed it on his lap. "Wh, wha, okay. What's the steps in getting a lawyer because I don't have one?"

He had lost him. Clark knew it was over. Twitchell had lawyered up.

The interview trailed on for a further half-hour, but Clark couldn't get his suspect back on point. It was all pleasantries.

Clark watched as Twitchell walked out of the interview room, spoke to a lawyer on the phone down the hallway, and then decided to leave. Clark jumped to his feet and followed, escorting him out of the building. Murphy stayed behind and looked over his notes.

The pair took the elevator to the ground floor in silence. Clark was fuming. He had thrown everything at the guy all night and he didn't get a confession. As the elevator doors opened, Clark turned to Twitchell. "I know you killed that guy," he spat. "And I'm coming to get you. It's just a matter of time."

Twitchell stared back blankly. They walked out the main door together with wheels turning in both of their heads.

It was a chilly dawn on a Monday morning.

Clark could see his breath. "Is that your car right there?" He pointed at the Pontiac Grand Am parked on the west end of the parking lot.

"Yeah."

"I'm seizing your car."

Twitchell's face went pale.

Clark beamed. After all, Twitchell had given him ample justification: he admitted to having Johnny's keys in the vehicle during the interview. "I'm seizing your car and I'm taking it right now."

"I just need to get something out of my car."

"You're getting fuck-all out of that car."

"I just wanna get my cell phone."

"You get nothing." Clark was smug. He was planning on getting a search warrant and he'd have the forensics team comb through everything inside. "You can either give me the keys or I will just call a tow truck down and we'll break in. Either way, it's gone."

Twitchell dug the keys out of his pocket, slapped them into Clark's hands, and stormed off down the street. Clark stood there for a moment and watched him hurry toward City Hall and the downtown core.

Clark jumped in the maroon vehicle. It was a mess and smelled like gas, but he had to leave the detailed search for his colleagues in forensics. He drove the car to the police warehouse two blocks away to keep it secure.

Clark was getting a second wind. His heart was pumping. Fresh ideas rushed into his head with the crisp outside air. He was thinking twenty-four-hour surveillance. His gut was telling him this file was something big.

Another thought had him break into a dead run back to police headquarters. Clark wanted to drive up to St. Albert and seize Twitchell's house too. With a story this fishy, Clark believed his new suspect would probably be racing back there right now, planning to burn or destroy evidence as fast as he could.

ON THE ROAD

AT THE START OF his early Monday morning shift, Acting Detective Dale Johnson passed Clark in the hallway as he walked to his desk on the other side of homicide. Clark double-backed and tapped him on the shoulder. They were in his car and speeding off to St. Albert before Johnson even had a chance to check his email.

Hungry and grumpy, hands on the wheel, Clark talked fast as Johnson listened. He was in his thirties and six months into the homicide beat, though he was coming off a stint in the gang unit, so he was no rookie. Relatively young compared to the rest of the team, Johnson had yet to develop the gruff attitude and sly expressions veteran cops like Clark liked to slide into their conversations. He was pale white and skinny, still sporting a head of red-brown hair that had begun receding on his temples. And while Clark was known for speaking his mind, sometimes even getting in trouble for it, Johnson was part of the next generation of city detectives who were far more measured in their public speaking. He was neatly dressed, wore glasses, looked far more book smarts than street smarts, more middle class than working class. But the pair shared one thing in common at this moment: both of them were excited, feeding off the energy of a new file. These were moments homicide detectives lived for.

Their car sped in the direction opposite the Monday morning traffic, weaving through each lane. By 7:45, they were pulling up to 30 Dayton Crescent on the north side of St. Albert. Clark rang the doorbell, then peeked through a window. It was a tiny home of bricks and blue siding on a corner lot. Seeing nobody inside, Clark rang the doorbell again and knocked. Johnson stood beside him, adjusting his glasses.

Finally, Clark saw movement through the curtains. A young woman with light brown hair came down the stairs and opened the front door a crack. Standing before them in pyjamas and a housecoat, Twitchell's wife, Jess, seemed hesitant.

Clark could hear a baby inside. "Oh, I apologize for that," he said.

Jess opened the door a bit more and gave him a look.

"I'm Detective Bill Clark." There was no easy way to say it. "We're investigating a disappearance and your husband's name has come up."

"My husband has already called me." She was abrupt and looking annoyed.

Clark bit his lip. "Oh, really?"

"Yeah, he called me from a lawyer's office. He told me not to talk to you guys."

"Well that's fair, I can understand that." He bobbed his head, thrilled they had at least beaten Twitchell back to his home. "But don't you want to know what's going on?" Clark was assessing how much to tell her. "Listen, there's a chance this guy that's missing is *dead* and your husband may have killed him." He threw his hands up. "We're investigating and we don't know where this is going to end up."

It took a few minutes, but she let them in.

Clark and Johnson stepped over baby toys as they walked up into the front room. Both detectives suspected Jess didn't entirely trust them, but she likely didn't believe what her husband was telling her either. Both cops darted their eyes around the house, taking it all in. They asked simple questions. *Are there any DVDs in the house? Where does your husband produce and work on his films? Where's his office? Would he keep hard drives there?* Jess told them his computer gear was in the basement office, except for a laptop, which he usually kept with him.

Clark and Johnson hurried back to the car and called Anstey, who told them they likely had enough for a warrant.

Jess was told the bad news: the police would be seizing her house. And Clark saw her shock from these unexpected circumstances suddenly spill out of her in streams of tears. She trembled. "I don't know what's going on." She looked vacantly ahead, mumbling to herself. Both detectives knew her quiet suburban life was about to change. Her husband was now under police scrutiny and everything she had was potentially in peril because of him.

Johnson attempted to soothe the distraught young mother, offering to let her stay while police searched her home. It would take a couple of hours, maybe longer. They'd just have to watch her while the police were doing the search.

Jess shook her head. "No. I can't be here," she said. "I'm leaving." Her pace quickened as she gathered up her clothes and her baby's things. With her child in her arms, tears in her eyes, she fled to her mother's, never to return to that house and call it her home again.

BACK AT HEADQUARTERS, ANSTEY hammered out search warrant requests on his computer. He had four on the go: Twitchell's car, Johnny's car, the rented garage, and Twitchell's St. Albert home. His fingers jammed up on the keyboard a few times. He was a two-fingered typist. Scanning the police notes, writing down all the information they had so far, he let out a loud whoop when he spotted the licence plate number for Twitchell's Grand Am. He'd have to tell the boys about it later.

Anstey had been a cop for three decades, a member of homicide for nearly six years. And from all that experience he knew crime, including all the motives for trying to kill someone – money, sex, jealousy, to name a few. Murder investigations seldom were the riveting whodunits of detective lore, featuring ingenious killings and elaborate deceptions. People were predictable. But already he knew this case had veered off the track murder cops were used to following and into the extraordinary. He therefore made his search warrant requests as broad as possible. Was this murder, manslaughter, assault, or kidnapping? Was Johnny alive but being held against his will? Was he seriously injured or had he been brutally murdered? He simply didn't know. But he had a wild theory. Clark and Anstey had been building on it all night, with Twitchell giving out enough hints to convince him to pursue this unusual angle. It was time to see if something so sinister, born out of urban myth, could possibly be coming true. On each warrant request, Anstey wrote that he was looking for anything related to the film industry, including records or books "pertaining to the production of graphically violent horror and pornographic films."

In short, he was looking for a possible snuff film, directed by filmmaker Mark Twitchell. Somewhere within one of those four locations, Anstey believed there could be video footage: something involving an online date, lots of blood, and Johnny Altinger, an innocent victim of an unclear motive and an unknown plan.

———

IN THE DAYS THAT followed, Twitchell's film crew saw their lives turned upside down, each one facing questioning from a team of homicide detectives. *How much blood was used for that short film? Have you ever heard of Johnny Altinger? What about Jen? What do you know about snuff films?* The police put their normal sleep patterns on hold. Clark was back in headquarters after a four-hour catnap. Mike Young and Jay Howatson, Twitchell's two production assistants, and David Puff, his director of photography, were interviewed one after another. All were young guys in their late twenties, baffled and astonished by the sudden police attention. None of them knew anything about a red Mazda 3, and they hadn't been near the garage since a few days after the film shoot. The crew had spent sixteen hours filming at the location on Saturday, September 27.

Mike Young was confused. When he stopped by the garage a few days after filming, it had been fairly clean. Certainly there was no fake blood left behind from the shoot requiring a big clean-up effort. He didn't understand why Clark was asking. Footage of the short film was likely downloaded on to Twitchell's home computer. The eight-minute film, called *House of Cards,* was a *"Dexter* spoof," as Mike remembered it. Based on a series of books by Jeff Lindsay, *Dexter* had become a popular television drama on the cable network Showtime. Both the novels and the show are told from the point of view of Dexter Morgan, a fictitious blood-spatter expert for the Miami police who helps homicide cops investigate murders. In his spare time, however, he kills criminals he believes the justice system has failed to control. It was Dexter's own unique moral code to kill only bad people. Many victims were placed in sleeper holds and later stirred awake to find themselves either shrink-wrapped or duct-taped to a large table inside a darkened "kill room" entirely sheathed in plastic sheeting. Victims were frequently dismembered and dumped in the ocean in garbage bags. And Twitchell was a fan of the show. He wouldn't stop talking about it.

One promising detail of Twitchell's life did come out early in the investigation. Many of his friends remembered that he had met Jess through the dating website plentyoffish.com – the same website where Johnny had met his own date.

—

DETECTIVES DIDN'T TAKE LONG to locate Scott Cooke, a set builder Twitchell had mentioned in one of his police statements. A big and tall man who sported a goatee and liked to shave his head, Scott was open to questions from officers. The details of Twitchell's filmmaking background slowly began to emerge.

Twitchell had sent out an email that August asking for help with a short horror film he planned to make while assembling funding for his next big project. The filmmaker's take on the genre was to adapt Dexter Morgan's method for his own purposes. Twitchell's version would feature a cop-turned-serial-killer whose own moral code would see him lure cheating husbands off dating websites with fake female profiles. When a married man arrives at his date's house, he is confronted by a man in a mask who knocks him out with a stun gun. The man wakes up duct-taped to a chair, his eyes covered in more tape, only to be tortured for his personal banking information and social-networking passwords before he is eventually killed.

In one of the first drafts of Twitchell's script, the victim is decapitated with a samurai sword. Twitchell had two swords on set. The higher quality blade was rarely touched by anybody but Twitchell. He became furious if anyone used it without his permission.

The script played off the theme of having the killer get away with a murder by making it appear as if the victim is still alive. Once he has his victim's personal information and passwords, the killer sends out emails from the victim's account, telling his friends and family that he's merely on an extended leave. "They'll just assume you ran off with one of your hussies and decided not to come back," the killer says in the script.

The man's real demise is far more gruesome. The killer dismembers the body, packs the chopped body parts into garbage bags, and then hauls them away in the trunk of his car.

But at the end of the film, there's a twist.

It's revealed that the entire plot of the film is being written by a writer at his computer. Yet, the writer also has a fake female profile on a dating website, which is visible on the screen for a brief moment before he packs away his laptop. Within the writer's bag is a hockey mask with the lower jaw section cut off and a stun gun. The implication is that the writer is about to re-enact elements of his script in real life. The film finishes with a rather ominous conversation between the writer and his wife.

"Off to the gym, honey?" his wife asks him in the script.

"You bet, gotta relieve some tension from sitting so long." He kisses her goodbye.

"How's the story coming along?"

"Really well, sweetie," he replies. "It's true when they say the best way to succeed is to write what you know."

TWITCHELL'S CAR HAD BEEN parked in a police warehouse for more than a day before the forensics team had time to examine it. In the late morning of Tuesday, October 21, the car was circled first with a video camera and then photographs were taken.

The car was a piece of junk. The Pontiac Grand Am's maroon paint was dull and caked with mud. A sticker on the car revealed that the four-door vehicle had been purchased from a place called John Keady's GM Superstore in Davenport, Iowa – a sale yard located more than a thirty-hour drive away in the American Midwest. There was no engine block heater in the car to help it start during bitter winters, another sign it was purchased outside of Edmonton.

The front bumper was cracked and splintered on one side, with deep gashes on the other. The rear bumper was crushed on the driver's side. Just below the spoiler, the taillight had been punctured. A piece of clear plastic tape covered a gaping hole.

A decal on the trunk prompted a few laughs. A Jesus fish was being mounted by another fish titled "Evolution." Dusting for prints revealed nothing of interest. But now that the forensics team had a signed warrant, issued by a judge just hours earlier, they could finally tear the car apart. This was typically a mundane task; it often took days to catalogue everything in a vehicle or other potential crime scenes, assign exhibit numbers, take photos of each item, sign the paperwork to maintain continuity, and write a detailed report. At times, this task could be as fruitless as it was monotonous.

But not this time. It was "the gold mine" for every detective on the file. As an exhibit handler, Constable Nancy Allen finally had her work cut out for her compared to what little she had to do in the search of Johnny's condo. Her discoveries within the car started off slow: a receipt for the movies, a duffle bag, an unpaid speeding ticket, a roll of black hockey tape, and a record of employment. Twitchell had a business card in the car that revealed his film company was called Xpress Entertainment, its motto "Independent Film At Its Finest." But then the search quickly descended into the bizarre and unbelievable.

With her red hair held back in a ponytail and wearing gloves, Allen spotted a key for a Mazda 3 left behind in a cup holder. Pressing the button on the key chain made a car horn beep on another vehicle in the impound lot – Johnny's red Mazda 3 parked nearby.

Allen found neon-yellow Post-It notes littered around the messy interior of Twitchell's vehicle. At one point, they must have been pasted on the dash. Some contained detailed maps. One sticky note included directions from St. Albert to the south side of Edmonton, noted later by detectives as a map leading straight to Johnny's condo building. Another series of maps scribbled on three sticky notes provided directions from St. Albert to an address in Wetaskiwin, a city about an hour south of Edmonton. Twitchell obviously had a short memory or a need to write everything down. The other stickies were reminders of all the things he had to do:

Ship phone while it's on (return addy of vic)
Destroy wallet contents
Use laptop general WiFi for email

And another note:

Ship eBay items
codpiece
helmet

Ending with the cops' favourites:

Kill room clean sweep
Fuck Traci senseless

Behind the driver's seat was a copy of *Dearly Devoted Dexter,* one of the *Dexter* novels by Jeff Lindsay. There was also a receipt for a hockey mask, purchased a few months ago from an online retailer.

In the front of the car was one of Allen's most startling discoveries. She lifted a backpack off the floor of the passenger seat and found that a military blade had been tucked inside. It was a weapon typically used only by combat marines. The rubber-handled, seven-inch carbon-steel blade was still wedged into a black leather holster that could attach to a belt. Red stains appeared to be caked on the handle. Working slowly, Allen grabbed a white marker and began circling each stain. She gently held the knife closer to her eyes, trying to handle it as little as possible. She squinted until the stains soaked into the rubber came into focus, then outlined these in white as well.

Her gloved hands pulled the blade out of its sheath, inch by inch. There were three or four red spots on the knife. From far away, it looked like rust, but a closer examination showed the stains were patterned in blotches close to where the blade meets the handle. Red stains were also soaked into embedded lettering printed into the steel, detailing the brand as a KA-BAR knife made in the United States.

Allen found a few more suspicious spots on the handle and the sheath. She then dabbed each spot on a plastic strip from a Hemastix bottle. They all turned dark from the chemical reaction, revealing a suspected bloodstain was behind each one.

A large red stain had soaked deep into the grey carpet lining of the trunk. A photograph was taken. It looked like the liquid had been transferred on to the carpet when an object was placed inside. The trunk also contained a half-empty plastic jerry can of gas. When the wheel well was popped open, Allen found a dirty steak knife tucked beside the spare tire. There were stains that looked like blood on both sides of the blade.

A second look at the duffle bag revealed it too had suspected bloodstains on the handle, along several zippers, and within the inside lining. She returned to the backpack that contained the military blade and discovered a Toshiba laptop covered with Spider-Man stickers. There appeared to be blood on the keyboard.

Allen delivered the laptop to Constable Michael Roszko, a computer forensic analyst in the police tech crimes unit. Given time, he could unlock the laptop like a treasure chest.

The car had held an unexpected haul of disturbing evidence. Two knives and a trunk covered in suspected blood, sticky notes about sex and cleaning up kill rooms, maps leading from near the suspect's house to the victim's – but none of this would compare to what Roszko would pull from the digital files of Twitchell's computer.

A FEW HOURS AFTER the car had been searched, Acting Detective Dale Johnson cruised south down the highway, a copy of the yellow Post-It note map leading the way. Another detective from homicide was riding along with him. Having grown up in St. Albert, Johnson was familiar with all of the streets in the area. Reading the map, he recognized the street names written down as leading from the address of Twitchell's St. Albert house to an unknown home south of Edmonton. After driving an hour in that direction, their car rumbled across railway tracks as the two detectives made it into the centre of the small city of Wetaskiwin. They were looking for the street address from the sticky note, not sure what they'd find at the end of their journey.

They finally reached a quiet street with a row of trailers on one side and located the address. Just as they were walking up to the front door of the trailer, a young woman in a car pulled in and parked in the back. Seeing them waiting on the doorstep, she hurried to a back door, walked through the trailer, and opened the front door. Two little dogs came racing up with her, barking and nipping at the feet of both detectives. Over the noise Johnson told her they were police officers and he asked for her name.

Stunned by the sudden presence of detectives on her steps, the woman meekly replied, "I'm Traci Higgins."

Johnson shot a look at his colleague, recalling one of the Post-It notes Twitchell had left in his car, thinking things were suddenly getting interesting.

"Do you know Mark Twitchell?" Johnson asked.

"Yes, I do . . . He was my boyfriend and we went to university together." She invited them in.

The three of them sat at a small wood table near Traci's kitchen, about halfway down the trailer. Traci had glasses, her brown hair with blond highlights touching the edges of her frames before her bangs fell down the sides of her face, curling to an end just under her chin. She seemed taken aback from having police officers in her home but listened carefully. The detectives told her they were investigating a missing persons case and Twitchell's name had come up. Johnson asked her broad questions before slowly moving into her history with Mark Twitchell and when she last saw him.

"Yeah, I've seen him. I've seen him recently." Traci began clarifying before they could even respond. "But it was all platonic. It was nothing sexual. He's married and I'm going through a divorce." She stopped for a second, then launched in again. "We're not *those* type of people."

Johnson pressed her on that point. "Can I ask why he would then write this?" He pulled out a copy of the sticky note from his binder and showed her what was written on it: *Fuck Traci senseless.*

"Oh." Her lips tightened as she huddled closer to the table. "Uh, I have no idea. Maybe that's just his weird sense of humour or something."

She remembered going to the movies with Twitchell, meeting him at a theatre in Edmonton one or two weeks ago. "But he's never been to my house," she added. "We've always met up in the city."

"Then why did he have a map from his house to your house?"

"Well, I had my address on Facebook for a while. He must've got it off there."

Johnson was skeptical but didn't pursue it. He was more worried about her safety. If she was telling the truth, then what were Twitchell's intentions with this woman? What did it mean to have her address, a map, and a plan written down to have his way with her? As they got up to leave, he asked Traci if she felt safe. He offered to notify the local police about the investigation so officers could be nearby if she felt she was in danger.

"No, no. That's not a problem," said Traci, trying to reassure them. "I'm fine."

The two detectives drove back to Edmonton, but before returning to headquarters, they took a detour to the South Edmonton Common movie theatres. After a few hours they found what they were looking for: security camera footage of Mark Twitchell and Traci Higgins. The time matched the movie stub receipt found in Twitchell's car. They had footage of Twitchell buying tickets to a film and leading Traci into the theatre. It was a matinee showing on Friday, October 10. The movie had ended around 5:15 p.m. – less than two hours before the time period when detectives believed Johnny had died in Twitchell's garage.

THE SURVEILLANCE TEAM HAD spent more than a day trying to find Twitchell – an eternity when a suspect is considered to be a potential threat to the community. He hadn't been spotted since he left police headquarters at dawn on Monday. The team had followed his wife to a Wal-Mart, watched his sister buy groceries, but saw nothing of the suspect.

Twitchell was gone.

By late evening on Tuesday, October 21, with Twitchell unaccounted for over the past thirty-nine hours, a worry began to fester within the investigation. Clark thought Twitchell could have gone to his parents' place. In the darkness, approaching 9:30 p.m., Clark decided to get the confirmation the team needed. He strolled up the sidewalk to a house in north Edmonton and knocked on the door. It was a single-storey modest home, overlooking a park.

A man whom Clark assumed to be Twitchell's father answered. The mood was bright until Clark told him who he was. That tended to sour any atmosphere of cheer.

"Is Mark here?" Clark asked. "I'd like to talk to him."

A woman came rushing up to the door to join them. Clark thought it was likely Twitchell's mother. "I know where he is, but I'm not telling you," she snapped.

Clark expected this reaction. He was the bad guy, going after their son. Any parent would behave the same way. "Listen, a couple things are happening here," he explained. "I am going to come back and arrest your son. It's just a matter of time. I believe he's involved up to his neck in this thing." Clark had four boys of his own, so he tried to engage them as parents. "But if this was *my* kid," he stressed, "I would sit him down and *talk* to him, find out what's going on . . . That would only make sense. You'll know as a parent if he's lying."

Clark saw Twitchell's father start to nod while his mother still looked suspicious.

"Well, he can't talk," she said. "He's been told by his lawyer that he can't talk."

"And doesn't that seem a little odd to you?" Clark figured by now that Twitchell was probably inside and maybe listening to their conversation from the staircase. Just in case he was there, Clark spoke loud enough to make sure he heard too. "He is a suspect in the disappearance and possible murder of a male. He was found in possession of the missing man's car. . . . But I'll give him a chance to turn himself in." He paused and tried again. "Will you tell me where he is?"

"I know where he is," his mother repeated. "But I'm not going to say."

Clark and Twitchell's father kept talking as his mother walked away. "Look, if he gets charged with this, you're the ones he's going to come to for the legal bill. So let me give you a piece of advice: I wouldn't be paying for no lawyer bill if I thought my son did something bad. If there's a grey area, *maybe* you would . . . I bet you this house is paid for?"

Twitchell's dad nodded. His mom walked back up to the door and began glaring at Clark.

"So they'll come to you because your son has no money. But he can get legal aid so you don't have to worry. But they're gonna try to get you to mortgage your house, and I'll tell ya, I wouldn't be standing here right now if I didn't think your son did this. I take my job seriously. When you have homicide detectives come knocking on your door, there's some serious –"

Twitchell's mother cut him off. "Enough talking to him," she said. She turned to Clark. "I want you to leave our house." She pointed behind him.

Clark got the message. "Okay, okay," he said, throwing his hands up in the air. "I'm gone."

SPELLING IT OUT

THE HOWL OF A late autumn breeze had ripped away the yellow leaf canopy from the city's trees, exposing the naked bark beneath like a network of veins. The grass was turning brown. The October sky faded to a light blue as the sun reached midday. Wednesday, October 22, was a suitable day to begin the search of Twitchell's residence. Police activity would draw far less attention during the afternoon, when neighbours had deserted their homes for work in the city, far away from this quaint St. Albert crescent. The last thing the detectives wanted was the media to start sniffing around the investigation.

Pulling up and parking, forensic team members Randy Topp, Nancy Allen, and Gary Short arrived at the Twitchell home to begin their usual routines of documenting and gathering evidence as the chilly air warmed with a rising sun. It had been two days since Jess had fled her home. The team would have been here earlier, but they were caught off guard by the scale of work in searching Twitchell's vehicle.

Topp opened the front door and slowly climbed the stairs. As the videographer for the team, he entered first to document the undisturbed state of the property before the rest of the team walked in and started moving things around. The home was quiet and the air inside had turned stale. The only sounds now were Topp's breathing and his soft footsteps as he wandered through the rooms with a video camera, barely uttering a word.

He passed a baby gate and a vacuum on the landing leading toward the living room. On the messy coffee table were an empty baby bottle, a diaper, and a few Cheerios piled in a mound on a tissue. A big flat-screen TV hung in the corner, hooked up to a PlayStation 2. The kitchen counters were littered with empty glass bottles. A half-eaten chocolate chip cookie had been left near a stack of dirty plates on the stove.

Topp moved deeper into the residence, descending the stairs to Twitchell's basement office. There was a second bedroom and bathroom down there. Twitchell's clothes were crumpled up near the bed. A shaving kit rested on the bathroom sink. In the furnace room, Topp found a medieval sword hidden behind paint cans and, later that day, a black samurai sword.

Twitchell's desk was cluttered with empty cans of energy drinks and juice bottles. A half-eaten bowl of noodles sat by the keyboard. Topp spotted an external hard drive and the tower for Twitchell's home computer. Both would have to be seized and examined. The computer monitor was still on, flickering under the harsh glow of fluorescent lights. Above the monitor he noted stacks of DVDs and an unusual possession: a single handcuff key. Among Twitchell's computer desk shelves were burned copies of all twelve episodes of the second season of *Dexter*.

His desk stretched out along the basement wall to an adjoining sewing table that was partially buried by a collection of fabrics, string, and costumes. A *Star Wars* alien mask with three eyes watched Topp from a corner. Next to a black "JEDI" baseball cap, he noticed a street hockey mask. It had been painted black with three stripes of gold shaped to form a vicious animal claw. Topp moved his video camera closer. The bottom of the mask had been cut away. Underneath the sewing table he found an air pistol handgun in a cardboard box.

As Topp circled each room, it became evident how two very different lives had come together in this marriage. All one had to do was examine the living room bookshelf. On the top shelf, Twitchell's love of fantasy had merged with the practical realities of Jess and the baby. Women's magazines, baby books, and a photo of Chloe seemed jarring beside *Power vs. Force,* a text that analyzed human behaviour, and *Troy: Shield of Thunder* by British fantasy writer David Gemmell. The shelf below was stacked high with hardcover editions: *Dexter in the Dark,* another Dexter Morgan serial killer novel, and *Sweetheart,* a novel by Chelsea Cain about an icy-eyed female serial killer. There were *Star Wars* books, an IKEA catalogue, books on what to expect as a new parent, and DVDs of violent movies and video games like *Kill Bill* and *Grand Theft Auto.* One of the lower shelves contained several travel guides, notably a 2007 Frommer's travel guide to Costa Rica. A stack of blank postcards from Costa Rica was found as well.

With Topp done filming, Allen and Short walked in for a detailed search and uncovered two more samurai swords tucked into the front entrance closet. Other items the team noted were a book titled *The Crime Scene: How Forensic Science Works* and a stash of DVDs and VHS tapes, many violent or horror-themed like *Fight Club* and *Predator.* There were a few home videos too.

Later on, when Allen examined the hockey mask they had found, she noticed two spots on the bridge of the nose that looked like bloodstains. She circled them with a white marker. A more detailed sweep of the home over the following hours also uncovered a pair of men's faded jeans with a single red spot just below the knee. The pockets on both sides were covered with what also looked like bloodstains. It appeared as if someone had been rubbing their hands on their thighs. Allen made a note of it.

Another odd discovery in the home, however, prompted a call for a special police expert. In the basement laundry room, the forensics team had found a strange stain in the interior bowl of the washer. It wasn't dark red in colour, which was of course expected if it was blood. Instead, the stain was more of a soft pink and stretched out in a long streak like a comet, circling the glossy white universe inside.

BACK AT HEADQUARTERS, CLARK began packing up his things scattered across his desk in a cascade of papers and trinkets. Clark liked to keep knickknacks under his computer monitor, whether it be a stuffed crab or a little kitten statue, which contrasted with police reports detailing brutal acts of violence.

It was half-past five on October 22. After a couple of long days and late-night interviews, Clark was getting ready to head home when one of the steel doors to homicide creaked open.

Anstey walked in with a huge grin. Behind him was Jeff Kerr, another detective on the Twitchell investigation. Clark took his eyes off his desk as the two of them approached. Anstey was beaming. "Bill, you won't believe what we've just found."

"What?" His ears perked up.

Kerr had a stack of paper in his hands. He lowered them briefly so Clark could read the top of the first page he was holding:

This story is based on true events. The names and events were altered slightly to protect the guilty.

    This is the story of my progression into becoming a serial killer. Like anyone just starting out in a new skill, I had a bit of trial and error in the beginning of my misadventures. Allow me to start from the beginning and I think you'll see what I mean.

Clark's jaw dropped.

Anstey couldn't contain his excitement anymore. "It's a diary of how he killed the guy!"

"Holy shit!" Clark smacked his head. "Gimme a copy! Come on! Come on!"

Kerr yanked the papers away from Clark. "No, no, no. Hang on, hang on here. This is the *original*. We've gotta be careful how many of these we make."

Eventually a few photocopies were made – on Clark's insistence – but only enough for all the major detectives. They wanted to keep this unexpected development very quiet.

The text had been pulled off the laptop found in Twitchell's car. Constable Michael Roszko in the tech crimes unit had found two temporary files buried in the hard drive and stitched them together. Both files had been made automatically in Microsoft Word by a user logged in to an account titled "Xpress Entertainment." One temporary file was likely created when the text was copied to the clipboard; the second was likely made during an auto-recovery backup. The original Word document, however, had been deleted. There were thirty-five pages of writing. The document appeared to have been saved as "SKConfessions.doc."

Clark huddled around his copy at his desk, reading as fast as he could.

    I don't remember the exact place and time it was that I decided to become a serial killer, but I remember the sensation that hit me when I committed to the decision. It was a rush of pure euphoria. I felt lighter, less stressed, if you will, at the freedom of the prospect. There was something about urgently exploring my dark side that greatly appealed to me and I'm such a methodical planner and thinker, the very challenge itself was enticing to behold.

"This is incredible!" Clark kept repeating as he read, at times covering his face in disbelief or clutching the back of his head. "Wow!"

The first page described the decision to begin killing as the "hand of fate," an idea taken from a fantasy book by David Gemmell. The second page detailed the method: targeting men through online dating websites. At first, the diary stated, the plan had been to lure cheating husbands, a way of "taking out the trash" – a line borrowed from the fictional Dexter Morgan, who justified his actions because he only killed bad people society already held in contempt. But the plan of targeting married men was too risky, the diary concluded, so it was changed to luring "middle-aged single men who lived alone." The writer reasoned it would be easier to get away with killing such men undetected. With no roommates or wives to worry about them, a victim could disappear for longer before people would notice. A fake female profile would do the trick: an attractive girl, using photos of a real woman's profile living in another city, but under a fake name and fake personal details. The girl would be flirty, toying with the man until he was so eager his guard would drop and he would fall for the trap.

The document revealed that a "kill room" had been chosen: a double-door detached garage with a dirt driveway in the south end of the city. All the killer had to do was remove the address sign from the back wall of the garage and give out strange directions so nobody would know the physical address. The diary detailed the killer's disguise: a black hockey mask, the forehead painted with gold streaks. It served the "double purpose of facial protection and identity shield to give the victim a false sense of security in thinking they would be let go." Then he picked out his "kill knife" from a military surplus store to help with the "nasty mayhem" about to transpire:

> The trap was set, and now it was time to bait the hook . . . My kill room was perfectly prepped. Plastic sheeting taped together and around my table; a large green cloth screwed into the drywall ceiling to shield view of it from my guest's line of sight, and to shield me too, of course. I now stood but a few feet way from the front door, which I had locked of course. The plan was to wait in the shadow of my curtain until he approached the door and shock him with the stun baton followed by a

sleeper hold that would sap away his consciousness so that I could tape him up and set him on my table.

Clark's eyes flared as he kept reading. He knew what was coming next: Johnny was going to show up at that garage and be killed by Mark Twitchell.

But that wasn't what happened.

Apparently, Johnny wasn't the first victim.

The document described another attack on October 3, the Friday *before* Johnny disappeared. During the earlier attempt, the attacker's stun baton had failed and the victim had fought back, reached for the man's gun, and somehow managed to escape.

Clark realized they had to find the surviving victim. And the Twitchell file had suddenly become something much bigger: a serial killer investigation. Thank God the detectives had the foresight to order twenty-four-hour surveillance, he thought. Now that the surveillance team had confirmed a positive sighting of Twitchell at his parents' house shortly after Clark's visit, he was at least being watched while they gathered more evidence.

AT THE OTHER END of the office, Johnson drew his own conclusions as he read the diary. About halfway through the text, he noted how the author began paying homage to a young woman:

> *Oh my sweet Laci. Just in case you are wondering, Laci is not my wife or my daughter. Laci is my ex-girlfriend. On paper she's the complete opposite of everything that should be my perfect match. She has two small dogs that she treats like children and those people usually drive me up the wall . . . But I love her uncontrollably and always will.*

The diary described his encounters with "Laci" at the movies while his wife, "Tess," was at home and caring for their baby, "Zoe." He later received a speeding ticket on the way to the woman's home for a late-night rendezvous. The diary then evolved into an erotic narrative with an entire page devoted to the extramarital affair.

Johnson thought it was pretty clear what was going on: Twitchell simply changed the names, but everything else was true. It meant Traci had been downplaying her contact with Twitchell. Perhaps she was embarrassed about having an affair with a married man. Little did she know, however, that the object of her affection was secretly writing about being a wannabe serial killer with a lust for blood and violence.

CLARK TOOK THE DIARY home with him that night, as did every other detective on the file. For the first time in his thirty-year career, he was overwhelmed with evidence in a homicide file. Reading the diary was an odyssey, a startling descent into the criminal persona, with the depths of human depravity presented to the reader in the form of entertainment. A detective usually never knew this level of detail about their suspects. Eyewitnesses were unreliable, even an admission from an accused was often embellished or twisted in some way. But what Clark and the team believed they had found this time was a virtual blow-by-blow account, an honest and full confession, relishing in every sordid detail. They had total insight into what the killer was likely thinking. Twitchell had written an extremely comprehensive account of how Johnny was killed. The descriptions were disgusting, some too graphic to repeat, words strung together about unspeakable and grotesque acts. Twitchell wrote at length about the difficulty in trying to hide Johnny's body. He had scoured the river valley for the perfect spot, but there were too many people around so he had to think of another plan.

Clark made it to the last section, hoping for a big conclusion.

> *Once again necessity is the mother of invention and my need to get rid of this evidence brought the solution to me like a child showing a parent their latest pencil crayon drawing.*
>
> *The sewer. Of course, how obvious. No one ever goes down there. The body would rot away completely before anyone ever discovered the bones and by then it would be way too late to identify the person.*

Clark flipped the page. "Where's the rest?" he asked out loud, pinching the paper, trying to see if a couple were stuck together. But there was nothing else. "Where's the body?" Either Twitchell had left out the ending or tech crimes had failed to locate it. "It doesn't say where the body is!"

—

ANSTEY'S INVESTIGATION RAMPED UP quickly. They had a potential serial killer on the loose, a surviving victim to find, and likely a body hidden in a sewer somewhere in the city. He was granted use of thirteen homicide detectives. Before he was finished, at least 112 officers would be involved in the case in some way, far more than any typical homicide investigation.

He littered his desk with sticky notes as he tried to cover off every angle. Anstey read the diary hundreds of times. He had no doubt that it was written by Twitchell and that it told the truth. It was found on his computer, under his company name, and the content matched details they already knew about his life. But with no body, it would be unheard-of to lay a murder charge. These were just words after all, and with no physical remains, a court could find there was reasonable doubt in the case. How could the police be sure Johnny wasn't still alive?

Anstey knew he would have to prove that the diary was a full and truthful confession to prevent the case from collapsing at trial. As he read the diary, he kept saying to himself, "Can I prove that this is true?" When he could, he marked a sentence down as a task to prove and assigned it to a detective to complete. By the end, 301 tasks would be assigned. Acting Detective Dale Johnson took on many of them.

Everyone saw how the various threads led back to the rented suburban garage. But the forensics team still hadn't gone inside because the officers were still busy processing evidence from Twitchell's home and vehicle.

It became a growing point of suspense. What could be in there? What secrets could be uncovered within the garage-turned-film-studio where Johnny Altinger had vanished and another man, identity unknown, had escaped with his life?

———————

IT WAS IN THE early evening of October 23 when police phone calls expressing concern for Johnny's well-being finally prompted comments to drift on to the Internet.

One of Johnny's old friends from Vancouver decided to post a message online about the strange disappearance. He signed in to Facebook and wrote on Johnny's personal profile page: "Edmonton police (homicide) are looking for John. He was last seen Oct. 10th."

Then something quite odd occurred. About an hour after the message was posted, Johnny logged into his Facebook account and did one simple task: he added a friend. And then, just like that, he logged right back out again. It was very odd indeed.

A PEEK INSIDE

CRUISING THE NORTH SIDE of the city along 137th Avenue, Clark talked shop with his new partner, Detective Paul Link. He had been brought in from the polygraph unit down the hall from homicide on Anstey's insistence. Someone had to do Twitchell's arrest interview when he was finally hauled in, and many cops considered Link to be one of the experts at interviewing murder suspects. There was some concern that Clark's interrogation tactics had alienated Twitchell. He was no longer the first pick for the job. It hadn't helped that whenever Clark retold the story of seizing Twitchell's car he added a handful more swear words and colourful insults. Anstey cringed at this, thinking he needed a cop whom Twitchell would trust, not despise, so they'd have a better chance of getting a confession. Link, who was tall with salt-and-pepper hair, could play the good cop role with ease or quickly switch into another mood if he felt the tactic useful. He knew how to deal with any kind of killer, but it also required a great deal of preparation before the planned confrontation.

Clark and Link spent hours at headquarters going over the evidence to bring the detective up to speed. On some nights, they'd cruise around Twitchell's parents' house, the radio traffic from the surveillance team buzzing through the speaker like background music.

It was during one of these northside drives when Link revealed he wasn't entirely convinced that Twitchell was guilty. "I'm fifty-fifty."

Clark was floored. "How can you be fifty-fifty with what we've got?"

"I'm trying to not get tunnel vision."

"Well, I don't have tunnel vision, but I'm ninety-ten," Clark said. His tone was more jesting than hostile. "Until we get the body we can't be one hundred, but come on!"

"I just wanna keep an open mind." Link didn't see how the man who killed Johnny and left behind all this evidence could be the same man who wrote the diary, which made the killer sound like a genius who could commit the perfect murder. In Link's mind, there was a disconnect. "It's too bizarre to even believe."

But the teasing continued for days. Whenever Link walked by a homicide detective, they'd ask for an update. "Still fifty-fifty, Paul?" And they'd share a quick laugh at Link's expense.

THE GARAGE WAS DREARY. Realtors would have called it a classic "worst property on the best street." Surrounding the garage was the neighbourhood of Greenview, a small subdivision crowning the north end of the suburb of Mill Woods in the city's southeast. Those that lived here liked to make the distinction. Mill Woods was working class and recovering from a spate of shootings and Molotov cocktail fights that had earned it unpleasant nicknames like "Kill Hood." But Greenview was nestled beside a golf course and attracted a slightly more pretentious middle class who liked their weekends quiet and their evenings predictable. The property in question sat on a crest of a small hill, elevated slightly above a neighbouring home to the west. The road in front of the garage curved past a park with short-cut grass, a baseball diamond, and an outdoor hockey rink, just waiting for the icy winds to blow. Beside the road, a walking path meandered through trees and grass, giving the neighbourhood the feel of a leafy English village.

The aging house on the corner lot, with the detached two-door garage and falling-down fence, certainly didn't match Greenview's desired image of comfort, quality, and wholesome values. Neighbours had complained about the property for years. The house tenants changed often and were frequently a problem. When the current tenants moved in and barely made a peep, the neighbours were relieved, thinking things in the neighbourhood had finally settled down. They didn't realize that the claim to the community's worst tenancy had merely been transferred from the house to the garage, which had been made all the more suspicious by the sudden presence of yellow police tape wrapping the back of the property like a plastic cocoon.

On Friday, October 24, the forensics team arrived in the late morning, expecting the worst considering what horrors the diary had disclosed.

Armed with a search warrant, they would be working out of the garage for at least four or five days, processing the scene. Everything of importance would be packed up and taken back to their office for a detailed examination.

Topp, Short, and Allen slipped on white coveralls, the disposable paper-plastic "bunny suits" worn by forensic teams. They snapped blue latex gloves over their fingers and peeked in the back doorway of the garage. They flicked on the light, using the key Twitchell had handed to detectives at the beginning of the week.

The garage was fairly empty. The floor swept and dry. The air was thick. Boxes were pushed to the side walls. After Topp had recorded his usual walk-through with his video camera, Allen began gathering exhibits. She started with a tall wood storage shelf, painted with several coatings of blue paint, standing just to the left of the back door. Allen worked her way down from the top shelf, where she found two rolls of duct tape beside an emerald-green plastic case, about the size of a briefcase. The case had a hard plastic handle and felt heavy, as if it contained many items, like a tool box. A single drop of what appeared to be blood had soaked into the textured green plastic. Allen put it aside to examine later.

She turned her attention to a pair of black handcuffs that had been stashed behind the duct tape. The key taken from Twitchell's home office desk was retrieved and inserted. It turned the lock.

The lower shelves were blanketed in a thin film of dust and sand. There were two bottles of red food colouring, a roll of garbage bags, and a blue case. Allen opened the case. A handgun shimmered in the light. Silver with a black grip. She picked it up and knew immediately that it was fake. The gun weighed half of what it should have. A sticker on the case identified it as a gas-powered BB gun.

Another storage shelf contained a plastic juice jug with a sticky red substance inside. A layer of red goo was gathered at the bottom and splattered around within it. Beside the jug was a strange find. The object had a black plastic handle and when a button was pressed a metal shaft extended into a baton. The end glowed blue. It appeared to be some kind of stun weapon.

The forensic team's focus shifted to the other side of the back garage door. Behind a little wooden table they found another shelving unit, containing a discarded television and a worn car tire.

On the first shelf, Allen discovered two long metal pipes. The end of one of the pipes was charred black, the soot gradually fading to a light grey at the opposite end. Allen reached for the second pipe. She quickly recognized the great importance of her find – it was a possible murder weapon. She wanted to handle it as little as possible. Nearly half of the pipe had been wrapped in black clothlike hockey tape that was stained a deep red. It was dry. Allen thought of a term to describe it and settled on "blood-soaked." The other end of the pipe was exposed, revealing a ring of bare metal threading. Each groove on each thread was filled with tiny pools of what she suspected to be blood. Inside the mouth of the pipe, resting just in from the tip, was a collection of plump shapes, no bigger than grains of rice. A laboratory later determined their exact nature: fragments of skin, fat, skeletal muscle, and bone.

The discoveries began piling up: a bottle of ammonia spotted in suspected blood; a jug of gasoline; sewing scissors spattered in blood; a metal table with its edges stained in blood; a steak knife in the dirt, possible blood on the handle; a bloody tooth fragment sitting on the concrete. The forensics team found blood on the wood table and the sticky substance from the jug plastered on a metal chair. There was an oil drum next to the metal table, to be examined later, and an extensive inventory of cleaning supplies:

> *Paper towels.*
> *Dust masks.*
> *Industrial-strength liquid cleaner.*
> *Three pairs of gloves.*
> *Full-body disposable coveralls.*
> *An empty package for a plastic drop cloth.*

The team noticed a plywood board resting near the garage door. When they turned it around they could see it was painted white on the reverse with big black letters: 5712 – 40 Ave. They grabbed the board and took it outside. It was held up high against the face of the garage, between the two garage doors. There were screw holes in the address board that seemed to line up with holes in the front of the garage. Short pulled out his camera and took a picture.

Before the team left, they scanned each interior wall. A closer look at the two large bay doors took several minutes, but it was worth it. What they found was something the forensics team could *not* examine. An expert would have to be called in, someone they could trust to take the time to analyze the discovery properly. The process could take days and it might involve complex math, physics, and dozens of photos – whatever was needed to make a judgment call on what this mysterious finding could possibly mean.

Two days later, Clark and Link pulled up to the garage. They had a meeting with the man brought in to assist the investigation, someone who could hopefully explain the unknowns the forensics team had discovered.

His name was Fons Chafe. He was a constable in the Edmonton police force, but his rank revealed little of his skills. He had been called as an expert witness in court cases more than forty times. He was gifted in what he did and had recently returned from Miami, where he had been training others in his unique specialty. What he knew so well, just like the fictitious Dexter Morgan, was blood-spatter analysis. It was his passion.

Like a teacher, Chafe gave Clark and Link a rundown of his conclusions. He had been studying the garage for days, focusing primarily on the two bay doors.

Clark saw that Chafe had drawn hundreds of little black circles all over the interior of the doors. Each circle had a tiny drop of suspected blood inside, like a bull's eye. By the time he was finished, Chafe had counted 222 possible blood impact stains on the inside of one of the doors. Most of them were located near the floor. He found that some were in the shape of a teardrop, others were round. The teardrop shapes sometimes pointed up, other times they faced down.

This meant nothing to most people, but to Chafe it was a clear road map. The shape of each drop allowed him to determine what direction it had been travelling when it splashed against the door. All he had to do was follow each drop's trajectory on an invisible string back to its source.

There was one hiccup. He noticed there was blood spatter outside the garage too, both on the garage door frame and sprayed across the concrete pad that stuck out into the elements. Another problem emerged. One particular stain had struck the door as if travelling upwards from the floor at a high angle, but when he traced its path he found it ran straight into the metal frame that held the garage door wheel tracks. It didn't make sense.

Chafe pulled the garage door open. He noticed that the door had to be raised about 80 centimetres, or 32 inches, for the spatter stains on the outside of the garage to match the ones inside. The one confusing stain could also be explained away when the door was raised. By doing so, the wheel movement exposed a hole in the frame, which matched the trajectory of the stain that had struck the door. It must have splashed in through the hole in the frame while the door was open.

Chafe ran calculations for several days before he began making conclusions. The blood-spatter pattern could be traced back to more than one originating impact site. He thought there were at least four, perhaps more. For such a pattern to occur, there had to be some event that caused blood to exit the body and multiple impacts to cause that blood to spray out and onto the bay door. That's as far as Chafe could take the math.

Clark and Link, however, were able to fit Chafe's physics into their investigative theory: Twitchell had likely swung the metal pipe at Johnny repeatedly, striking him at least four times. It explained the bloody pipe; it explained the blood spatter. Clark figured Twitchell had likely struck Johnny moments after he ducked his head under the opened garage door. Twitchell probably closed the door after the attack, not knowing or caring that some of his victim's blood had already sprayed outside.

———

IN THE WEEK SINCE becoming a suspect, Twitchell's life had descended into the meaningless. The surveillance team had been on him for days, and their notes made clear he was a man with nothing to do. Twitchell had been staying with his parents, in the house where he had grown up, but he tended not to stir before the early afternoon. Even then, he rarely left the house. Detectives were relieved that at least he wasn't hunting for more victims.

He took a bus and a train to his downtown lawyer's office one day, walked to a 7-Eleven on another, checked the mail. Once the search warrant on his house expired, Twitchell's parents drove him back to St. Albert to pick up some clothes and, later, to deposit a cheque before taking him back to their home.

On Tuesday, October 28, as the evening settled in after 7:00 p.m., Twitchell received his first visitor. His sister, Susan, had stopped by for the first time since he took up residence with their parents. She drove Twitchell to a coffee shop in the city's northwest.

Sitting inside the café, the siblings, separated by only a few years, talked for more than an hour. No one else joined them. They returned to their parents' place. For fifteen minutes, brother, sister, mother, and father sat talking in the living room until Susan rose to her feet, walked out of the house, and drove away. The home plunged into darkness about an hour later.

The surveillance team had been watching in silence from outside, having followed Twitchell all day and documenting his every move in their notes.

What Susan discussed with her brother was not known, nor was the conclusion the family reached. Had Clark been successful in convincing them to confront Twitchell? He wasn't sure. All that became clear with the passage of time was this evening visit and coffee shop conversation would be the last time Susan saw her brother before the police dragnet would finally close in.

THE SCIENCE OF WAITING

As the investigation stretched into its second week, Anstey sat at his desk and looked over the case notes, now spilling out of more than a dozen thick binders. There were more facts and evidence gathered for a single homicide file than most cops had seen in their entire careers. Despite this rare thrill, it was quickly pointed out they had nothing to celebrate. They still didn't have enough evidence to lay criminal charges.

Anstey had several conversations with the prosecutor's office as he was preparing for Twitchell's arrest. He was told the same concerns each time: "How do you know that it's Johnny's blood? What happens if it's not a DNA match or it comes up as someone else's blood? Then where are you at?" The prosecutor's office was right. Without DNA, the case became an elaborate trail of circumstantial evidence that led to nowhere. It didn't help matters either that Anstey's relationship with the head of homicide was worsening. Things with his boss had been tense for some time, but their disagreements were becoming more frequent.

So Anstey was forced to wait for the lab results before he could act. He had two types of tests on the go. One was from a stained carpet sample ripped from the trunk of Twitchell's car. That would be used to build a profile of the victim. Then Anstey needed a DNA profile to be built off the items taken from Johnny's apartment. If the two matched, he would have enough to lay a charge. He could complete the DNA testing on all the other exhibits later.

Crime lab scientists aren't normally too fussed over standard DNA sequencing, a routine and daily procedure these days, but detectives saw how this particular file had the lab unusually excited. The results had come back early after the lab worked through the weekend. But the detectives would be disappointed by what had happened.

The lab had created a profile for the blood in Twitchell's car, but for some unknown reason, the materials Allen had pulled out of Johnny's condo were insufficient to extract a DNA profile. They had only solved half the puzzle. Without the rest, the police remained powerless to lay a charge and Twitchell could continue living at his parents' house a free man.

ON MONDAY, OCTOBER 27, Constable Nancy Allen from the forensics team swung open the door to Johnny's condo, bringing along two people from the crime lab to help her. They weren't taking any chances this time.

The three scoured the place for everything Johnny might have touched to secure a DNA sample. Swabs were taken from a glass in the bathroom, nail clippers, and inside Johnny's razor; from a bottle on the floor of the living room, Johnny's keyboard, a straw in a cup, and three forks. Another swab was taken from a grapefruit juice container and a Mike's Hard Lemonade bottle on the kitchen island.

Allen hoped that would be sufficient.

They would need DNA from Johnny's relatives eventually. But for now, this would at least prove that the DNA for whomever had access to Johnny's condo, assumed to be Johnny himself, would match the DNA found in Twitchell's trunk.

———————

THE MEDIA HAD PICKED up on the case. The *St. Albert Gazette* broke the story. Twitchell's neighbours had found the police activity "unsettling" and "wished there was more information about what was taking place," the newspaper reported. Nobody knew why Twitchell's house had been seized. The local police, a detachment for the Royal Canadian Mounted Police, weren't saying a word.

Farther south in Edmonton, Johnny's name appeared in print for the first time. A routine police press release had been sent out suggesting there were concerns for his safety. A few of the local newspapers had published a small article on the missing man, but no one was pursuing the story further. At least, not yet.

But down at the garage, anxious neighbours were calling newsrooms. A police car had been parked in their alley for more than a week. Neighbours saw officers in white jumpsuits. But the officers at the scene refused to say what was happening.

Journalists told them not to worry. It was Mill Woods. It was probably a drug house or the cops were seizing some gang member's car. Typical police activity.

But the neighbours wouldn't let up. The oddest things were happening. Homicide detectives were dropping off flyers, looking for information on a movie filmed in the garage. "A couple, believed to be living in that neighbourhood, may have observed what appeared to be a struggle between two men inside or just outside that garage," the flyer stated.

The story gained some traction. But it would be days before the media finally realized that all three stories – the missing man, the activity around Twitchell's house, and the seized garage – were all one and the same.

———

IT WAS A BRILLIANT idea from the investigative team. Anstey was thrilled. A call was made to the hate crimes unit in late October to make it happen. There was an officer there who was skilled in using the Internet and in undercover work. Twitchell would have no idea what they were up to.

The officer had a little experiment to conduct, a way of testing human behaviour. All he had to do was sign up for plentyoffish.com and design a few fake female profiles of his own.

The first woman the officer created was looking for romance. She wanted a relationship, to find the right guy. The second woman was looking for sex and nothing more. The officer sat back, waited an hour, and then recorded the results. He would later state, as diplomatically as possible, that "the results were markedly different." No one had contacted the relationship-seeker, but the woman wanting casual sex had her profile viewed nearly four times more often and had received more than fifty instant message requests. "There were a number of repeats as well, guys that were repeatedly trying to get a hold of me," he said.

The experiment didn't say much for men, but it said a lot for the investigation: it proved another fact in Twitchell's diary was true. The document had stated the very same differences in responses based on the type of interaction the woman was seeking. The officer could cross that one off the list of 301 tasks from the diary to prove.

But this was just one of the two duties assigned to the officer by homicide during the Twitchell investigation. The other would require an elaborate plan. The cop would need to be cunning and determined. It was to be a covert operation, requiring him to get as deep into Twitchell's life as possible while remaining completely undetected.

———

THE SURVEILLANCE TEAM HAD been given orders to arrest Twitchell only if he tried to flee or commit a crime. Sometimes officers crawled into the yard at night to peer into a window to confirm he was still in the basement. But twenty-four-hour surveillance was expensive. The team had to include a half-dozen officers at any given time. After only a few days of steady monitoring, a decision was made to pull the night crew. Surveillance started leaving at 1:30 a.m. and returning at 5:30 a.m., giving Twitchell a four-hour window each night when no one was watching.

They could only hope he was staying put.

———

ANSTEY HAD BEEN WAITING for lab results for three days, trying to be patient, but he was frustrated. Detectives started each day rolling their eyes when told the lab results for the new items taken from Johnny's condo still weren't back. They would joke that lab techs from television crime shows like *CSI* could get DNA results in an hour. In real life, there were city cases that had been stalled on DNA analysis for weeks, sometimes months. Even with a case as high priority as Twitchell's, it would still take time. No one knew how long.

Anstey passed Clark in the hallway. "I've changed my mind," he said. He wanted Paul Link's role in the case changed. "If he doesn't believe this guy did it, then I can't have him interview him. You guys decide amongst yourselves how you wanna do it."

Clark talked it over with Link, and they figured they would work as a tag team when an arrest interview took place. Clark would bombard Twitchell with the facts and see how he responded. Then he would introduce Link as the biggest cop in town. He would be addressed as an "Inspector," the top dog in every criminal investigation. They thought Twitchell may think it was beneath him to talk to a detective; they would stroke his ego by making him think his actions had attracted the attention of the most senior officer in the city.

But the truth was, they didn't know the man at all. They had a lot of evidence, but they still didn't know what really made him tick. The guy was weird, some kind of *Star Wars* and horror film fanatic. He was a father, a businessman, and a wannabe serial killer? It didn't make any sense. What was his motive?

The police theory was that Mark Twitchell had decided he wanted to become a serial killer, documented that decision in writing, and embarked on that career by luring strangers to their deaths. No one knew why. It started with the shooting of a short film called *House of Cards,* about a killer who attacks cheating husbands for their infidelity. The movie plot was then replicated in real life, but with single men as the victims. According to the diary, Twitchell failed in his first attempt on Friday, October 3, and the man got away. But he must have learned from his mistakes when he lured Johnny Altinger to the garage exactly one week later on Friday, October 10. From the forensic evidence gathered at the garage, it was clear the film plot had been amended slightly – a stun gun baton replaced with a metal pipe. It all reeked of Dexter Morgan, the fictional serial killer: there was that metal table in the garage and Twitchell's own references to the character in his movie script and the discovered diary. Was he the inspiration for these acts?

They still hadn't found any evidence of a possible snuff film. Roszko in tech crimes was looking through all of Twitchell's computer gear. Already, he had found hard drives full of video footage from various movie projects. But even if there were some record of a real murder, it could be hidden anywhere within that footage and searching through it all could take weeks. Some of the cops thought that if a snuff film existed, it could be at Twitchell's parents' house. They would need a search warrant for that house too.

Anstey was stuck on the motive. He wondered what kind of market there might be for a snuff film. With Twitchell's background in sales, he figured money could be a driving force. A detective was assigned. To his surprise, they found a buyer for a real snuff film on the Internet. Anyone who could provide proof of a real murder on video would be paid a handsome sum: $1 million.

The case had other loose ends.

Anstey needed to find the first victim. He assumed he was a married man who was concerned that phoning the police would expose his cheating. Why else would he have failed to report the incident after being attacked by a man in a mask?

He also needed to confirm whether Johnny was alive or dead. The team still had not found any trace of his body. Johnny could still be alive somewhere. It was looking unlikely, but with no body, he couldn't rule it out.

How much could he trust what Twitchell had written to be the truth? Maybe he wrote about the sewer to throw them off the real location. Maybe there was no dump site at all. Without a body, it would be difficult to prosecute him for a planned and deliberate murder. He could argue Johnny simply ran away after a fight – instant reasonable doubt.

As Anstey kept working, another thought crept into the investigation: what if this was all just a hoax?

It was Friday, October 31, 2008. Halloween. In the sub-zero chill of early morning, a man left his house for a walk with his dog. They rounded a large park a few blocks north of where Twitchell was staying with his parents and cut across the moist grass. Under a grove of trees, the dog walker spotted a strange shadow. When he moved closer he realized it was a man lying down.

His dog pulled ahead and scampered up to the man. The dog licked his face.

But the man didn't move. The dog walker leaned down and tapped the man gently. No movement.

He touched his clammy hand.

The man was dead.

It was clear this person had died some time ago. The body was cold and stiff, likely dumped in the shelter of the trees during the night.

The police were called. Schoolchildren were rushed inside away from the horror. A forensics team arrived and took photographs. Police tape went up. Homicide detectives arrived at the scene.

They turned the man over. He was black, in his early twenties.

The body had surfaced less than ten blocks away from Mark Twitchell, the biggest suspect in town. But to the relief of many officers, it was quickly determined that there was no connection to their ongoing serial killer investigation. Pulling the night crew hadn't given Twitchell an opportunity to commit another crime.

The homicide office had been emptied with the discovery of the body, but most of the officers dedicated to the Twitchell file had stayed behind. Including Anstey.

He wasn't going anywhere. Anstey had been waiting on lab results for four days now.

He had been trying to concentrate on his work but was constantly distracted by anticipation of the phone call that never came.

Anstey felt like an expectant father.

It was frustrating.

He was willing that phone to ring.

With every call he jumped to pick up the receiver, and when he realized it wasn't the call he was waiting for, he got off as quickly as possible to free up the phone.

He just needed that one call.

Just one ring.

Whenever it came.

PART TWO

ORIGINS OF MADNESS

SUITING UP

OCTOBER 26, 2007: HALLOWEEN drew near and the moon was full. Ghouls and revellers, zombies and princes, men seeking cheap laughs with cheap costumes and the scantily clad – all had gathered along with Mark Twitchell in a long line descending the covered steps of Edmonton's Shaw Conference Centre, snaking into one of its vast halls. Rock music pounded. Concert lights burst in shards of purple and green. Alcohol flowed. Loud talk and laughter rose against the backdrop of pumpkins, skeletons, and cobwebs. It was the night of the Howler, the city's largest Halloween celebration. There was an energy in the air. The electricity of youth was channelled into dressing up, dancing, and losing control.

The party's annual costume competition was underway with a cash prize on offer. Thousands were in attendance as Twitchell awaited the announcement of the winner – and his own chance at becoming a star. It was a weekend he had dreamed about since moving back to Edmonton from the American Midwest. Now his fantasy of winning the contest was close to coming true.

At this moment, at the age of twenty-eight, Twitchell believed he had it all. He was enjoying his first year of marriage to a wonderful woman, Jess, who was at home and six months' pregnant with their first child. His film career was looking promising. He had wrapped up shooting *Secrets of the Rebellion,* a *Star Wars* fan film that had taken over his life for the past two summers. He was now finalizing a script called *Day Players,* a buddy comedy he hoped to produce with investor funding. He had steady work in sales to pay the bills too. The coming weeks would prove to be some of his happiest.

But it was all about to crumble. The next twelve months would see him embark on a journey leading from suburbia to bedlam, from expectant father and filmmaker to serial killer suspect. Until then, a year away from his destruction, he was still an unknown, a prospect on the cusp of a potential greatness he had worked so hard to achieve in film, in business, and, now, in costume design.

"Wow! Did you make it yourself?" a curious woman asked about Twitchell's costume.

"How long did it take?" another queried.

A girl brushed past and pinched his ass.

Twitchell enjoyed being the centre of attention. Eager admirers took pictures of him and his costume. And anyone walking past could see why: he stood nearly two feet taller than everyone else, his head high above the crowd like that of a proud warrior guarding the lobby of the main hall. His mask was hiding a beaming smile with every new inquiry.

His interest in costume-making had begun more than a decade earlier in classes with his aunt, who ran the fashion program at his high school. In his spare time during those teenaged years, Twitchell made a trench coat and designed his own Peter Pan costume. Later efforts included Spider-Man, Darth Vader, and Wolverine. But if he was going to get noticed this year, he knew his costume had to be spectacular. He decided on a *Transformers* theme since most attending the party would remember the recent summer movie release based on the series. He then settled on designing a costume of the character Bumblebee, the sporty yellow car that turns into a playful robot. If he pulled it off, he could win the Howler's coveted cash prize.

In preparation, Twitchell had bought thick sheets of Sintra, a brand of plastic foam board that can be boiled in hot water or heated with a hairdryer to bend in various ways. Over a period of two months, he cut through sheet after sheet of foam to shape the robot's gigantic body. He used a motorcycle helmet, parts from a Chevy dealership, props from his own *Star Wars* film, hockey gear. Everything was painted yellow and black. The costume required multiple fittings, adjustments, and the construction of large robot feet that amplified his height like stilts. "What kind of masochistic weirdo does this?" he asked himself as he toiled away. His pregnant wife could only shake her head as she watched her husband lock himself in the basement for hours at a time, fiddling with his creation. He was like a big kid when it came to Halloween. It was his Christmas. And after weeks of work, he was finally ready for his public debut.

His sister, Susan, stood beside him in the lobby as the crowd grew in size. More pictures were taken. She had played along with his theme and came dressed as "mini-Bumblebee." Her long brown hair held back with cute antennae, she was wearing a black-and-yellow-striped sweater, fairy wings, and holding three sunflowers. It looked like a last-minute costume, but it was in good fun and received a few chuckles from passers-by who noticed how she was playing off her only sibling's massive effort.

As the night rolled on, streams of partygoers circled and strolled around them. Twitchell didn't drink or dance. He chose instead to soak up the attention in the lobby, watching the party from the sidelines and away from drunkards who could destroy his costume. But even in the lobby, a few people brushed past and accidentally knocked off pieces of his foot or his fake metal parts. Susan became an impromptu assistant at times, using tape for makeshift repairs on her brother's outfit.

His friends soon arrived, squeezing through pockets in the crowd. One of the first was Rebecca, a business student whom Twitchell had met on plentyoffish.com. While it was primarily a dating site, she had not been looking for romance and viewed Twitchell as a big brother, nothing more. After several get-togethers, Rebecca thought he was a tad arrogant, a loud talker, and too much of a geek. But she also discovered they both knew Joss Hnatiuk, one of Twitchell's closest buddies, and the random connection made her uneasiness subside. They began hanging out as friends at the movies, car shows, and coffee shops.

Twitchell spotted another friend, Mike Young, bouncing along in his own robot costume. "Hey, what's going on there, robot buddy?" Mike shouted as he strolled past in his cardboard Bender outfit from the TV show *Futurama*. He was off to dance, "throwing the horns" with his fingers as he rocked out to the blaring music of the hall with a group of girls.

Rebecca dragged her girlfriends over and they too were stunned by Twitchell's costume. "What's it made out of?" She took a photo of him, and then the two of them posed for another one together. Rebecca noticed how Twitchell was loving the attention. "He liked feeling like a famous person," she later recalled.

But the huge party came with a whiff of anxiety for Twitchell. After several hours, he was still waiting for the winners of the costume competition to be announced. He began to doubt his efforts. Twitchell took off pieces of his *Transformers* gear, preparing to leave and give Rebecca a lift home, when the speakers pumped out the one word he had been waiting all evening to hear.

Bumblebee!

Giant TV screens broadcast a photograph of his yellow costume as an announcer screamed the name of the winner. The crowd erupted in cheers of appreciation. For a second, Twitchell did not believe it. As the big win slowly sunk in, his smile grew until his teeth finally bucked out like a horse.

He was elated.

The next evening, Twitchell was still bathing in the afterglow. He dragged Susan to West Edmonton Mall to repeat their Halloween experience and hopefully win another prize. He stood inside a massive nightclub, once again dressed as Bumblebee.

As the night reached its peak, Twitchell rose to the stage. A large audience before him was left to decide the costume winner with a screaming vote. The chanting swelled as he gazed at the sea of hands and faces. The howling and whistling mixed in a blur of tones. And it didn't take long for the announcer to proclaim the crowd's favourite.

It's Bumblebee!

The nightclub exploded in excitement.

Twitchell's face bloomed once again in a sublime grin. He had secured two wins in two days.

He was a hero.

Between the two Halloween parties, Twitchell had won a Harley-Davidson motorcycle and thousands of dollars in cash. He quickly sold off the bike and his costume, earning a total of $16,000 from a handmade effort that cost him a mere $300 to build.

He had won a small fortune. Adoration. New-found respect.

Finally, he felt like he was on top of the world.

———

Born in Edmonton on July 4, 1979, Twitchell had shown a passion for costume-making, performance, and fantasy from an early age, reaching its pinnacle when he was nearing thirty and still dressing up to win money.

Both of his parents were equally encouraging of his creative pursuits. His mother, Mary, was a career graphic artist; his father, Norman – or "The Normster," as Twitchell liked to call him – was a maintenance worker for one of the city's downtown office towers. Both grew up on Alberta farms outside of Edmonton, and Mary was one of twelve siblings. His parents met in their twenties and had now been married for more than three decades. And Twitchell viewed his childhood as a "textbook upbringing" with parents who did everything right and gave him a stable and positive home. They were the typical suburban family: mom, dad, two kids, and a dog.

His sister, Susan, had been a close friend for many years, though they fought as teenagers, as siblings usually do. Twitchell viewed his sister, four years his junior, as an "Amazon" woman. She was tall, always active in kick-boxing, skiing, or mountain climbing. Susan was a tomboy and probably had more muscle than him. And she was smart. Growing up, the family used to watch *Star Trek: The Next Generation* after dinner, which led to Twitchell calling her "Q" as a nod to one of the show's omnipotent, genius characters. It was no surprise to the family when she decided to pursue a career in engineering.

The family had always lived in the north end of the city. Their single-storey home had been built during the 1950s when the city expanded rapidly in all directions, creating a new grid of picket-fence neighbourhoods. Their small house sat near the outer edge of the Killarney suburb, 132nd Avenue separating it from a nearby Catholic school. It was a home Twitchell would return to as an adult, when the police were watching his every move.

Despite how ordinary the family seemed, Twitchell's childhood best friend remembered how Twitchell craved attention while getting noticed at school for all the wrong reasons.

Kirk Paetz met Twitchell in the fifth grade, when they were both ten years old. Back then, Twitchell was a socially awkward Catholic school-boy with reddish-brown hair, big glasses, and ears that stuck out. Before he underwent corrective surgery to flatten his big ears, Twitchell was often taunted for his nerdy appearance. One classmate recalled how he was even nicknamed "Twitch Hell." He tried to diffuse the teasing with his wits, but his various passions ensured negative attention: *Star Wars,* video games, comic books, science fiction, drawing and dressing up in homemade costumes. He was never part of the "in-crowd," never joined a school group or sports team. He was an outcast.

Twitchell appeared happiest when he was playing make-believe. He doodled in his notes, drew fantasy characters frequently. After class, he would rush home to hang out with Kirk, who had been transferred in junior high to another school. As teenagers, they would goof around with a video camera and make up stories.

It soon spawned the creation of *The Video,* Twitchell's first effort in writing and filmmaking. As a compilation of various skits and short film ideas, Twitchell used *The Video* to take established concepts or shows and change them slightly to make them his own. One summer video project concluded with a parody movie trailer for the comic book icon Judge Dredd. Twitchell tried to copy the character's signature helmet – which hid his entire face except for the chin and mouth – by using an old street hockey mask and cutting away the jaw. While Judge Dredd was a character from a dystopian future where he acted as the police, judge, jury, and executioner, Twitchell turned him into Judge Fred, from *The Flintstones,* and played it up for laughs. "I am the law!" Judge Fred shouted in the video. "Yabba-Dabba Do!"

As his family watched the trailer, Twitchell would giggle and his parents would burst into hysterical laughter. "From that point, a reaction from them or any audience was what drove the rest," Twitchell wrote years later in explaining his progression into filmmaking.

Later skits became more violent. A parody of *Wheel of Fortune* became *Wheel of Torture,* with contestants spinning the wheel to determine which painful scenario they would be subjected to next. Kirk liked making these videos. Twitchell, however, often treated these efforts far more seriously. Kirk thought his friend was becoming too attached to his hobbies, more than any normal person should, until they became all-encompassing ventures. If something interested Twitchell, he never seemed to go halfway with it; the new hobby would take control.

When Twitchell felt inspiration strike, it was like a rush of blood to the head, something he began calling his "Internal Creative Genius" (ICG). When it hit, he had to keep writing, filming, or drawing as his mind was flooded with new ideas. Twitchell began writing so frequently that his friends and classmates thought he was bordering on obsessive-compulsive. He wrote stories about a world like Earth but with little blue aliens. A girl who sat behind him in high school was handed an expansive two-hundred-page report he had written on the *Star Wars* universe. "He wanted me to read it. He wanted to get me interested in *Star Wars*," she recalled.

Twitchell also had a rebellious streak. He'd lie to get his way or tell tall tales Kirk knew couldn't possibly be true. Twitchell started stealing money from his mother's purse to buy junk food. He was arrested twice for shoplifting at grocery stores but dodged a criminal record through the court's alternative measures program for first-time offenders. "He was a storyteller and a liar. There's no doubt about that," said Kirk.

In his twenties, Twitchell began sympathizing with darker characters as his love of fantasy storylines continued. He was especially fascinated with Anakin Skywalker, whose progression into becoming Darth Vader is the major turning point of the *Star Wars* prequels. "It's so easy for someone on the outside looking in to judge why Anakin's choices were stupid, but it's different when you're the one in the position," he wrote on theforce.net, a website hosting the popular online messages boards used by the most dedicated *Star Wars* fans around the world. He penned long and plentiful posts about *Star Wars* through the years on the same website under multiple accounts. He watched each prequel film at least a half-dozen times while they were still in theatres. He was even moved to tears. When the message boards began discussing the pure evilness of Anakin, who, in one scene, slaughters innocent children in a fit of rage, Twitchell wrote: "I know, isn't it sweet? The pure calculated precision of it all. It's admirable how he manages to have the stomach for it. I wonder what was going through his mind?"

He assumed other identities online as his interest grew in communicating with others through the rapidly expanding Internet. On his favourite *Star Wars* websites, he became Grinning Fisto and Achilles of Edmonton, an allusion to one of his favourite mythological characters. For months, he also identified himself online as Psycho Jedi.

Twitchell enrolled in a diploma program in radio and television production at Edmonton's Northern Alberta Institute of Technology (NAIT). By this time, his reddish hair had darkened and he had ditched the glasses for contacts. He met a woman. Traci Higgins was a few years older than him, taking the same upgrading classes, and quickly became his first love. They had a raw attraction to each other, despite protests from friends that they were incompatible. The couple's romance was heated. But Traci slowly noticed that her new boyfriend told her lies. He had lied about his age and things that seemed pointless to lie about, like details about his family background. After a year together, she ended the relationship. Traci felt she couldn't be with someone if she couldn't trust him completely. He was heartbroken.

Kirk and Twitchell stayed close until their mid-twenties. The pair even lived together for a year during this time before they drifted apart. Twitchell was succeeding in sales jobs and liked to call himself "Logan" at work – a reference to Wolverine, the brooding comic book character and member of the X-Men whose alter ego is James "Logan" Howlett.

In 2001, as a recent college graduate, Twitchell met an American girl through an online chat room. He quickly married her and moved to the American Midwest. The couple lived in Iowa and Illinois. He hoped the move was an opportunity for him to gain an American work visa while getting out of the snowy city in which he had spent his entire life. But he ended up spending most of his time away logged on to the Internet. He started making fake online profiles, accounts for Satan, Jesus, and even a woman. His new wife would watch him pretend to be a girl online, chatting with random men, just to mess with their heads. He thought it was a laugh.

Four years flew by. Kirk barely stayed in touch with his old friend, even when he returned to Edmonton in 2005, a divorced man seeking a new relationship and a new start as a filmmaker. Twitchell was putting together a fan film, telling everyone that he decided to return to Edmonton because the *Star Wars* fan community was strong in the city and could help him complete the ambitious project. But Kirk had no interest in the film effort. He stopped hanging out with Twitchell altogether or even returning his calls. Kirk didn't attend Twitchell's wedding when, in 2007, he got married for the second time, his new wife, Jess, becoming pregnant within months of their nuptials. "We had totally different interests by then," Kirk explained. "Every time we got together, all he wanted to do was talk about *Star Wars*."

It was a slow end to a close friendship that had begun in childhood. Kirk still fondly remembered walking to his friend's house as a child and playing basketball with Twitchell at the community hoops across the street. It was during one of their regular get-togethers when Twitchell, then a teenager, had revealed a secret to Kirk, who at the time was his only real friend. "He told me he had a little hit list for people who he hated," Kirk recalled. "He was very descriptive about how he would do things to people who bullied him." For each of his enemies, Twitchell had imagined a unique way to end their life. "He had come up with some pretty good ideas on how to kill people," said Kirk. "He was going to get rid of a body in a trash compactor in the grocery store where he worked."

At the time, Kirk didn't think anything of it. He accepted that his friend was a bit weird and he knew teenagers talked tough and can be prone to bouts of rage.

It just seemed like another one of Twitchell's bizarre and comical fantasies. But his fantasies were far more elaborate and far more gruesome than Kirk could ever imagine.

MAGNUS

Johnny Altinger held a diamond ring in his hands. He twirled it between his fingers, pressing the metal into his skin. When he saw it for the first time, the stone had sparkled so brightly, the light reflecting into his silver-rimmed glasses. It had brought him such joy and filled him with promise. But now, many months later, he leaned back into his chair, eyes drifting to his computer screen. And with a heavy sigh, his fingers rested on his keyboard. "Silly me," he typed. "I jumped the gun some time ago and thought I was ready for marriage. Well . . . I am . . . just not to her. So here I am, single again and have no need for this ring."

The relationship had ended over the issue of children; his girlfriend had insisted on starting a family while Johnny thought otherwise. Now, in 2007, he knew it was finally time to face this final reminder of his failed relationship. He kept typing. The ring had been purchased with help from an oil royalty cheque given to every man, woman, and child living in Alberta, paid out from a budget surplus so big the provincial government didn't know what to do with it. Concluding his thoughts a moment later, Johnny published online what he had just written. Someone over the Internet could read this, take the burden of what the ring had meant to him long ago, and turn it into something more meaningful in their lives. The ring was now listed for sale.

It was like Johnny had come full circle.

Born on April 28, 1970, in an Edmonton hospital, Johnny had spent more than a decade away from the city before returning as a grown man. As a child, his only brother, Gary, had asked for a baby Johnny, so that was what his parents named him. His mother, Elfriede, thought he was "pure joy" as a child. Her second child had not been blessed with the best of looks, but that never mattered. She watched him grow into a caring, quiet, and trusting man. He was tall and thin. Johnny may have been bullied as a child, but he had a gentle soul. He cared little about what others thought of him.

"Everyone does as they will, in their own time, for their own reasons," he had written down as one of his favourite quotations.

When Johnny was a teenager, the family of four headed to the West Coast and settled in White Rock, a town just south of Vancouver and perched near Canada's border with the United States. The community was a convenient two-hour drive north of Seattle and one of the few spots along the Lower Mainland of British Columbia that tended to remain sunny year-round.

Johnny's father was of German heritage and had worked as an auto upholsterer. The family garage in their new coastal home was often crammed with tools and men tinkering under car hoods. Johnny was inspired by the family love of mechanics and quality European engineering. He even called his kitten "Diesel" because it purred so loudly. After high school, he owned at least a half-dozen vehicles – all German brands like Volkswagen, Audi, or Mercedes-Benz – but some were more than a decade old by the time Johnny placed his hands behind the wheel. Frequent problems plagued these purchases. One of his cars had a heater that would never turn off, blasting scorching air at his feet as he drove. "In summer, I'm gonna bake!" he used to exclaim. Despite the difficulties, Johnny adored his aging cars. He polished metal or rubbed in leather cleaner, making sure his vehicles always looked their best.

Johnny grew up within an emerging world of online communication. He had been raised with a keen interest in computers, often helping his brother with a word processor to write university term papers or playing games on his Commodore 64. But now, with technology rapidly expanding, he could finally connect with likeminded computer geeks without even leaving the house. His first modem, a clunky, archaic plastic dial-up, ran the phone line hot for hours at a time. Back in the 1980s, he became a daily contributor to virtual bulletin board systems where users could read or post messages on newsgroups. Writing back and forth with others, reading their posts on cars and music, Johnny made friends across the Vancouver area – the original social network. One bulletin board system he used frequently was called Shoreline. He played online fighting games and donned the nickname or handle "Magnus" in honour of his favourite *Transformers* character. It was a name he used online for years. Whenever he won a game, other players scattered across the region would have to shout out

"Hail mAgNUS!" They capitalized a few letters as a teasing parting shot at his supposed greatness.

His extended network of Vancouver friends proved to be pioneers of the Internet age. Many went on to become video game or software developers. And their personal lives were featured in newspaper articles as examples of "e-romances" that were sweeping through singledom as couples met through their computers and married in real life. No one had the foresight then to realize that the trend of online encounters would transform the dating scene and become a normal and accepted practice for millions, not just computer geeks.

When his father died, Johnny moved back into the family home to care for his devastated mother. His presence gave the new widow much comfort. But after three years in the house, the draw of returning to his birthplace of Edmonton soon became too great. In 1998, Johnny left a pharmacy warehouse job for a new life in the booming prairie capital. He drove inland with a few buddies, hoping to become a helicopter pilot. Through mutual friends, Johnny reconnected with an old elementary school classmate, Dale Smith. He even convinced Dale to buy a computer as the two drew close, often talking on a daily basis and playing paintball together.

Johnny soon complained of the financial cost of getting a helicopter licence and his dreams found a way to change. After taking courses at NAIT, he landed a steady job at Argus Machine. He toiled in quality control at the manufacturer, a career spent confirming that the steel pipes and connections being hauled out the door were of the correct dimensions. "Measure measure measure . . . and measure some more" is how he described his usual 4:00 p.m. to 2:00 a.m. shift.

He was now in his late thirties. He often shaved his head to hide the fact that he was balding. Johnny had two good friends at work, Willy Stanic and Hans-Wilhelm Adam, who heard all about his dating exploits, often occurring online through websites. His failed wedding engagement, however, was one detail he did not share widely among his workmates. Having met after the relationship ended, Hans never knew his friend had once been so close to marriage.

In selling the ring online, Johnny returned to the newsgroup bulletin board services he had grown up using. Staring at the posting now available across the Internet, Johnny knew he had reached an end – and a new beginning.

Of course, a relationship dissolves for more than one reason, but the issue of children, as he explained to a long-time friend, was central to the breakup and the return of the ring. He had made the decision long ago never to experience fatherhood.

Remaining childless, however, would have nothing to do with his own decisions. It would soon depend entirely on a complete stranger, a man who would enter his life swiftly and leave just as quickly, ripping every option from his grasp along the way.

UNINTENDED DISCOVERIES

As THE FIRST SNOWFALL was dusting sidewalks, a winter chill taking over as 2007 neared its end, Twitchell was told of an exciting, controversial new show on television. It was several weeks after he had won the Halloween costume prize. The novelty was fading, the money being spent, as his life returned slowly to the normal routine.

His friend Joss Hnatiuk had discovered the program. The web designer by trade recommended the show to Twitchell. "It's called *Dexter.* You *have* to watch it," Joss insisted. "I think you'll love it."

But he brushed off his friend's suggestion, having always been skeptical of recommendations and especially hard to impress when it came to TV shows. He looked up to Joss as a "big lovable dude" but privately found him to be far too "gullible." For one, he regarded Joss as religious. It was a passion Twitchell did not fully understand. His interests lay elsewhere. Twitchell had just uploaded a sample movie trailer to YouTube for *Day Players,* which he had produced to help sell the potential film project to investors. He was thinking of his future – his wife, Jess, a child on the way, the fact that he needed to secure funding for his comedy feature and complete post-production on his recently wrapped *Star Wars* fan film. He just wasn't interested in introducing another element into his busy life just yet.

Members of his film crew, however, had joined Joss in following *Dexter's* violent storylines. Joss kept praising the show, thinking weeks of prodding would eventually convince his pal to take in the program. Finally, there came a day when Joss shoved a pack of DVDs into Twitchell's hands. He had studiously copied all twelve episodes of the first season of *Dexter* on to the pack of discs and presented it to his friend as a gift. With a sigh, Twitchell finally agreed to give the show a look.

Back at a rented townhouse, where Jess was nearly bursting as her due date neared, Twitchell chose to watch *Dexter* for the first time in secret. He settled into his couch alone to give the show his undivided attention.

In silence, Twitchell watched every episode in only four days.

He was mesmerized.

Dexter focused on the bizarre double life of the fictitious Dexter Morgan. He was a blood-spatter analyst for the Miami police and a vigilante serial killer, going after criminals he deemed deserving of death. He had little empathy and would keep a blood slide of each victim as a souvenir. He liked to use a kill room, wrapping everything in plastic to contain all the evidence. All Dexter had to do was strap his victims to his table, perhaps torture them a bit, and then cut them into pieces, tossing their remains in garbage bags into the ocean. His knowledge of forensics, and his presence inside the police force, helped him continue killing largely undetected.

In one episode, Dexter stood in a comic book store shocked by the realization that his killings had become a motivation for storytelling. On the wall, a poster was tacked up for *The Dark Defender,* a graphic novel based on the unsolved killings in the region. The character had a hoodie pulled over his head. Most of his face was cast in darkness, except for his mouth and chin. He wore leather gloves and held an army-style blade. Dexter was intrigued that his own actions were inspiring others.

Twitchell was enthralled by the way *Dexter* presented a philosophical debate about justified murder. Sure Dexter was a monster, Twitchell thought, but he's "a self-aware one." He appreciated the fact that Dexter was still a charming and witty character, even though he was deeply flawed.

Episodes were watched closely and repeatedly. Twitchell then bought the *Dexter* series of novels, by Jeff Lindsay, which had inspired the TV series. He saw how Dexter Morgan in the books wore a silk mask to hide his identity from his victims.

He thought the show was better than the books. Twitchell admired the writing, thought the show gritty and not too flashy. He adored the cliffhangers. The main actor, Michael C. Hall, was impressive in the role. His Dexter was more believable and more dynamic. Twitchell wanted to see Dexter's pathology transform. He felt the books kept him too static as "always the same old sociopath." The books explained Dexter's "dark passenger" – his internalized desire to kill – as a near-supernatural force, while Twitchell liked how the show treated it more realistically as a psychological condition.

The discovery of *Dexter* complicated Twitchell's life. He suddenly had a new interest and he knew he had a tendency to dive deeply into his passions until they consumed him – as it did two years ago when his fan film dominated his schedule. Back then, in 2005, Twitchell had met Joss through the message boards on theforce.net. Twitchell had written a post asking for help with a fan film he was trying to create. He had written the script for *Star Wars: Secrets of the Rebellion* with a friend from the Midwest, and having moved back to Edmonton, he planned to shoot the feature-length film at his old college, NAIT, in front of a studio green screen. He was spending $60,000 of his own money to do it, hoping it would be a calling card for the industry. There was talk of top-notch costumes, computer-generated special effects, and plenty of lightsabers. It was a rare chance to get the *Star Wars* fan community in the region together, working on a single project. Joss read the post and loved the idea. He was in.

On the set of the fan film, Twitchell became good friends with Joss and others he had drawn in for the *Star Wars* experience: Mike Young, Jay Howatson, Scott Cooke. Some were associates from Twitchell's various sales jobs while others were from the sci-fi community. It wasn't long until the four of them became Twitchell's go-to film crew and his tiny circle of friends. David Puff, a local cinematographer and editor, was brought into the fold. Jason Fritz, an avid *Star Wars* fan and his roommate at the time, joined the cast to assist with fight scenes. Together, they would formulate ways of making Twitchell's large-scale concepts a reality. They also bonded over their shared sarcastic sense of humour and love of outlandish pop culture and fantasy. Some of them even carried lightsabers on their belts, breaking into pretend battles when the urge struck them. Growing up, they had been the fanboys on the fringe, finding acceptance not in the classroom but in online message boards. Twitchell had become a standout star among them. When his new friends gave him the nickname "Twitch," he was more than thrilled.

The *Star Wars* project was elaborate and took years to film. Over the summers of 2006 and 2007, actors and performers from across Canada and the United States flew to Edmonton to star in the movie, news of the project spreading among sci-fi fans through the Internet. Eventually, Jeremy Bulloch signed up too. The cast was amazed because he was a living icon from his role as bounty hunter Boba Fett in the original *Star Wars* trilogy. Twitchell had somehow convinced the actor to make a brief appearance in his fan film.

Twitchell's dreams were rising faster and higher than his crew could ever imagine. A confident man with a charm that drew others closer, Twitchell imagined his film career looked to be heading to Hollywood. His only demand was that he wanted to remain in control. His production company, Xpress Entertainment, would be behind his efforts and he would be the producer, the writer, the director – a triple talent. He felt he was born to deliver provocative content to the masses and considered himself to be "a young George Lucas." His crew was brought along just to build sets, hold lights, work as production assistants, and follow his lead.

As shooting wrapped in the late summer of 2007, Twitchell declared how significant an achievement it had been. "It's going to be a surreal experience bringing those long awaited incredible stories to the screen and I'm blown away that it gets to be me to bring it to the world," he wrote on his blog. "It feels like destiny."

He also wrote of being a believer in fate. So what destiny was there now, if any, in stumbling upon Dexter Morgan at this exact moment in his life? Twitchell needed a team of 3D graphic artists working for free to finish his masterpiece of *Star Wars* fandom. He needed to convince investors to give him thousands of dollars so he could film *Day Players*. And with 2008 approaching, he was mere weeks away from becoming a father. He would need to keep working in sales to support his growing family with a regular income. But now, there was *Dexter*. The show engaged him deeply and ran the very real risk of taking up all of his spare time.

He was confident his efforts would be worth it. Television networks had already come down to his *Star Wars* film set and interviewed him, boosting his crew's belief each time that he could become something big with all this media attention. "A lot of people take it very seriously and they decide to go all the way with it and make it screen accurate," Twitchell explained of his filmmaking philosophy to CBC television, the nation's public broadcaster.

At the end of shooting, he became even more upbeat and assertive as another TV news crew visited his production. "Word has gotten around that I'm making a one-hundred-million-dollar movie for sixty grand and some production and directing jobs have already come my way," he told the CTV network with a smile. "I'm going to be very busy. And everyone here who has shown their work ethic with me on this project? I'm taking them with me on a ride!"

With Dexter Morgan now in the picture, none of his friends realized just how foreboding his declaration would one day turn out to be.

———

AT THE END OF January 2008, Twitchell became a father. Together, he and Jess had been thinking of baby names before they were even married. They settled on Chloe when the child was born. Jess let her husband pick one of the baby's middle names, even after she learned his choice was taken from the expanded *Star Wars* universe. At least it was a name only hardcore fans would recognize: Jaina, the daughter of Han Solo and Princess Leia.

He celebrated the new arrival with a mass email. His happiness was clear in his prose. "She's remarkably easy going (just like her dad) and pretty much popped out already presentable with no conehead or misshapen body parts of any kind," Twitchell wrote with his usual humour. "Welcome to the world kiddo." He attached a photo of Chloe with Jess and another of his mother, Mary, giving a look of wonder only someone holding their first grandchild can give.

It was a joyous start to their new family for a couple who had been swept up in a speedy romance. In the beginning, having met on plentyoffish.com, Twitchell had actually forgotten about their first date and was heading to the movies when Jess called, wondering why he wasn't at the restaurant. After the shaky start, Twitchell became enamoured with her. Jess was a smart woman with a university degree who was three years older than him. He liked that. Yet, they appeared to be opposites. He was a big-picture thinker while she was detail-oriented; he was spontaneous and Jess was more of a planner; he saw how organized she could be while his life had always been more like organized chaos. She didn't share his intense passion for filmmaking, *Star Wars*, or fantasy. Jess cringed at the thought of violence. Despite these differences, they fell in love quickly. On a stroll through a park only months after meeting, Twitchell pulled out a ring and surprised her with a proposal. He had picked out a diamond with a platinum band worth around $7,000. He later joked that he had given Jess "a promotion" to fiancé. The couple was in the highest of spirits. She moved in to his rented townhouse while his roommate, Jason Fritz, moved out. Theirs was a small wedding, with his sister, Susan, serving as best man. Their honeymoon took them to Costa Rica. And Chloe was born just after their first anniversary.

Early on, he had faltered. His first love, Traci Higgins, had found her way back into his life through Facebook and they had later kissed. Just once. He knew it was a foolish and hurtful thing to do and he regretted it. Twitchell wanted to keep a pledge to never lie to his wife, so he quickly confessed. The couple worked hard to sail through their first rocky patch. The incident had been all the more devastating for Jess, however, because she had been a couple months' pregnant at the time, suffering through morning sickness, the infidelity catching her totally off guard.

Chloe was the grounding Twitchell needed to finally put an end to his impulsive lifestyle and erratic actions. He was supposed to be growing up and becoming a responsible father. But it wasn't working out the way he had hoped.

Twitchell was doing all the things that new fathers do, even expressing the same worries and concerns. But deep inside, his stomach was in knots. He wasn't actually experiencing any of the feelings for his child that he understood other new fathers felt. He was acting. He wrote about his struggle in his personal writings, wondering what to do. But publicly, he remained jovial. He had only offered possible hints through the years that he was different, hiding his emotions through humour or double meanings.

"Sometimes I just don't understand human behaviour," he once wrote online.

Quoting *Star Wars,* of course.

DREAMS

JOHNNY HAD BEEN SEARCHING for meaning. Becoming single again at his age tended to put one's life in perspective. He wanted to meet someone special, but his transition into the dating scene in his late thirties was also providing time to explore within.

He believed there was more to life than the day-to-day grind. He wanted to understand himself and others – not just who they were, but to look beyond and see deep inside, to become self-aware.

For hours each night, he searched online for answers to these big questions of the universe. He read New Age books and watched movies examining philosophy, spiritual enlightenment, and the world's religions.

He found achieving such enlightenment was proving difficult. He was no hippie. He had never listened to psychedelic music or smoked pot. He rarely drank. The extent of his alternative lifestyle included dabbling in herbal teas and spices to assist in meditation.

As his interest grew, he pushed himself a bit farther by importing South American herbs. Some had been used by Aboriginal groups to stimulate hallucinatory experiences. Grinding these herbs into a steeped tea, Johnny sat on his couch, sipping the mixture for a couple of hours. But he became frustrated. "I got a little drowsy, but that's about it," he wrote online of the experience. "Is there something I did wrong?"

His spiritual quest faltering, Johnny enlisted the help of a hypnotherapist. One day, he relaxed at her home office for a one-hour session, leaning back into her couch. She slowly lulled him into a deep trance. His breathing slowed. His muscles loosened. Shapes formed within the darkness under his eyelids. He saw a blurry image moving toward him. The shape slowly focused at it approached. It was an old man. He appeared serene and wise. Johnny's mind was flooded with peace.

His vision crystallized.

Johnny's eyes fluttered open. He turned to the hypnotherapist and asked her what he had experienced. She gave him a knowing look. He had been visited by his spirit guide, who appeared to be an ancient tribal medicine man. And his soul dated back over twelve thousand years.

He felt like he had just seen something profound and he couldn't wait to share.

NEW DIRECTIONS

THE HISTORIC HOTEL MACDONALD stood under Edmonton's downtown office towers like a little French castle, its copper roof rising to peaks out of limestone walls. Walking into one of the hotel's meeting rooms, Twitchell and Joss scanned a gathering of a dozen business executives. The pair of young men weren't used to such an ornate setting, but Twitchell didn't let it bother him. He met each person's gaze with a smile and soon launched into a polished speech that demonstrated both his salesmanship and passion.

In the previous weeks, in late April and early May of 2008, he had worked his way through a screening process for Venture Alberta, an umbrella group of angel investors keen on hearing about new business opportunities. Out of two hundred applications a year, about thirty to fifty were given the chance to pitch to the group. Barely a quarter of all entrepreneurs who entered the room would find someone at the table willing to hand over their money. These were professional investors. Many ran multi-million-dollar companies, had heard hundreds of pitches before, and were a notoriously hard audience to impress.

Twitchell and Joss had come prepared. Their friend Rebecca had tried to help since she was in business school, but Twitchell was convinced he could do it better on his own. Joss had spent a great deal of time designing a comprehensive website for Twitchell's production company and their fan film project. The public face of the business looked slick and professional, like they had been making movies for years.

As he spoke, Twitchell projected enthusiasm. In a way, it was no different than selling electronics or office supplies, as he had done thousands of times before. He flicked on a PowerPoint presentation explaining Xpress Entertainment and his new movie, *Day Players*. He smiled once more.

The proposed comedy followed two movie extras and their often silly and outrageous lives. It was a lot like the British sitcom *Extras,* starring

Ricky Gervais, but in Twitchell's script an undertone of sex and violence filtered through the narrative. There were subtle references to slit throats, duct tape, and being restrained to a chair. In an early scene, a woman complains about a man who had deceived her with a fake online dating profile. But most jokes in the film were corny and clichéd. One scene featured "screaming crazy athletic sex" waking up the neighbours. And a key gag involved an actor who fools someone into thinking he's a criminal by using props from a movie set.

The Hollywood filmmaker portrayed in Twitchell's script was also adept at magic, able to correctly guess a playing card chosen from the deck. The secret to the trick required him to influence people's choices through the art of suggestion. And Twitchell compared this ability to telling a story; both magicians and filmmakers rely on persuasion, slight of hand, and misdirection. "A convincing storyteller takes you on a journey and makes you feel like you're the one willing it along when, in reality, you're not," he wrote in the script.

Twitchell's investment pitch centred on securing plenty of cameos from Hollywood stars to guarantee a big box office draw. All he needed was some financing, he said, to get the exciting project rolling.

Twitchell paused. A big photograph of actor Alec Baldwin flashed up on the screen.

Investors rubbed their chins. Eyebrows were raised.

Each potential investor had been handed a two-page document:

> We produce independent feature films on low budgets with high production value and generate profit from their distribution. With an investment of $1,500,000 in the first round, we will start a production schedule of two projects per year for a five year run that will result in an overall return on investment of approximately ten times the original investment amount.

Twitchell was reassuring, explaining how his company used completion bonds, or an insurance policy, to protect investments if the movie project failed to be signed by a distributor. Getting investors signed, he said, also opened up access to six-figure government grants.

Attached to the fact sheet were revenue forecasts. Based on his research, he envisioned Xpress Entertainment would generate $26 million in revenue within twelve months. The following two years would see the figure balloon to $33.9 million annually.

Joss listened closely as Twitchell weaved his way through the difficult parts of the pitch. He came across like a seasoned performer. Articulate. Engaging. Charismatic. By the end of Twitchell's presentation, Joss saw a few investors pick up their pens and scribble their names down on the "gold sheet" for the company, showing they wanted to know more.

The pair walked out of the investor meeting feeling like they had won an award. Twitchell would repeat his performance two more times as he headed south to the cities of Red Deer and Calgary to make the same sales pitch. The experience invigorated him. He began pushing everyone he knew to invest in his film project. With such a positive response from professional investors, he believed he could get a deal locked up quickly.

And it couldn't have come at a better time.

Twitchell had just been fired from his latest job, where he was supposed to be selling outsourced IT systems to corporate clients. Instead, he spent most of his workday talking about *Dexter* and filmmaking. His work email account showed no messages sent to clients in nearly three months on the job. Twitchell resorted to taking on another sales job, selling home security systems, as he waited for his chance to transform himself from a wannabe big-shot filmmaker to the real deal.

Joss was the first to respond to his urgent financing requests. He saw Twitchell as a "glorious leader" who was guiding him and the rest of the film crew toward dream jobs and untold fortunes. Joss had been designing websites with his own company, Mandroid Inc., but now his friend was promising him a huge slice of the production services pie if the *Day Players* deal went through. Seeing Twitchell work a room simply confirmed what he already knew: his friend could be a star. Joss's parents handed over $30,000 in three installments. The next to fall into line was Twitchell's brother-in-law. He had money saved up from working in the oilfields. On May 23, 2008, he signed over $30,000, but only under the strict condition that his investment "be held in trust" for the film project.

With so much potential brewing, Twitchell began to believe that if he quit his job to focus on securing funding full-time, he could be producing a major film within weeks. The very thought of it was tantalizing.

Twitchell talked it over with his wife. While Jess was happy his film career appeared to be taking off, she didn't want him leaving his day job just yet. She urged him to keep a steady paycheque coming in until he had all the money for *Day Players* in the bank. They had a daughter to raise, after all.

But her pragmatism made him angry. Twitchell took her concerns as an ultimatum, an attack of his life's work by pitting his passions against their relationship. With more money in the bank than ever before, Twitchell simply couldn't wait any longer after dreaming of this chance for years. Twitchell decided it was finally time to take the plunge, to shed his old life and embrace the new. But he wanted it both ways too, so he found a way around the dilemma: he quit the job and kept it a secret. Having an open schedule would enable him to sign up the remaining investors he needed more quickly. Jess would never know.

The day he quit, his brother-in-law handed over his money and signed a film investment contract. Twitchell sat down in front of his computer and logged into the message boards on theforce.net. Under his Achilles of Edmonton account, he began typing a post with the subject line, "How to parlay fan films into a career." It was a chance to brag – and to say goodbye – to the *Star Wars* community that had embraced him for years. "Sweet zombie Jesus. I did it!" he wrote in elation. "I did my homework, made sure that all my ducks were in a row before hitting up the big boys and now we're there." He explained how this meant he was likely weeks away from being fully funded. "It's my first multi-million-dollar feature and we're looking very realistically at getting Alec Baldwin and Jeff Goldblum on board. . . . Without my fan project to prove my crew had what it takes to get the job done and do it right, this would not be happening right now."

It would be the last words he ever wrote on the *Star Wars* boards. A lifetime of fascination and three years of writing more than sixteen hundred messages on the fan forums came to an abrupt end.

He had a new life, a new career. A new Mark Twitchell had emerged.

"No one's going to stop me but me," he later mused.

FANTASIES AND DESIRES

AFTER WORK AND DURING his weekends, Johnny was often filled with anticipation. He had been going on dates again, looking for someone to spend his life with. He preferred the convenience of online dating and was relying on several sites. He gave his co-worker Willy, who was also single, updates on his lovelife. While Johnny didn't go on too many dates, the people he did meet were often impressive and lovely girls. Things were looking up.

Johnny had noticed a good-looking brunette on plentyoffish.com one day and sent her a message. Debra Teichroeb read his message and replied. The registered nurse found she had a few things in common with Johnny and agreed to meet him for a coffee. He introduced himself as "John," preferring to shorten his birth name these days, as the two talked in a restaurant. Debra thought they could be friends. Soon they were phoning each other regularly. She would sign into MSN Messenger and type him messages on the chat service as the weeks flew by.

But Johnny found very few women shared his deep interests in New Age philosophy. He believed in reincarnation and had become fascinated with out-of-body experiences. He was practising methods of separating the mind from the body through meditation. He once tried placing a metal pyramid above his bed, a practice meant to focus and heighten his energy. This behaviour appeared bizarre to those not accustomed to discussing such grand theories as the meaning of life and spiritual consciousness. He discovered a group listed on meetup.com, however, that understood his interest in the unknown.

On couches in the Students' Union Building, a tower near the western edge of the University of Alberta's main campus, Johnny met a half-dozen likeminded people taking the same spiritual path. Discussions revolved around concepts like chakras, intuition, and dream travelling. Across from him sat a man with long brown hair and glasses. Darcy Gehl had studied such ideas for most of his adult life and Johnny found him to be an inspiration. The two became fast friends and Johnny regarded him as his teacher.

Darcy found Johnny had already been studying many spiritual theories. He had a very open mind about the world around him. While he didn't adopt any particular religion as his own, Johnny did believe in a higher power. He just didn't know what to call it. Darcy thought his new friend was a bit reserved at times but confident in who he was. He appeared relaxed and easygoing. He loved music, especially the singer Elton John. When they went to a rock concert together, Darcy was impressed to see how Johnny could focus on just the lyrics or the ability of the guitar player. He knew how to appreciate life by just looking at it from a different perspective. The pair stopped going to the group meetings after a few months but continued talking to each other online and through their Facebook profiles.

Johnny invited Darcy over to his condo to show his friend his amassed collection on everything from secret societies to meditation. While he had been archiving what he had found online on his computer, he also wanted to share it. The student was becoming the teacher.

One of Johnny's most treasured possessions was a copy of the movie *What The Bleep Do We Know!?* The film examined connections between physics, neuroscience, and spirituality to explain the origins of the universe. A major concept was the waking reality, the lucid dream. It was something Johnny desperately wanted to achieve. The film relied upon an analogy from the work of author Lewis Carroll to explain this deep desire. Just like Alice in Wonderland, Johnny wanted to take a tumble down the rabbit hole and see what lay on the other side.

KEEPING PACE

DRESSED IN BUSINESS ATTIRE, Twitchell jumped in his Pontiac Grand Am and cruised the streets of the city. He had nowhere to go, but he had to leave the house each day to convince Jess that he still had a job. On most days he'd end up at a coffee shop, fiddling on his laptop, working the numbers on his cell phone like a real film producer. Other days he'd stop in at his parents' house while they were at work. He had his own set of keys. Lunches tended to revolve around fast food and greasy spoons. He'd break up the routine by turning to *Dexter,* either reading the books or watching more episodes. He was soaking up the series like a sponge. At the usual time, he'd then drive home, creaking open his townhouse door to greet Jess, pretending to be recovering from another hard day of appointments and meetings. He'd give Chloe a cuddle.

Getting more investors signed on the dotted line wasn't going as quickly as anticipated. By July, with little new business coming his way, he was getting impatient. After lunch one day, he stuck his WiFi card into his laptop and logged into his Facebook account, entering a new status update: "Mark is getting pretty tired of depending on unreliable people to get back to him." Over the following days, around the same time, he continued to post updates or crack odd jokes: "Mark is set to evil." It was a reference to one of *The Simpsons* Halloween specials. "Mark is always on." With no job, money was running out fast. He was forced to use around $1,800 from his business account to pay off debts. And now there was another financial worry on his plate.

Jess hated the townhouse. She wanted to move.

Their rental lay beside rail tracks. The freight trains would start up early, loud engines rumbling, sending clouds of dust and toxic fumes into the sky as it chugged across the city. With a new baby, it was time to buy a house, get a mortgage, and stop paying rent for a home Jess despised.

Twitchell feared their living situation would continue to deteriorate if they didn't move, placing greater strains on their marriage. Their fights were already escalating. Talk of leaving the marriage became regular ammunition as bickering rose above calm reasoning. Yet, he knew it would be impossible to get a mortgage without a job and Jess, who was on maternity leave, would be unable to secure a mortgage on her own. He couldn't exactly tell his wife the real reason why he couldn't be approved for financing either.

His lie would need more lies.

Twitchell drove to the mall and picked up a second cell phone, registering it under a fake name. When the mortgage broker called, he'd answer the phone, disguise his voice, and pretend to be Jim McDougal, HR manager, an imaginary boss who would confirm Twitchell's fake employment details.

Twitchell's chequing account became flooded with $15,000 from his Xpress Entertainment account – money meant for funding *Day Players*. Another $5,000 was transferred a few weeks later. Bank statements were then forged to hide where the down payment funds had originated. "It fooled everyone," Twitchell would later explain. "Presto, mortgage approval."

In her ignorance, Jess was pleased that her husband had delivered. It wasn't much, but it was a start: a little blue and brick bungalow, their first real home. It sat on a corner lot on the north end of St. Albert. They moved in August 1, 2008.

For Twitchell, finding and buying the house was a relief. He could now focus on securing a movie deal. The whole ordeal had been a huge unwanted distraction for him and he let the world know about it on Facebook: "Mark is finally free to move shit forward."

RANDY LENNON HAD DIPPED his hands into plenty of business deals, but seeing Mark Twitchell tell his story in front of a room of hardened invest- ors had perked his ears. He was skeptical that the filmmaker apparently had a major star attached to his project, but the kid had moxie, at least. The sheer confidence of the man encouraged Randy to meet him for lunch. He wanted to explore what Twitchell really had lined up for his big movie project, and he wanted to put him in touch with a friend in the film indus- try, who could advise the entire group of investors as to whether this deal was worth pursuing.

Meanwhile, another investor, John Pinsent, who had sat a few seats away from Randy during Twitchell's pitch, thought it could be an interesting opportunity too. Over the course of the summer, he maintained contact with Twitchell, but the financial details of the film project never seemed to be completely clear. He was waiting on a formal pitch from the filmmaker before he would make a decision.

JESS HAD KNOWN NOTHING about it for months, but then there he was: Dexter Morgan, the likable serial killer. Darkly and deviously, the character had captured her husband's attention, something she only became aware of as they unpacked and settled into their new home. Seeing the books and DVDs, she assumed *Dexter* was a new interest of her husband's. *Dexter* novels were placed on their bookshelf in the front room. Written in the first-person, each page revealed that Dexter's day-to-day interactions existed as elaborate lies:

> Being careful meant building a careful life, too. Compartmentalize. Socialize. Imitate life.
> All of which I had done, so very carefully. I was a near perfect hologram. Above suspicion, beyond reproach, and beneath contempt. A neat and polite monster, the boy next door.

Their marriage was still on shaky ground. Twitchell seemed distant. There was some kind of wall forming between them. He had set up an office in the basement. A spare mattress had been thrown on the carpet nearby. Jess was sleeping upstairs, near the baby.

Twitchell's fake employment routine continued on in the new house. Every weekday morning, he'd put on his work clothes, pretend to drive to the office, and then reappear at home eight or nine hours later. Jess had no idea what he was really doing.

As time opened up between investor meetings, Twitchell found himself drawn deeper into Dexter's world. He got his hands on the second season and, just like the first, watched every episode in under four days. By mid-August, he was sharing his love of the series with virtually every everyone he knew. An old acquaintance in America had been in contact with him about raising funds for *Day Players*. But he received an odd email that veered off into subjects totally unrelated to those efforts:

> *I've been catching up on the Showtime series* Dexter. *That is far and away, leaps and bounds the single best TV series I have ever seen. The writing, the pacing, the casting, the performances, all of it absolute solid gold. . . . It just sucks you in so well. It's one of the most inspiring pieces I've seen as an artist too. Engaging does not begin to describe it.*

Twitchell told the man that he had spent the weekend directing a local movie:

> *It's this intense action thriller short about a guy who's sleeping with his best-friend's wife and then brings him out to the woods to kill him during a hunting trip. It was fun as hell and I really felt that I contributed greatly to maximizing the strength of the dialogue and creating one hell of a tense situation.*

His acquaintance had no idea if the story was fact or fiction. He had never heard of the project before and never received more details. In truth, Twitchell was thinking a lot about broadening his range. *Secrets of the Rebellion* had stalled with non-existent post-production work; *Day Players* needed serious financing. He wanted to try his hand at writing and directing his own short film, something small to pass the time with his film crew while he waited on these two big projects. He had already tried his hand at science fiction and comedy. And he was curious about a genre he had been exploring lately: the psychological thriller.

It was a deepening thought.

But he was running out of cash. His business account had dropped to under $7,000. Nearly all of the investment money from Joss and his brother-in-law was gone. If he was going to make a short film, it would have to be on the cheap.

The next two days became a blur as he thought more about the potential short horror film. Cruising in his maroon car, Twitchell found himself drifting between St. Albert and Edmonton, stopping in at coffee shops and convenience stores along the way. When he finally came home at night, he found himself restless. A heat wave was beginning. The August sun burned hot for the next four days, a late-summer fever trapped under the canopy of lush elm trees and blankets of clouds. Chloe was put to bed and Jess tried to sleep. But Twitchell stayed up late as twilight turned to black.

The silence of the suburban home was broken only by the light tapping of his fingers on the keyboard. He was on the Internet again. He had written something that was sure to provoke a response. But when his friends read his comment in the coming days, they kept their questions to themselves. Some thought it a very odd joke to make. Others did not know what he was referring to.

Just after two in the morning, Twitchell had updated his status on Facebook. It was one sentence that would take on a far more sinister meaning as the months rolled by. He had written: "Mark has way too much in common with Dexter Morgan."

SEARCHING

JOHNNY'S SCHEDULE FILLED QUICKLY, his weekends spent playing paintball with his close friend Dale, and many evenings busy with work, yet through the summer of 2008 romance never veered too far from his mind. He drove to a coffee shop to meet Debra, their friendship having grown closer these past few months. Pulling up a chair, he sat and stared across the table at her, sharing how he really wanted to find someone. In fact, he confessed, he was falling for her. "Would you give it a shot?" he asked with a smile.

Debra met his gaze. There was a lot to like about Johnny. He had interests that crossed the spectrum, whether motorbikes or camping, sitcoms or spiritualism. She thought he was a great person and she knew he had a big heart. But she had to be honest too. She felt no romantic chemistry between them. She wanted only to be friends.

But Johnny didn't seem to get it and just kept asking, "Why won't you just give it a try?"

Debra realized their discussion was going to end badly. She told him she didn't think it would be appropriate for them to keep hanging out all the time if he had these intense feelings for her. "It would be too unhealthy for the friendship," she said.

It wasn't what Johnny had wanted to hear. They departed knowing they would be taking a break for a time, hopefully for the betterment of their friendship.

But as the summer continued, Debra had trouble keeping Johnny out of her life. Returning home from her long shifts as a nurse, she checked her home phone's voicemail and often heard a familiar voice on the other end. "Can't we just talk about this?" Johnny pleaded. She shook her head and rubbed her temples, knowing it was for the best if she just ignored these messages and made a determined effort never to respond.

CONSTRUCTION AND DESIGN

PLANNING AND PLOTTING, TWITCHELL'S mind raced as he sped through the city. He had to stay organized as he checked off his list. He needed a practical effects artist to pull off his idea for a short film and had no clue where to look. But at least he had secured a location for the film shoot. The property was renting for $175 a month. It wasn't much, but when he saw it, he knew it was all he needed: a double-door garage surrounded by high fences and detached from the home. He liked how quiet it was, despite being in the middle of a suburb. The current renters of the house were from Mexico and spoke little English, which suited him fine. Twitchell knew they'd leave him alone. He signed the lease that morning.

Now sitting in front of his computer, pretending to be at work for another day, he read over an email he had written. He clicked through his address book, adding the names of his film crew – Mike, Jay, Scott, Joss, David – and a possible backup for camera duties. A woman who did makeup was included. He hit send:

> *What up bitches,*
> *. . . I have a month to kill so I decided we should produce a short thriller. This one is about a serial killer who gets his kicks from taking out people who think they're getting away with something. The shoot dates are Friday, Sept. 26th and Saturday, Sept. 27th. . . . The actual main portion of the short will be shot in a garage I have rented at 5712 40th Ave which has power but no heat so if the weather is being nice, great, if it's a bitch, we'll bring space heaters.*
> *Look forward to having some fun.*
> *Mark Twitchell*
> *Xpress Entertainment*

He was searching for an actor who could deliver the killer's cold and intimidating tone without being too "corny" and overdoing it. The film's victim, Roger, was meant to be a working man "who considers himself quite smooth at hiding things from his wife but loses all bravado when he's tied to a chair in a dark room."

His email to the crew included a description of his desired special effects:

> I need a severed ear. And there's one shot I'd like to get of the victim's decapitation. The more realistic the better. . . . It's a darkly lit scene so minor detail is not as important as overall weight and trajectory of the head falling from the body and the believability of the blood spurting afterward. The shot I have in mind is practically a silhouette of the victim.

He told his crew not to worry about props. He had already bought a few the previous day, some contained in a green plastic briefcase. Twitchell wanted a stun gun for the shoot but discovered they were only legal for purchase in some American states.

His crew proved eager to help. Mike, Jay, and Scott all replied within four hours. Having formed a business partnership after the *Star Wars* fan film, the trio thought it would be a good chance to show off their new company, Apocalypse Arts, and their set-building abilities.

But Twitchell didn't need their input. He already knew exactly what he wanted.

He asked for a large rectangular table, longer than a grown man, and turned to Scott to build it. "It needs to be sturdy, strong as fuck," he wrote the trio in another email. "This is not to be built for temporary use. . . . This has to be precision quality." Twitchell wanted a thick wood top and six big table legs, all cross-braced. "The table must be surfaced and edged in stainless steel."

Next, he demanded a custom-made chair. "Not just any chair though," he explained. It had to be metal. Twitchell had drawn sketches of what he wanted and sent them on to some of the crew. Mike would help in this building effort. One of Twitchell's drawings showed the "killer chair" and the "victim chair," looking like it had been bolted to a concrete floor. "I'll gladly pay for all materials used for this, as long as you shop wisely," Twitchell wrote, finishing his email on a joke. "And then the hookers and beer on top of it."

The film crew did as they were told. Mike and Jay would help build the set pieces, but couldn't be there for the filming. Scott would be there for both, however.

Mike picked up a set of keys and drove to the newly rented garage to begin working. One of the first things he did was pick up a padlock. Twitchell had insisted that one be attached to the back door as soon as possible.

———————

On Friday, August 29, Twitchell had taken until mid-afternoon to reach the U.S. border, a seven-hour drive straight south that ended at the mouth of a security checkpoint. Sitting in his car, Twitchell had been caught in a lie and refused entry. He wasn't sure why he did that. Sometimes he lied for no reason at all.

He had planned on driving to Montana to buy props and supplies for his new movie project but had told Jess he had scored work on a music video shoot over the Labour Day long weekend. Keeping the ruse going, he had told the customs officer the same story. The officer then asked Twitchell if he had the required U.S. work visa for such a project. He did not.

The mission failed, Twitchell pointed his Grand Am back north and hit the gas. By the time he reached Calgary a few hours later, he was tired and pulled in to a hotel. He needed a break from his life for a few days.

In his hotel room, just after 9:00 p.m., Twitchell flipped open his computer and surfed the web for solutions to his movie problems. After a few clicks, he found an option. A seller was offering to ship one of his desired props to Canada. He thought it would be perfect for a horror movie. Listed as a "Telescopic Stun Gun Baton," the weapon could collapse into a black handle and even came with its own holster. "Just the sound of this unit should stop most people," the seller boasted on the online advertisement. "It is loud, sparks bright and is very intimidating. If that doesn't stop them, the 800,000 volts will." Twitchell pulled out his credit card. Minutes later, he was back on Facebook and asking for help: "Mark needs a headless mannequin to complete the effect. Anyone know where I can borrow/rent one?"

His secret weekend in Calgary included many online purchases: a meat cleaver, a pair of handcuffs, software to prevent tracking of his Internet activity through his web address. But alone in his hotel room he found his mind drifting from movie plots to personal plights. He was thinking of his failing marriage; he was thinking of other women. His thoughts returned to his first love, Traci, who was never far from his heart. Twitchell flipped through another type of listing, one more discreet than those for knives and stun guns. It was something exotic, an unrushed service that attended his needs: the city escort or courtesan.

———————

INVESTOR JOHN PINSENT, A chartered accountant by trade, thumbed the dozen pages in a business proposal Twitchell had finally sent over to his office. The sales pitch had changed considerably over the past six months. There was a Hollywood veteran attached to the project, who was identified as a co-producer behind the blockbusters *Old School* and *Ocean's Eleven*. Twitchell had lined up big stars like cult movie director Kevin Smith, musician Justin Timberlake, and actors Jeff Goldblum and Alec Baldwin:

> *We have been in contact with the representation of each of these performers and the feedback has been the same in each case. They like the script, they love our offers, they appreciate the logistics and none of them can foresee anything getting in the way of getting them signed on to play supporting roles or themselves.*

Twitchell stated he had gathered $500,000 in escrow and signed a $1 million production services contract with a company called Mandroid Inc. The remaining financing terms were now all cleared up. The filmmaker was asking John for a temporary loan. If Twitchell could get investors like him to buy ten units at $35,000 each, he could unlock a line of credit with a gap financier to cover the rest of the movie's budget. Once that happened, each investor would get their money back, plus a slice of profits, estimated at $170,000 for each unit purchase. The initial investment would be held in trust for a few months. "With the production values, level of talent and low cost of our budget that we have," Twitchell wrote, "the movie would have to bomb beyond all comprehension to present any real risk."

———————

LEANING INTO HIS DESK and staring at the computer screen, Twitchell talked into his phone in his home basement office. He had been back from his solo trip to Calgary for a few weeks and was once again busy searching the Internet.

Jess came in from the backyard and headed for the stairs. As she turned the corner in the basement, she spotted her husband at the computer. He didn't see her as he blabbed into his phone. She glanced at the screen around the back of his head and, seeing what he was looking at, she suddenly felt sick. "Get off the fucking phone!" she exploded.

Twitchell jolted back in his chair and whipped around to meet her gaze.

"What *are* you doing!?" she screamed.

The computer monitor displayed a page from ashleymadison.com, a dating site tailored for extramarital affairs.

He flicked off his phone and gave her a quick answer. "I'm doing research for a freelance article about Internet dating." He sounded calm. "I got the job by convincing the editor that I would sign up on some of the sites undercover to get first-hand material."

Jess scowled. "What publication?"

"It's an online company."

"I don't believe you."

"I can prove it. My editor is going to be calling to discuss the article and my payment."

Jess stared at him.

"You can listen in on the conference call if you'd like," he added.

Raising a doubting eyebrow, Jess put her hand on her hip. "What's his name?"

"Phil Porter."

Two days later, sitting in the upstairs living room, Twitchell talked on the phone as Jess listened in. Her husband was discussing an article with a man whose voice she didn't recognize, a man who identified himself as Phil Porter from an online magazine. Twitchell hung up after a few minutes.

"It still doesn't make any sense to me," Jess sighed, shaking her head. "I don't believe it."

Twitchell didn't know what else to do. He shrugged. "The only other thing I can think of is when the money comes in, you'll know they are using the article."

It wasn't enough for Jess. She was terribly confused. He had never written a piece of journalism before. And thinking back to the distance growing between them, she feared her husband was having an affair. He eventually handed over his passwords to his email account to ease her suspicions, but they both knew where their relationship was heading. With trust between them rapidly deteriorating, they would likely need marriage counselling. Jess was wondering if her husband needed his own personal therapy as well.

Sulking around the house, Twitchell told Jess about his little horror movie he was making. She was immediately worried about the cost, but he assured her it would be of no concern. In fact, a draft of the script was complete and he explained how it had been an outlet for him during their recent problems. He had been inspired by their marital difficulties and mixed it into his interest in psychological thrillers. It was only a few pages long but he had come up with a title: *House of Cards*.

His proposed ending for the short film, however, had Jess horrified. The thought of a man being decapitated was revolting to her. She demanded he change it. Twitchell resisted, having planned that specific ending for weeks. But Jess persisted and in a huff Twitchell eventually assured her that he would think of something else.

AMUSEMENT

STANDING IN HIS CONDO in a black T-shirt, Johnny showed off his huge flat-screen television and custom-built computer to his house guest, Marie Laugesen. He was nearly as pleased with his integrated home entertainment system as he was with having Marie finally visit.

She had called recently to say she was catching a ride from Vancouver to Edmonton for a late-August weekend and the time together could help repair their strained friendship. They had known each other for more than a decade, from their time on Vancouver's online bulletin boards, but had later fought and stopped talking. Johnny had finally called to say sorry. While she accepted his apology, Marie was going to make him grovel a little.

Johnny was a gentleman and gave her his bed while he pulled out a mattress on the living room floor. She was in town for only a day, so he asked her what she wanted to do. Everyone had told her it was a lame idea, but Marie confessed in excitement to wanting to experience one of the city's only attractions: West Edmonton Mall.

The pair jumped in Johnny's red Mazda 3, a departure from his usual beloved German cars, but one he was willing to make as his age tipped closer to the big four-o. Marie started taking pictures as they pulled into the mall's giant parking lot. Johnny couldn't stop snickering as Marie snapped away.

The mall offered new discoveries for Marie along every vast corridor of marble and brass, mirrors and skylights scattering the daylight. They strolled past fountains, a lagoon once home to a fleet of submarines and an indoor water park, simulated waves rolling across a fake tropical beach. The pair stopped at the ice palace, watching skaters twirl on the rink surface. Stores were stacked in long rows around these amusements.

During her trip, a lull in conversation prompted Johnny to make a confession to Marie. "You've inspired me, you know?"

"What?" she asked, puzzled. "How?"

"Because you chose never to have children."

"I shouldn't be an inspiration for that." Marie tilted her head. "It's from within that you make this decision."

Johnny nodded. He told her about his journey of self-discovery by studying New Age philosophy. "It's made me a happier person."

The pair soon found their way wandering under the vivid colours and flashing lights of Galaxyland, the mall's indoor park of roller coasters and fairgrounds. The main entrance opened to reveal a spinning carousel, children bumping along on hard plastic horses. From the purple flooring they saw a giant swing lit up with red twinkling lights. A funhouse and haunted castle loomed in the corner. They toured the grounds of painted-blue space rocks as nervous screams echoed from visitors thundering by on noisy rides overhead. Ahead lay a winding bed of red and yellow tracks. Marie's gaze was lifted high as she saw the rails twirl into a triple-loop across the sky. The ride was aptly titled The Mindbender.

"Let's go on it!" she smiled, tugging on Johnny's arm. The pair climbed into one of the three cars, holding a total of a dozen souls aboard a steady climb to the top.

They clasped the safety harnesses around their shoulders as the track clicked higher and higher. Upon reaching the summit, the cars seemed to hover for a brief moment before suddenly plunging in a freefall and banking hard to the left. Racing at an incredible speed, the cars tore back up the track before plunging again and curving upwards, rolling upside-down as riders screamed through the ride's triple loops.

The entire ride lasted about a minute but was forever burned into their memories. Screaming and hollering, stomachs in their chests, Johnny and Marie climbed out of the car and decided quite quickly: they would ride the roller coaster once again.

Marie left Edmonton the next morning knowing the trip had been worthwhile. Driving back to Vancouver, staring out at the evergreen forests, she realized her bond with Johnny remained strong. Despite their distance and brief period of difficulties, she knew he would remain a loyal friend for the rest of his life.

FATE MACHINE

PLACED ON MULTIPLE WEBSITES, Twitchell's casting calls for *House of Cards* had achieved much success. One actor, a local comedian, would be playing the victim, another was flying in from Toronto to be the killer, and a young woman agreed to portray the wife in the script. While they would be working for free, Twitchell was promising them potential roles in *Day Players* alongside stars like Alec Baldwin for their efforts. All were excited by the coming possibilities.

Twitchell's search for movie props had been successful too. A military surplus store had a variety of knives, for which Twitchell had personally selected a sturdy KA-BAR blade as his killer's weapon of choice. He also bought a large oil drum to help dress the set, hoping to give the garage the gritty look of a serial killer's lair. Joss had urged Twitchell not to buy it since the drum would cost more than $150 after shipping, but Twitchell was adamant that he own such an item.

One of his most striking props brought back memories of Twitchell's childhood video efforts. In an online sporting goods store, he had found a hard plastic hockey mask. It looked steeped in a horror vintage from the *Friday the 13th* slasher-film franchise, like something a goalie for the original-six NHL team the Detroit Red Wings would have worn. All he had to do was cut out the jaw, maybe dress it up with gold and black paint.

Far darker concepts were also brewing as he prepared for the film shoot, but like many aspects of Twitchell's life, he was hiding them in plain sight. For no one, save for his suspicious spouse, was looking very closely at what was really transpiring. On Facebook he revealed his biggest clues, often wrapping them within his love of the double entendre.

He had already become Dexter Morgan on Facebook. He had opened an account under the fictional character's name and included more than a dozen photos of the actor who played the role. He was gathering friends who were pretending Dexter was real. Twitchell would then communicate with his followers, responding as Dexter would with every reply. "Dexter is thinking deep these days," he wrote.

Twitchell continued to update his own account. At the time, some users of the social-networking site were making references to themselves in the third person. Twitchell played along. It was just like a narrative technique used in *Fight Club,* one of his favourite movies. "Mark feeds on the souls of his defeated foes," read one of his September offerings. "Mark is making the magic happen." And as month's end neared and the film shoot drew closer to reality, his excitement became quite evident: "Mark is gearing up for a crazy weekend of filmin' action."

Although *House of Cards* was only a short film, Twitchell had been spending a great deal of time researching the psychology behind his killer character – anything that could be used to describe the motives and personality of such a troubled man. He read books on psychological disorders and the kinds of diagnosed conditions that define a rare breed of uncaring, real-life criminal who can kill with as much emotion as required to slice bread. It was like a fundamental part of what it means to be human was missing from these people, a quality that made others uneasy.

What Twitchell was surprised to discover during his research was that he actually shared some of these undesirable personality traits with such monsters: an emotional detachment, a tendency to lie. At times, he was selfish. He sat down at his computer, struggling with the horrible self-discovery he had just made, and began typing a long passage that began with an admission that his continued lying to his wife was spiralling out of control:

> I feel no remorse for this whatsoever, maybe because I feel like I'm entitled. I often find myself justifying my actions based on overarching loose philosophy like life is too short, or what she doesn't know won't hurt her. I've set up an intricate and elaborate web of lies around my entire relationship that I would claim is to protect her from stress, but all I seem to be doing is protecting her from truly knowing who I am.

He expanded on this point later:

I feel like I have to fake it the whole time. . . . If my family and friends ever knew the real me, it would damage many of them, some irreparably. I think I would rather continue faking it for their own benefit than watch several people's worlds, including my own, unravel completely. I know they'll survive, but sometimes happiness is more important than mere survival.

Twitchell was worried his exploration into the depths of the killer instinct had uncovered a startling, unexpected portrait of himself. Twitchell picked up the phone and called a therapist. He also visited an on-staff psychiatrist at his nearby hospital. But both mental health experts, he later claimed, insisted that he was fine. After all, the beasts he was using as comparison never sought treatment because they insisted nothing was wrong with them – it was the world that had the problem. The fact that he visited a therapist was all the proof he needed to believe he was fine. "After a much wider series of probing questions that weren't closed ended or leading, we discovered I have no deficiency in this area," he later wrote, brushing off the incident. His fear of what could lie beneath found a way to subside.

Twitchell returned to designing what would make his killer tick. He was a fan of Batman's Joker, especially actor Heath Ledger's portrayal of the warped, sadistic prankster. Twitchell wrote how he loved the same concepts the Joker had exploited in the movie *The Dark Knight*:

The Joker is about theatrics. He wants to shake up the status quo, put the wildly invigorating thrill of uncertainty and imbalance into the public's mind. He sees masses of drones living their worker bee lives and losing large sections of themselves to monotony. How do we solve this problem? Adventure. Mayhem. Chaos. That's how.

And, of course, Dexter Morgan had always been top of mind:

Anyone who takes out the trash in such a way as the depiction of Dexter, or the killer in my film, is fine by me. Vigilante or not, the thought that there could be random citizens eliminating the dredge of society by hacking up pedophiles, rapists, killers of the innocent, and other vermin is a warm, comforting thought, and we should be so lucky to have anyone like that in the real world, let alone working for the police with their resources and education.

The concept of fate was of interest too. Twitchell had been struck by a passage in a book by fantasy writer David Gemmell, in which an assassin views himself as simply the "hand of fate" at work. As Twitchell would write days after the film shoot: "Not only does fate exist, but I am very important to this fate machine, and it has gone out of its way to teach me a valuable lesson so that I may continue carrying out its inevitabilities."

After all his research, a composite of his killer character, blended from his various passions, was finally complete.

Twitchell had actually been honest with his wife when he confessed that *House of Cards* took inspiration from his personal life. In fact, the film focused on the concept of "self-hatred," an admission he would later make to a total stranger drawn to his Dexter Morgan profile on Facebook. And as the years passed, Twitchell would continue to reveal how far more sinister themes had also played a role in the plot of his short film.

After all, at the very heart of his project, a film he was scheduled to begin shooting in a few short days, was a story of deception. Twitchell stayed quiet on this front, especially during filming when he appeared subdued, even slightly detached from his film crew. But the brutal violence of his serial killer came almost secondary to his film's premise of a man living his life as a performance – perfecting day-to-day motions to mask his real identity and to fool the world – just like Dexter Morgan.

BEHIND THE SCENES

CHRIS HEWARD SAT HUNCHED over in the darkened garage, strapped to a metal chair in the middle of the musty wood building. His wrists were duct-taped to the back of the chair, his ankles strapped to its legs, his stomach spilling out over the sides of its narrow frame. It had been welded together out of angle iron. He was the victim trapped in the victim's chair.

Before him stood Mark Twitchell in a dark hoodie and jeans, a studio light glowing behind his head, throwing a soft hue onto the grease-stained walls. Joss was nearby, checking on the sound equipment. David huddled over a rented digital camera mounted on a tripod. Scott, who towered over everyone, was fiddling with a light.

The crew had already unspooled a roll of duct tape across Chris's chest. It tugged tight on the navy blue dress shirt he was wearing, squeezing his arms into his sides. Twitchell took a step back and looked down at the captive Chris, completely restrained from his shoulders to his feet. Twitchell's lips pouted a bit as he tried to hide a brief smile of pride.

"Okay," David announced, adjusting the camera a little. "We're ready for the killer stuff."

It was several hours into the second day of the *House of Cards* film shoot and aspiring actor Chris was not enjoying the experience. The acting job seemed exciting at first, but after being strapped down for hours he was feeling the cold drip of uneasiness. Chris began to wriggle his wrists and ankles, trying to loosen the tape.

Chris had met Twitchell only once previously, over coffee, and he was starting to realize just how little he knew of the director's filmmaking background. Their meeting had ended with a job offer and no formal audition – just a joke or two from Chris's repertoire of amateur standup. While acting was a newer endeavour for Chris, Twitchell's enthusiasm and promises of future work with Hollywood stars had him hoping the low-budget mystery thriller could be his big break. But when Chris showed up at the film set on the morning of Saturday, September 27, he found it wasn't a professional studio but a rundown two-door garage. Its cream-coloured doors had been pulled down tight once filming began. Hardly any light could escape it. The air hung heavy with sawdust. And it was freezing cold. Everyone had their sleeves pulled down. Chris was regretting not telling his agent about what he was doing.

It had been a tense morning for the crew. They had taken longer than expected to get organized and continued to stumble over one another. Many of the finer details of the film shoot, from set pieces and props to the script, had been planned weeks in advance, but some of the very basics of filmmaking seemed to have been forgotten, almost treated like an after-thought. Mike and Jay had helped Scott clean out the garage and build set pieces, including perfecting Twitchell's desired table and chair. But the camera Twitchell had rented didn't come with a power adapter, forcing the crew to go hunting for one when the internal batteries died. Joss had to drive to St. Albert at the last minute to pick up a pair of samurai swords that Twitchell had forgotten at home. Disagreements broke out among the crew. At one point, Twitchell became upset because the crew was using too much of his duct tape. He wanted the tape rationed for some reason. He had also snatched one of the samurai swords out of the hands of his actors when they touched the sharpened blade between shots. "Don't put your fingerprints on these!" he snarled. He explained how it was a higher quality blade of folded steel. "The oil on your hands could wreck it."

With the final prep work for the next scene complete, Chris fidgeted in the metal chair, trying to get comfortable. He had read the script a few times and was worried about how the next scene would play out. Chris was playing the part of a cheating husband who uses online dating web-sites to arrange liaisons with other women. Only this time when he thinks he's meeting some sexy date, he is confronted by a masked killer. "He's about seven steps from the door when the unmistakable sound of a stun gun being fired explodes from the darkness," the script read. "Before he has time to comprehend what's going on he gets clubbed in the back of the head and is knocked unconscious."

Now Chris's character, strapped to the cold metal chair, was awaiting an interrogation by the masked stranger. The killer was being played by Robert Barnsley, another inexperienced actor who was so excited by the chance of landing a role in Twitchell's next movie that he paid for his own flight from Toronto. Robert was skinny, only twenty years old, and looked young for his age. Some of the crew had wondered how he was going to pull off the performance of a threatening and crazed man. At least his youthful appearance would be hidden behind the modified hockey mask Twitchell had made. Robert slipped on the killer's black mask, tightening the white straps behind his head as his nose pressed against the plastic, cupping his forehead. The lower section of the mask had been cut away, leaving his mouth and chin exposed. Twitchell had outfitted him with a hoodie, which covered his hair and ears, making him look sinister while still hiding his appearance.

Moments before they were to begin shooting the interrogation scene, a strip of duct tape was suddenly slapped across Chris's mouth.

Twitchell disappeared behind the camera.

Joss, the sound man, held up a microphone.

David pressed the camera's record button. "And rolling."

It was Twitchell's call. The sound of the camera humming, the buzz of the lights, a pause. Twitchell had given both of his actors very little direction throughout the shoot beyond minor instructions. Robert took a breath as he readied himself. Chris could only wait helplessly like a stuck pig, lips sealed tight with the fresh piece of tape.

Twitchell finally spoke: "Action."

"Boo!" Robert hooted with a fiendish delight reminiscent of Batman's Joker, his opening line rolling into a sadistic cackle. "Heeheeeheehehehe!" The noise startled his captive awake as Robert emerged from the darkness as the film's killer, standing tall under the harsh glow of the light.

"Okay, welcome to a little game of live or die," the killer declared, greeting his victim as he paced in front of him. "The process is really quite simple, so pay very close attention because I don't enjoy repeating myself and if you make me do that, well . . ." He pulled out a knife.

Chris snapped himself into character, staring at the killer, a dark shadow falling off the nose of the mask. Remembering his cue, Chris began to whimper. He tried to scream, but the duct tape muffled the sound. He started to sweat. Chris knew it was a real knife taken off the metal table.

And as the killer drew near, the knife's sharp edge was inching closer toward his nose. Chris felt a lump in his throat and he didn't have to feign fear.

"Okay, settle down." The killer spat like he was disciplining a child, pulling back and twisting the knife in the light. "You have to take stock of your situation. You don't know where you are, and I'm hiding my identity from you." He spun on his heels, scraping a bit of dirt on the concrete floor. "Now, why would I bother if I was going to kill you?"

He glared and started pacing again. Chris stared back, noisily sucking air through his nose.

"I'm going to ask you a series of questions, and you're going to answer me truthfully," the killer continued. "I'm going to check your answers while you're sitting here." He looked over to the laptop on the table. "And if I find out you lied to me on any particular point . . ." He stopped his pacing and swung his masked face closer to Chris. "I'm going to cut something off."

Chris tossed his weight from side to side and whimpered.

"Now I don't mess around, and I don't give second chances, so if anything comes out of your pie hole that isn't a polite direct answer to a question, you'll go home missing pieces. And that will be really hard to explain to your wife." The killer tapped the blade on his palm. "Do you read me?"

Chris nodded frantically. The metal chair groaned and squeaked.

"Perfect. Let's start with the easy one. What's your Cheating Hearts password?"

"Mmmpphhhpmhhh."

"Sorry, what? I didn't quite catch that?" The killer squinted at the duct tape sealing his victim's lips. "Oh right. Sorry!" He pinched his fingers and gripped the edge of one side, leaning in close to Chris's ear. "I realize this goes without saying," he whispered, "but I don't want any misunderstandings. If you scream I'm going to cut your windpipe out, which will cause an awfully huge mess and leave you unable to answer any more questions, so I'd recommend you restrain yourself."

The killer ripped the tape off and threw it on the floor.

"Ugghhh!" Chris grunted in real pain. His lips were stinging and he wanted to rub them, but his arms were still taped to the chair.

Twitchell stopped the scene. David and Scott relaxed and Joss brought down the microphone. The crew would need several more takes as they tried to make the tape less sticky, sympathetic to the pain Chris was suffering every time it was ripped off his face.

During a break, Joss asked about the dating site in the film plot. "Are there even sites like this where married people can hook up?"

"Yeah, I heard of one," Chris told the group. "I saw it in the paper the other day. It's called Ashley Madison."

Twitchell appeared to pick up on the conversation. But he didn't say a word.

As the Saturday film shoot stretched into the early evening, the crew moved on to one of the last scenes at the garage. After the killer tortures his victim into revealing his bank PIN numbers, email and dating site passwords, he deletes his fake female account and all the communication between the profile and his victim, then drives to the bank to withdraw his victim's money. Now in this scene, the killer returns, announcing he has changed his mind about letting his victim survive and will instead use the extorted personal information to fool his victim's friends and family into believing he's still alive. The perfect cover.

At Jess's request, Twitchell had altered the film's ending to remove a gruesome decapitation and power-saw dismemberment scene, but she probably wouldn't have liked his new idea any better: the victim would now be brutally stabbed and his body chopped into pieces with a meat cleaver. It was a departure from Dexter's preferred tools, but there were still references to the series littered throughout. The killer remained an employee of the police force in the script, and Twitchell made a "Power-Saw To The People" sticker promoting the TV show that appeared in the background of one scene. The victim's wife also reads a Dexter novel in an earlier shot. Throughout the weekend, Twitchell kept saying things were "just like Dexter," smiling and laughing boisterously.

His new ending required the killer to plunge the samurai sword into his captive's chest. Chris was relieved the crew could film this shot with him freed from the metal chair. As he stretched his legs and rubbed his wrists, the crew finished debating how to film the murder scene on such a low budget. Scott fashioned a fake torso by pulling apart an old couch the crew had tossed into the alley driveway. He ripped at the foam and placed the stuffing into an extra dress shirt Chris had brought with him, using duct tape to help form the belly and general shape of the actor's body. He dropped the newly constructed torso on the chair.

Twitchell returned from the grocery store with a bottle of corn syrup, red food colouring, and a juice jug. It was the film industry's recipe for fake blood.

Scott poured the syrup into the jug, added a bit of water and red dye, and then mixed it with an attached juice plunger. Within seconds he had created a glorious red liquid that looked just like the real thing. He dumped the fake blood into a Ziploc bag and made a few incisions in the foam chest cavity and inserted the bag inside. At last, they were ready for the final act of mayhem as a container was placed under the chair to stop the sticky substance from pooling on the floor.

Twitchell circled the chair, smiling in satisfaction at the foam torso, before he took a spot behind the camera.

Robert pulled one of the samurai blades out of its sheath and wrapped his hands around the handle. He pointed the long blade at the chair.

"Camera's rolling," David announced.

"Action!" said Twitchell.

The killer leaped forward and plunged the sword deep into his victim's torso. Grinding his teeth, he twisted the blade into his guts, taking great pleasure in killing his victim.

But Robert missed the blood bag. And the sword he was using, the cheaper stainless steel version, wasn't sharp enough to rip the shirt. On the second try, the sword sliced through the fabric, but it also pushed out foam, making it obvious that the victim was made of stuffing.

The crew gave up on the idea of the fake torso and decided to just hold the shirt in place. Scott and Joss stood on either side of the chair, dangling the blood bag just behind the fabric. "Thrust!" everyone shouted, encouraging Robert to ram the sword through as hard as he could.

The blade cut deep and the blood bag burst open. A pool of blood spilled out from the back of the shirt in a thickened stream. The liquid moved down the length of the sword, reaching the tip and falling off in drips of red.

The crew waited and watched in excitement, letting the fake blood flow for several minutes as the camera kept recording, making sure they had captured the perfect shot.

Chris was smiling, eyes bright. He thought the death scene looked fantastic. David and Scott were pleased with the special effect too. But Twitchell had gone silent, as if deep in thought. Crew members noticed his lack of reaction and wondered if he didn't care at all. After their day of hard work, it looked like Twitchell was unmoved or disappointed by their effort, but if he was, he wasn't saying.

The crew had been filming for two days for what was supposed to be a short eight-minute film, and they still had another day to go. That night, they were scheduled to shoot a final scene at the garage, an external shot showing the killer dumping large garbage bags full of body parts into the trunk of his car. But David was exhausted and looking for an excuse to leave. He turned to Twitchell. "We're not shooting that scene," he said. "It's too anti-climatic."

Twitchell listened to his complaints patiently.

"We'll do a really intense closeup of the guy being impaled," David continued, trying to get Twitchell excited. "And he's screaming from under the duct tape, the music is going to build up and, bam, it's going to cut to the computer typing scene."

"Okay," said Twitchell, nodding. "That works." He remembered the scene well. It had been filmed the night before – with him playing the starring role. For Twitchell, the "write what you know" reveal of the writer being the real killer was just like a major twist renowned film director Alfred Hitchcock would have used in one of his suspense thrillers. And as Twitchell explained years later, the last shot of *House of Cards* also perfectly explained the theme – and an important lesson – behind his work, demonstrating how easily real motives can be hidden from view. "Anyone can turn out to be a psycho," he wrote, "without being overtly obvious about it."

THE NEXT EVENING, TWITCHELL was cruising toward the freeway, slowing down on a yellow light, as he pondered the three-day film shoot. He had just left an east end steak house, where some of the crew had joined him for a *House of Cards* wrap party to celebrate the end of shooting. Over dinner, conversations had drifted into talk of follow-up projects, giving Twitchell a handful of ideas on where his little film project could be taken next. Of course, he had also pitched Chris on investing in *Day Players*. And while a $35,000 investment would be nearly all of his money, Chris was giving the proposal some serious thought. Twitchell just had to give him some time.

Twitchell stopped for the red light and considered how much more he was capable of doing. While *House of Cards* was an accomplishment, he knew something was missing. He thought back to the film set, his ideas, his script, his character pulling a narrative forward. He tapped the steering wheel, deep in thought.

Above the glowing streetlights a thin blue line of stars appeared through a rift in the clouds as an evening chill plunged the city close to the freezing point. He flicked on the car heater and waited as it coughed out a warm dusting at his feet. The light flashed to green. By the time he parked and reached his front door, he was on to a new plan.

That evening, the third season of *Dexter* premiered on television. The episode depicted the first time Dexter slays an innocent man in an act of self-defence. He covers it up, but the incident had him pondering his long-held code to only kill bad people. From now on, Dexter wondered if the code had been too rigid, and whether his targets for murder could be broadened to include more categories.

Nearing midnight, Twitchell sat at his computer in his basement office, unable to sleep. His mind was a mess of jumbled thoughts. Jess and Chloe had gone to bed long ago. Twitchell logged on to his Dexter Morgan account on Facebook and discovered he had a new message from one of his followers. A woman named Renee Waring had "kidnapped" him. It was some silly game people could play on the site, forcing a response out of a targeted profile. He checked her account. She was a total stranger and lived in Ohio. She had long dark hair and sparkling green eyes. Twitchell was intrigued and sent her a Facebook message while still pretending to be Dexter. "I had to ignore your request," he wrote, "because my only options were escape and ignore and if I were actually kidnapped by you, there's no way I would want to escape."

He logged out after his subtle online flirt but found he still couldn't sleep. His mind was lurching forward, and then an idea struck him with such a powerful force that he was staggered by the very thought of it.

It had happened a few times before, but nothing like this. His Internal Creative Genius was rising within, giving him the confidence he needed to think through his plans. Twitchell viewed it as a "savant power," a subconscious and random boost that helped drive his actions. "It's not something that I can manually control or manipulate," he explained later. "It's like if you had a faucet and the dials didn't work. And it just ran water when it felt like it, but you gotta get in there with a pitcher whenever it runs water to get a hold of it."

If there was a faucet, the water was now flowing uncontrollably. His mind could barely keep up. His heart was racing. He had an epiphany. At last, he was given the insight he had been seeking for so long.

This night would change everything.

Thinking about the film shoot, the conversation over dinner, everything he had been working toward over the past year, Twitchell had finally achieved some clarity of mind. He had a purpose, a new destiny. His next steps would impact the lives of countless others. But he wasn't thinking of them. Perhaps he never would.

Twitchell stared at the ceiling, realizing his maudlin suburban life was about to be blown apart. What he now saw in front of him was terrifying and exhilarating at the same time. It would be full of risk, but it would set him apart from everyone else, forever.

It would be his legacy. His claim to fame.

FREEDOM

ROARING DOWN THE HIGHWAY, Johnny grinned as he accelerated his motorcycle, feeling the speed of the road racing under his boots. His shaved head fit snugly in his helmet, the wind rushing past, tugging on his black riding jacket. Life was great.

He was enjoying the final days of summer on a solo trip through the mountains. Rolling hills were opening up before him as he approached jagged peaks still brushed with glacial snow. He had plans throughout August to see an old friend in Calgary and was hoping to visit family during his vacation too. He had located the perfect parkland camping spots. Days were remaining warm as nights in the mountain valleys cooled rapidly. Tall grasses became moist with dew. A sprinkling of yellow was turning in the forests, the stillness of nature only broken by the chittering of chipmunks and the thundering engine of Johnny's bike as he tore around a corner, full throttle, into the wild.

Johnny had been watching his diet lately and was losing weight. At thirty-eight, he was still on the dating scene, meeting new women online, and moving on from his failed attempts at beginning relationships. On a spiritual level, he had experienced some success in his journey to enlightenment. He had developed a diverse network of friends. And he leaned on the support of Dale and his work buddies Hans and Willy. He enjoyed his job. But most of all, Johnny loved his motorbike, a Yamaha FJR. The navy-blue sport touring model had been loaded up with a sleeping bag secured on the seat behind Johnny's back. A yellow tent became his shelter as he camped for several days. He had another bike parked at home. Both gave him the "mindnumbing" power and speed that he craved, and often expensive speeding fines. He could handle riding for more than seven hours a day, watching the picturesque landscape rush by.

For years, Johnny had loved cruising in his cars with the stereo cranked, often singing along to Elton John. Picking up an interest in motorcycles in his thirties, Johnny found he couldn't get enough. He posted a few pictures of his beloved machines on his Facebook profile as he returned to the city following his mountain vacation. To describe the motorbikes, he used only two words: "My children."

His enthusiasm had even convinced his buddy Dale to join the ranks of motorbike owners. Johnny was hoping to teach him how to ride. While they were running out of time with the turning weather, next summer was looking like a great opportunity to go cruising together. But for now, Johnny parked his bikes and headed back to work. His summer fun was over. Autumn had arrived.

PLAY TIME

IN THE BRILLIANCE OF Monday morning, Twitchell headed for his computer. Renee had already replied to his refusal to escape her little kidnapping game. "Or would it be that there would be no way *I* could escape?" she had written to his Dexter Morgan profile. "Hrmmm?"

Intrigued by her cheeky response, he quickly wrote her back.

Throughout the day, they would exchange five more messages, adding up to two dozen by week's end. He revealed his real identity. They flirted. It escalated into sexual vulgarity. She knew he had a wife, but he assured Renee he was living in an "open marriage." They became instant distractions in each other's lives.

Drawn together as strangers by their shared *Dexter* fandom, Twitchell and Renee discovered they had other interests in common. They both described themselves as geeks and Halloween fanatics, having social circles of costume-makers. But these were superficial connections. Their bond would soon go much deeper.

At first, he treated Renee as a sounding board. Feeding into her Hollywood dreams, he promised a creative partnership in a potential movie project, bragging about his company and coming fortunes. Renee was a dog trainer. She was thrilled to have stumbled upon a filmmaker offering a slice of his success. "Where do I sign up and what can I do to help?"

Photos were swapped, private details undressed, and long, rambling messages on failed relationships exchanged. It wasn't long until their communication turned confessional. They both admitted to having dark fantasies through the years. Twitchell offered the cover of fiction to broach this topic, telling her they could continue brainstorming film concepts. It would be their "play time" and if it led anywhere, she would of course be paid handsomely for her contribution. Renee dove in. "I carry my own dark demons every day," she confessed. "There are days when all I want to see is broken necks and blood, but it never happens."

Twitchell was reassuring, as if he was eager to hear more details. "There is nothing you could possibly reveal to me that would make me cease communicating with you," he wrote back, before making his own confession. "We all have a dark side, some darker than others, and you're not the only one to relate to Dexter. It sometimes scares me how much I relate."

Renee was an unexpected jolt of energy just as Twitchell was beginning his new journey. She joined his long list of enterprises. Between writing her each day, he was also resuming contact with Traci Higgins. He was flirting with her again, picking up where the two had left off with their one kiss the previous summer. They made plans to meet up, which Twitchell organized through his Dexter Morgan profile. He knew Jess was still monitoring his emails and personal Facebook account.

His eye was also drawn elsewhere, back to plentyoffish.com. He flicked on his software that blocked tracking of his Internet activity as he browsed the profiles of women in other cities. He sometimes looked for hours, scanning photo after photo of women seeking men.

It was a profile for a young blonde that captured his attention. He thought she was beautiful, able to instill a lustful craving in most men. He saved three of her available photos. One showed her posing in sunglasses behind the wheel of a convertible, giving a tiny smile.

Twitchell quickly created a new dating profile on the same site, using a new email address to open it. He then defined the particulars of the account holder: a woman, blond, seeking a man in Edmonton. He posted the three treasured photos he had just saved to his new account. He called it "Spiderwebzz" and gave the new woman the name "Sheena." It was the name of his old roommate's girlfriend.

Then he sat back and waited for the men to respond.

He couldn't wait to write about it. He had learned long ago that there was no better release than writing. He turned to his computer again, fingers above the keyboard, and typed in high spirits: *This is the story of my progression into becoming a serial killer . . .*

It was only the beginning. Over the coming days, the words would flow from his mind onto his computer screen in bursts of creative energy:

At first I considered married men looking to cheat on their wives. In one way I'd be taking out the trash, doling out justice to those who on some level, deserved what they got. But the logic of the situation denies this possibility. After all, people who are expected home at a certain hour tend to get reported as missing and there's other factors that would lead to an investigation I didn't want. No, I had to choose people whose entire lives I could infiltrate and eliminate evidence of my existence from on all levels.

He just needed a title.

Twitchell remembered a quote attributed to Mark Twain that horror novelist Stephen King had used in his novel *'Salem's Lot:* "A novel was a confession to everything by a man who had never done anything." Twitchell loved the quote nearly as much as he loved how *Stephen King* and *serial killer* began with the same letters.

He had found the perfect phrase. Twitchell called his new masterpiece "S. K. Confessions."

MIKE YOUNG TWIRLED THE dial on the padlock on the back of the garage. It clicked open and he swung through the door. Inside, the garage was fairly clean. A few pop bottles and discarded coffee cups were littered about, the only signs of the weekend film shoot. Of course, he could not know how crucial this observation would soon prove to be for the police. At the time, he was solely focused on using the space as a workshop. Jay and Scott were coming over later. Together, they were about to build a tank for a pet snake.

TWITCHELL AND JESS CONTINUED to fight, the distance growing between them, but a conversation one day pushed them even farther apart. Jess was still worried that his editor, Phil Porter, was a lie and her husband was cheating on her. And then he shocked her further with a startling admission that came with no warning.

"I'm not sure I can feel empathy like other people," he said.

Jess stopped what she was doing. Shaken by what her husband had just revealed, Jess tried to engage him in a long conversation about empathy. He was acting like it was a foreign concept to him, and she had to define what it meant. She thought back to an episode of *The Oprah Winfrey Show*, when a woman had revealed how she had forgotten her baby in a car, only to have the child die of heat exhaustion. As a new mother, Jess felt a great deal of empathy for the woman's tragedy. "That's the kind of situation," she said, "where I felt like, 'Oh my God, what if that happened to me?'"

"Yeah, that's sad that happened," he replied, "but that doesn't have anything to do with me."

Jess looked at her husband in confusion. She was amazed that something so serious was only bubbling to the surface at this stage of their relationship. Gone was his usual charm, replaced with a cold distance she did not understand. They had a daughter nearing eight months of age and just now she was being told her husband felt nothing?

"That's not normal," she said in sadness. If he couldn't feel empathy, she knew she couldn't stay in this marriage. "You need help."

He agreed it would be for the best. A marriage counsellor was called and another to address his personal issues.

Not long after the conversation, he told Jess he had a confirmed schedule with a therapist. He would be seeing a psychiatrist every Friday evening. In fact, he had wasted no time about it. He already had an appointment lined up for the upcoming Friday. A session was scheduled for October 3, 2008. He'd drive there straight after work.

THE INVITATION

WHAT A CATCH. SHEENA had straight blond hair, a curled cute smile, and her sparkling eyes flickered in a digital snapshot on Gilles Tetreault's computer screen like a flirty text message.

Online dating had made single life so much easier. And Sheena was a forward girl too. Here it was four days since their first connection on plentyoffish.com and she was already finalizing plans for their first date that weekend. Gilles didn't even have her phone number yet, but he was set to pick her up at seven o'clock on Friday for a dinner and a movie.

At thirty-three, Gilles was a new arrival to the city from a francophone prairie town so small it only had five streets, seven avenues, and one thousand residents. He had black, neatly trimmed hair and spoke in a country accent. He was quite short and terribly thin. Working at a casino, he was enjoying life during the latest oil boom, living alone and in search of city romance.

Gilles was thrilled that Sheena seemed to be so interested in him. The only thing that bothered him were the confusing directions she had given. He had told her online where he lived, but her directions seemed to assume he was coming from the other side of town. And she wanted him to drive down a back alley and park outside her detached double-door garage. She would leave one of the garage doors open a touch so he could enter through the garage and cross the yard to the back door of the house.

She then explained how there was no parking in front because of a bus stop, and the landlord padlocked the back gate. "Pull in to the only driveway on your left that isn't paved," Sheena had written in her directions, explaining the mess he'd soon see piled up near her fence. "Seriously, who ever heard of a driveway that looks like the Amazon? It won't swallow your car, I promise."

She didn't provide a street address.

Gilles could understand the girl not wanting to give out her phone number just yet – there were stalkers on the Internet, after all – but these directions struck him as a bit odd.

Having experienced little luck with online dating thus far, however, Gilles brushed it off and looked forward to his date, a bit tickled that he had charmed such a beautiful blonde so very quickly.

LITTLE CIRCLES

TWITCHELL FOUND HAVING ACCESS to Renee's dark mind was impossibly riveting. Never before had he shared such thoughts with such vigor, as if gorging himself on the darkest of chocolates. As the first few days of October passed by, he could barely resist spilling his own gruesome fantasies in return, but he maintained composure, at least for now, as if afraid of frightening his newest admirer.

Twitchell thought it best to begin with a *Dexter* analogy, a passion he knew she already shared, and then blend the words with his life experience. Messaging Renee through his Dexter Morgan Facebook account, he went back to his rejection at the U.S. border and told her of his reaction when the customs officer delivered the bad news. "I fantasized about wrapping her to the table, collecting the blood slide and then dismembering her so vigorously," he wrote, before adding an "lol" or "laughing out loud" as a light punctuation at the very thought of what he had just stated.

Renee bathed in this dark passage, soaking in each sinister word as she contemplated what she should share to top it. She didn't hold back. She unveiled one of her most violent fantasies, one that was deeply personal, full of visceral venom and rage:

> I relate totally to the dark fantasies of wrapping that bitch up and cutting her into pieces . . . I have many a dark thought about my ex-husband's current wife. That fucker couldn't wait four months for our divorce papers to dry (not even a whole year since we split) before he got married to a nasty, skeleton skank with a rod in her spine! . . . All I wanted, well, still want to do, is cut her up and draw little circles with her blood. Little circles on her face, on a window, on the knife. Just little blood circles. Like finger painting, but with only one colour. Slowly, watching the blood drip a bit. Watching the lines dry on the window.

Waiting for the knife to dip in again and create more paint. Little tiny
circles. Pretty much like that.

The vivid imagery of her story struck deeply. Twitchell viewed her
prose as smooth and romantic, like a piece of Gothic literature – full of
torment, lost love, and gore. He sat on her story for five hours. Then, late
in the evening of Thursday, October 2, thoughts turning to the day ahead,
he finally touched his keyboard. Swept up in the moment, he descended
into darker territory, exposing his elaborate insights on how to commit the
perfect murder. He warned Renee that she was "too close" to her victim
and could easily be caught. She needed a far stronger plan to dispose of her
ex-husband's new wife.

If you really want to make this happen and get away with it, prepare a
kill room the same way Dex does, wall-to-wall plastic sheeting. Kidnap
said anorexic girl, sounds fairly simple and easy considering her small
carriage, and get her to the room. In the US, stun guns are a cost-effective
approach, followed by a sleeper hold. This tactic leaves no forensic evi-
dence behind and renders your target unconscious quickly and silently.

The method for securing the body on TV is theatrical, but imprac-
tical to say the least. Tethering is useless. Tie the body up in duct tape
completely, feet together, arms to body, hands wrapped. Then tether to
prevent twisting.

Make sure you are head to toe in a disposable rain suit and that you
have plenty of hefties for the pieces and the plastic sheeting when fin-
ished. Pulverize the jaw bones and remove the teeth to avoid dental ID.
Also remove the finger tips and incinerate them.

Ideally you would want to incinerate the entire body, but this requires
exhaustive location planning and a suitable container as well as fuel.
Otherwise you can just dump the bags loaded with rocks Dexter style
into a large body of water. Isn't Ohio fairly close to the great lakes?
Hmm.

Finished with passing on his detailed suggestions, he called it a night and
settled into bed.

PREPARING

GILLES TETREAULT HAD BUTTERFLIES in his stomach as his first date with Sheena drew nearer. He still wasn't entirely sure how to get there and had to ask Sheena for clarification. Her response, however, made it all quite clear: "There's certainly no other driveways along our alley like this one, and the half-open car door is a dead giveaway."

He printed off her directions in case he needed them. After work on Friday, he knew he would have to rush home to slip on his best shirt and a jacket, a thin black one from Old Navy, in order to make it to her house on time.

He didn't want to be late.

ACROSS TOWN, TWITCHELL WAS preparing. He was spending Friday morning buying more duct tape, a new padlock, and two disposable coveralls. The possibilities that the evening would bring seemed impossibly appealing. The afternoon passed quickly. He stopped to pay the rent on his garage film studio, a courtesy he did not extend to his own home loan holder. The mortgage on his St. Albert bungalow had gone unpaid since the signing of the deed.

LYNDA WARREN HAD A curiosity about her next-door neighbour. On the weekend, she had spotted a crew making a movie in the garage. Several men she had never seen before had been joined by a man in a maroon car who had stopped by more frequently.

Their activities were unusual but explainable. Her suspicions had only been raised earlier, when a large table was dragged out of the garage and into the sunlight. The metal surface had been polished vigorously. She had seen such a table only once before, deep inside a medical examiner's office, where autopsies were performed.

—

TWITCHELL SLIPPED INTO THE garage undetected.

The walls deadened the sounds of his labourious work, his Friday preparations stretching on for hours with a staple gun and scissors in hand.

Tape was ripped. Plastic sheeting laid out. Inch by inch, the ceiling was covered, staples holding the sheeting in place. Walls were draped. The cement floor blanketed. Even the table was prepared, sheeting falling overtop. A thin green bed sheet was tacked up too, separating the two sides of the garage. He had made a dark sanctuary of which even Dexter would be proud.

The painted hockey mask sat nearby, close to the stun gun baton. A pair of handcuffs was at the ready. Joining the armoury was a firearm. Twitchell tucked the handgun in close, making sure it was never far from his reach.

With time to spare, he flipped open his laptop and checked his Dexter Morgan profile. His fans had no idea what he was really up to, which likely heightened the thrill of it all. A status update was entered: "Dexter is patiently waiting for his next victi . . . uh, play date buddy."

His message triggered a response. "Do this well, Dex," one fan wrote, "and it could be really really cool."

Twitchell closed the laptop, slipped on his hoodie, and lay in wait.

Time passed in silence.

A breeze rattled the partially opened bay door, but soon settled. The sky bruised purple. He finally heard a vehicle rumble down the alley, then the sharp sounds of wheels on gravel. Headlights beamed onto the garage bay doors, vanished, and the engine shuddered cold.

Fingers were clenched tight, gripping the stun gun baton.

Outside, shoes pressed into soil. A man was entering the property.

A pause, as if to enjoy this brief moment of calm, and then Twitchell rushed forward, racing across the kill room under a cloak of darkness. He approached his foolish arrival in full flight, drifting ever closer like the harbinger of terror.

THE DATE

GILLES HAD BEEN DRIVING fast, but when he pulled into the alley, parked his truck, and checked the time – fifteen minutes after 7:00 p.m. – he knew rushing hadn't helped enough. Sheena had told him not to be late and he already was, losing that good first impression.

Yellow leaves crunched beneath his shoes as he jumped out of his truck and ducked under one of the garage bay doors, left open a bit just like she said. His tardiness on his mind, Gilles tried to hurry through the darkened garage as he headed straight toward the faint outline of the back door ahead of him.

As he reached for the door handle, Gilles was suddenly embraced from behind. He thought Sheena was playing a joke on him. But then something caught his eye.

He saw an arm reach around with what looked like a cattle prod. An arc of electricity crackled and echoed against his chest. Again and again.

"What the hell is going on?" Gilles called out in pain. "What the fuck?" He spun around.

He was terrified to see a tall man standing behind him, his face obscured by a black and gold hockey mask. The jaw had been cut away, revealing the stranger's mouth and tightened lips.

This was no date. The masked attacker was holding the glowing shock device in his right hand. The blue arc of his weapon glowed in the darkness.

But the electrical pulse was more annoying than crippling. It felt like an electronic bug zapper. Gilles finally grabbed the man's arm and pushed it to the side, away from his own body, until the stranger stopped pressing the trigger and holstered the weapon.

Gilles started to run, but the attacker cut him off as he pulled out a gun.

"Get down on the ground! Put your head down!" The attacker roared, gesturing with the handgun.

Gilles thought he was going to die.

"Put your hands behind your back," the stranger's deep voice ordered, "and don't move."

He fell to the floor and tried to look up, but the stranger yelled at him repeatedly to keep his head down.

The next thing he knew he had duct tape over his eyes. Gilles was blind, lying on the cold concrete, feeling totally helpless, panicking. "Take whatever you want," he pleaded. "Take my wallet. Anything. Just let me go," he begged tearfully.

"If you cooperate, this will only be a standard robbery."

Gilles didn't dare move. All he could hear was a jingling sound. Horrible thoughts came in flashes of terror behind his taped-up eyes. *No one knows where I am. This man is going to rob me, abduct me, kill me.* The jingling continued. *Oh God. He's going to rape me!*

Gilles made a split-second decision. In desperation, he decided to fight back. *I'd rather die my way than his way.*

He ripped off the duct tape and jumped to his feet. "I can't go down like this!"

It startled the stranger. "Get back down on the ground! Get back down on the ground!" He swung the handgun toward him.

Gilles waited for the bullet. No time to react. His mind was racing. *Grab the barrel of the gun. You can do this.*

In that instant, in a space occupying no more than a half-second of time – although it felt so much longer – he saw the stranger's outstretched hand grasping the firearm, moving it closer to his head. Aiming.

Gilles lunged, palm toward the enemy.

His fingers touched the barrel. His eyes fluttered open in surprise.

Gilles realized the gun was a fake.

He felt the hard plastic in his hand, realizing with exhilaration the weapon weighed just half the weight of a real gun. It gave him a newfound hope. He wasn't afraid of the gun anymore. And his confidence suddenly exploded in rage, adrenaline fuelling a wild bout of courage: he could fight off this weaponless fraud.

Gilles ripped the gun out of the stranger's hands. He clasped on tight and tried to break the gun, crush it, smash it in two. He spotted black handcuffs on the floor and picked them up.

"Put those down!" the masked man shouted excitedly.

But Gilles ignored him. He tossed the fake gun into a corner and wrapped the handcuffs around his fist like a set of brass knuckles. Gilles took a long look at his attacker. Realizing the handcuffs wouldn't dent the stranger's mask, he discarded them and clenched his fists.

The two collided. They wrestled, arms and hands ripping, grasping. Their feet jostled as they pushed and shoved each other in the scuffle, both trying to gain the upper hand.

Gilles clasped his hands tightly around his attacker when the man lunged forward and head-butted him in the face. The mask struck hard against his nose, his eye, and he recoiled from the stinging pain.

The stranger sneered. "Because you're not cooperating, this is the way this has to be!"

The duo struggled and spun around several times in the near darkness. The stranger threw a hard punch at Gilles's left temple, but he was too high on adrenaline to feel its full impact. They continued struggling furiously, smashing from one end of the garage to the other. Arms flailing, fingers pulling and tearing, Gilles tried to rip his attacker's mask off, but the man kept dodging him.

Gilles lifted one leg and swung it as hard as he could at the groin of his masked attacker. But the man just ducked out of the way and he kicked nothing but air. The stranger tried to kick him back. Gilles kept punching the man in the chest, avoiding contact with the hard plastic mask.

Then, as they struggled, Gilles felt some kind of pouch on the man's waist. He shuddered.

His attacker could be armed with a knife. Gilles knew he had to escape quickly if the man had such a weapon on him. This brawl could end his life.

Gilles figured that if he let his attacker continue to hit him, he could slowly manoeuvre himself toward the bay door, each punch sending him closer to the exit.

The punches kept battering the left side of his head. But there seemed to be no method to the attack. It was unorganized, chaotic. He tried to focus on what he could see of the attacker's face, hoping to remember the details later. *Maybe freckles.* Gilles glanced again. *He could have red hair.* He was moving too fast for him to be sure, and the mask and hoodie covered nearly everything else.

Gilles stepped away, then took another baby step. The door was close. He pushed the man back, but his grasp held on tight, the stranger's fingers clawing into his jacket. Gilles slipped his arms out, letting the jacket slide off in the grasp of his attacker.

Freedom neared.

Gilles dropped to the floor and rolled under the partially opened garage door. He started crawling, palms pushing himself past the edge of the garage and down the driveway. He grabbed at soil and rocks. Out of breath and exhausted, he could barely keep going or even lift himself up. Maybe the stun gun baton had really knocked him out, he thought. All his energy was drained.

Gilles gasped for air, crawling feverishly through patches of dying grass and dirt. Behind him, the stranger was back on his feet. He ducked under the garage door and started walking toward his prey. Gilles could hear him drawing closer and he pushed himself forward again, fighting to keep moving, to find help. But the stranger was upon him, grabbing him by his ankles, and pulling hard.

Gilles struggled to hold him off, fingers digging and scratching into the ground. He reached for a rock, but just then the man pulled hard and the rock slipped out of his hands. He flailed his arms about uselessly as he was dragged all the way back to the garage.

As the attacker attempted to raise the garage door high enough for both of them to slide under, he released his grip on Gilles momentarily, giving him a second chance to escape. He pushed away and leapt to his feet, stumbling sideways and nearly crashing into the old maroon-coloured fence. But he steadied himself and bolted once again around the corner and down the alley, heart booming in his chest.

As he staggered toward the crossroads where the alley meets the walking path, Gilles spotted a young couple out for an evening stroll. "Please!" Gilles gasped, trying to find his voice as he stumbled again, collapsing at their feet. "There's a guy attacking me."

The couple looked down at him.

"He's trying to mug me!" Gilles cried.

Just then, his attacker emerged from out of the alley.

"That's the man!" Gilles groaned, holding his stomach. He slowly rose to his feet.

The couple looked on in terror at the approaching figure who looked like someone out of a horror movie, his mask still covering his face as he lumbered closer toward them.

"Oh, hey friend!" the stranger said cheerfully, trying to feign friendship.

But the young couple wasn't buying it. Terrorized by the sight of a masked stranger, the woman took off down the path. Her boyfriend stayed behind momentarily, before he also fled, leaving Gilles on his own. But their presence had been enough to make the stranger skittish and he retreated as well.

Gilles watched as everyone scattered. He was more angry than scared now and determined to return to the driveway to get to his truck.

He moved slowly, quietly. He placed each footstep silently on the alley pavement, looking all around him and wondering where his attacker had fled. As he neared his parked truck, he could see under the partially opened garage door. A pair of feet was pacing frantically back and forth. His jacket was still on the floor, but he wasn't going in there again to get it.

Gilles jumped into his vehicle and locked the doors. He jammed the key in the ignition, gave it a crank, and slammed the gas pedal to the floor. He was driving on adrenaline.

He was nearing a major roadway when the whole experience finally hit him, and then his heart really started to pound. It was like getting hit in the face with a sledgehammer: the shock, the fear, the panic. Everything started hurting, especially his ribs and the side of his face.

He felt sick to his stomach. He had to stop.

Gilles pulled over down a side street, got out, and dry-heaved. He grabbed a bottle of water he had in his truck, twisted the top, poured some over his burning face, and downed the rest.

He was exhausted. He laid down in his vehicle, motionless.

When he finally arrived at home, he saw in his bathroom mirror that he had a huge welt forming on his head. His clothes were torn. And he hurt everywhere. He grabbed a bag of frozen vegetables out of his freezer, wrapped it in a towel, and placed it on his head.

He fell asleep.

When he awoke a few hours later, it dawned on him to check his computer.

He rushed over to his desk. He started up his web browser and logged back on to plentyoffish.com. But "Sheena" was gone.

All her correspondence with him had been deleted. Details of their dinner and movie plans were now missing. All of her flirty messages had disappeared, along with all of his replies.

He tried to find her dating profile.

It had vanished too.

CHANGING METHODS

TWITCHELL CRINGED WITH EVERY phone call and spotted police cruiser. Each passing day, however, confirmed that the incident had likely – and remarkably – gone unreported. He felt his confidence bloom. He wrote about it later as he expanded on S. K. Confessions:

> *My fear subsided. . . . No patrol car would come to take me away bound in handcuffs to be brought up on assault charges, forever ending my serial killing career before it began, bringing down my marriage with it when my wife finds out what I really am.*

Deleting Sheena's dating profile minutes after the struggle had been a very good idea too, just in case police were ever called. But Twitchell was under the impression that Gilles had received the threatening message he had written, warning him that he would "hunt him down where he lives when he least expects it and finish what I started" if he ever went to the police. But deleting Sheena's account minutes later had also erased that message before Gilles had a chance to read it.

Twitchell's paperwork for a real firearm had not yet arrived. Joss had been his reference, as he requested, and the legal papers signed, authorized, and approved by the police but still delayed somewhere in the mail. Twitchell couldn't legally buy himself a gun. Not yet.

The fake firearm he had used was owned by a local movie prop company. Clearly, it didn't fool anyone. If he was to continue with his plan, he would need to change his tactics.

ON SUNDAY, OCTOBER 5, two days after her last contact with Twitchell, Renee sat at her computer in Ohio, cup of coffee in hand. "What were you up to this weekend?" she inquired. She had the whole day to herself, but her mind kept returning to Twitchell. She felt like he had awakened a part of her that had lay dormant for years. "Stun gun . . . that's a good idea," she told him. "But I think when it came to cutting her up in little pieces, I would choke." She thought his plan would leave too much forensic evidence behind. "Where's all the blood going to go when it's time to pull the plastic down?"

Renee viewed their discussions as intriguing, but upon reflection, she reminded him that an invisible line always separated her from the violence they envisioned together. She was never going to be a potential killer. "That's what dark fantasies are," she concluded. "Just a fantasy."

WHEN TWITCHELL READ RENEE'S message about stun gun batons, he must have chuckled to himself as he retracted his stated method. He warned her there were several unforeseen flaws:

> *Batons and the like are ineffective and sloppy. And in the rare event the wild card situation of the victim grabbing it from you should happen, not good. I'd go with a sturdy copper pipe. Lead is too heavy and the copper finish allows you to tape the base ends for good gripping.*
>
> *Two swift hard bonks of the back of the head, and out cold. And if not out cold, they come in handy for concise hits to the torso to wind the individual and knee cap them as well so the sleeper hold can finish the job.*
>
> *Tearing apart bone connections by hand is simply not done and too much work for anyone, male or female. A hunter's game processing kit comes with everything you would need to cut the body into nice manageable pieces, including a hand saw that will go through bone like butter . . . well, okay, maybe frozen butter, but still.*
>
> *As for what to do with the blood, that's easy too. We assume she's laying down on the table. With both her hands totally wrapped in duct tape, free one arm and slit the wrist, allowing the vast majority of the blood to flow out of the wrist and into a container like a garbage can with a hefty bag in it. The blood either gets dumped with the body, or poured into the nearest most convenient sewer drain. . . . After that, the body has barely any blood left and certainly wouldn't be enough to pool anywhere.*

Renee called him an "evil genius" for his fantasy. "Oh, the horribly awesome things we could accomplish together," she laughed.

"I'm perfecting a few of them, but don't tell anyone," he replied.

INVESTORS HUDDLED AROUND THE table of Venture Alberta. All eyes fell to Randy Lennon as he walked in and discussions returned to Xpress Entertainment. Having spent a few months looking at the *Day Players* film proposal from Mark Twitchell, Randy was asked for his advice.

"I recommend everyone against investing in this." The whole concept bothered him.

Another member pulled Randy aside with some uncomfortable news: at least one investor had already agreed to put his money in.

John Pinsent believed his investment was protected because his recently signed contract declared his funds to be "held in trust" and used "only for the direct purposes of assisting an independent gap financier establish a line of credit." He planned on handing over a cheque at the end of October, as per his agreement.

It couldn't come sooner for Twitchell. He now had less than $200 in his business account.

IT WAS NEARING 5:00 p.m. on Thursday, October 9, when Twitchell found he had time to spare before his marriage counselling session on the west end. He strolled into a Canadian Tire hardware store and scanned the aisles. Rows of auto parts stretched into sections devoted to camping, barbecues, gardening, sports, and home repair. Finally, he rounded a corner and spotted what he was looking for.

A father and his little girl were standing nearby, rummaging through a section of faucets, sinks, and the like. The girl, who was around five years old, had picked up the wooden handle of a toilet plunger and was holding it high like a Jedi with a lightsaber, striking a defensive pose.

Normally, children irritated Twitchell, but watching this scene unfold softened his hostility. The little girl blushed when she noticed he was staring at her. He smiled to assure her make-believe was okay and she gave him a bashful grin in return. Twitchell found the moment endearing, and he thought of his own daughter, who would be the girl's age in only a few short years.

As the girl scampered away, her father's arms filled with supplies, Twitchell turned his attention back to what he was looking for. In front of him was a pile of pipes. He wrapped his hands around two of them. He felt the cold metal in his palms. Passing a twenty-dollar bill to the clerk as payment, he walked back to his car and drove off to his south side garage, dropping the items off before he had to meet Jess to discuss their marriage. He made a mental note that he had to pick up hockey tape later. He'd need a roll to deliver a much better grip.

ARGUS

JOHNNY WALKED INTO ARGUS Machine late Thursday afternoon, ready to begin his ten-hour night shift. But it didn't take long until he was counting down the hours, eagerly awaiting the approaching long weekend. It would be his first four-day break since his late-summer road trips and he wouldn't be expected back in the shop until Tuesday afternoon. He had finalized plans to teach Dale how to ride his motorcycle over the Canadian Thanksgiving holiday. That activity would take up most of one of his days off. But Johnny's evenings were looking entirely free. He knew he would be back on his computer, hoping to find a date through an online dating service. Evenings as a single man could be so lonely.

Johnny had headed straight for his warehouse station to measure the steel pipes coming down the line. His friend Hans was on shift but working in another section.

As an inspector, Johnny held his digital caliper and examined the thread connections on the ends of each pipe. The instrument could measure the pipe's dimensions like a precise ruler. If it looked good, he would let it go. But if it didn't, Johnny slapped red tape on it and sent it back. Machinists like Hans would have to cut off the end of the pipe and do it all over again.

The shift was unremarkable. A usual routine took over, the flow of pipes rolling down the assembly line in a noisy and steady pace.

He took a break later while Hans enjoyed a coffee. They talked.

At around 11:00 p.m., Hans sighed as he faced a long drive to his apartment. Johnny had to stay in the shop for at least three more hours.

Hans left the building without saying goodbye to his friend. It was only in hindsight months later that this fact would bother him. It would bother him a great deal.

RELATIONSHIPS

An hour and a half after buying metal pipes, Twitchell watched as his wife cried, the couple discussing their crumbling relationship with a therapist. Twitchell had mixed feelings about seeing this psychologist, who was operating out of a clinic in a neighbourhood mall. There was a lot going on in his life that he certainly wasn't going to talk about in front of Jess or a professional, some of which he shared only in S. K. Confessions:

> *The last thing I needed to do was air out all my darkest fantasies and half-formed plans to someone who is legally obligated to contact the authorities if they think a patient will do harm to themselves or others. I'm not stupid.*

Twitchell's mind was also drifting back to Traci. They had continued to chat online and tomorrow they would finally reconnect during an afternoon rendezvous.

Still, as he sat in the therapist's office, he found he was learning how his disagreements with his wife could turn into fights. A key concern clearly revolved around the issue of trust.

"Tell me," Jess begged him. "Is Phil Porter a real person?"

"Yes!" he assured her, nearly rolling his eyes as she brought up the editor once again. "You *heard* me talk to him. He's real."

The couple left after sixty minutes with Twitchell shelling out eighty-five dollars for the session. Having spent the last of his cash on the pipes, he pulled out his business account bank card. His company funds had now dipped to only sixty-two dollars.

They drove home in separate cars.

Twitchell retreated to his basement office to check his computer. Tomorrow was another Friday, seven days since his first visitor fled the garage. Jess was under the impression he had another personal therapy appointment booked for Friday evening.

Sitting in the basement, far away from the prying eyes of his wife, he returned to plentyoffish.com and designed a new dating profile. He created a new woman, with a new name, and with new photos. A new email address was used. He liked coming up with names. Some of the online usernames he had used over the years included Kill 'Em All Twice, Night Stalker, Kill Mill, and Death By Flying.

He was having fun.

"This weekend I've got all kinds of shit planned," he wrote to Renee.

All week he had been writing Dexter Morgan status updates on how he was "reviewing possible candidates" and "contemplating selling his vics organs on the black market." As Friday neared, he simply stated: "Dexter is crouching killer, nervous father."

Fans of the show played right into it.

"You've been getting sloppy," a follower warned in reply. "Rule #1: Don't get caught."

DATE NIGHT

JOHNNY HAD BEEN HUNCHED in front of his computer all Friday morning, flirting online with a girl he had just met as he settled into his long weekend, trying to make plans for the evening. Logging into plentyoffish.com, he had noticed the woman's profile quickly. Her name was Jen and she had just joined the dating site. He thought she was beautiful and looked to be about thirty-five years old. She had included four photos in her account. One of them showed her on the beach in a bikini, her light brown hair teased around her face. And she was on the prowl. Jen wanted an "intimate encounter" with someone that evening. Johnny liked what he saw.

She seemed interested in him. When he happened to mention the kind of vehicle he drove, Jen was intrigued. "A Mazda you say," she wrote. "Zoom zoom!" Johnny told her about how he had the whole weekend off and an extra two days because of the Thanksgiving Day holiday.

Their messages bounced back and forth, their flirting escalating, until she offered her place as the meeting point for their evening. But she was concerned about safety:

> *Although this sounds exciting, I have to make sure you're not some kind of weirdo and so far you seem fairly well put together, but anyone can lie online right? So I have an idea for how both of us can be made comfortable with the situation, and by both of us, of course, I mean me. lol.*
>
> *I bought this . . . well let's call it a handyman special (I'm all about resale) and the back gate is a little screwed up so I locked it off and everyone's just been entering through the garage so it works out okay. When you see it you'll know what I mean. If you do this, I can direct you to the house from the alley without giving away the street address and see you before I let you in. Maybe this is paranoid on my part but I have to look after myself. My first instincts about people are never wrong and I know to trust them.*

*I want to play very much but I have to be cautious as I'm sure you
can understand. If you're okay with this let me know. If not we'll have
to miss each other.*

*On a lighter note though, if we really gel you said you had four days
off. How long can I keep you for if I choose? Maybe you should pack for
a few days. lol.*

Jen

Johnny read the message closely, thought it over, and told her he was
in. A few minutes later, Jen passed on driving directions. "Park in the only
driveway that looks like a forest," she wrote. "What did I say. Fixer upper."

She asked that he close the garage door when he entered – the button
was by the back door to the house – and to be aware of how the garage
may look inside. "I have a friend coming over to use part of it as a workshop this weekend, so he blanketed off where my car usually goes. Like I
need red spray paint on my car, right? Don't ask."

She planned to be home around 7:00 p.m.

PURE HOLLYWOOD

TWITCHELL THREW A ROLL of black hockey tape on the car seat and sped off toward the movie theatre. He was early, but Traci was already waiting for him at their meeting place in a bookstore. He spotted her near a stack of novels as he walked inside. And with one look into her green eyes, he knew the attraction between them was still strong. Their secret movie plans were like old times in college. Flirting was just the start of it.

Bracing against a cold breeze, the pair hurried across the vast, nearly deserted parking lot to South Edmonton Common's Cineplex Odeon. The theatre had a huge blue and silver front entrance with a boulevard of naked trees and red lava rocks. It was Friday afternoon and the matinee theatres all looked pretty empty. They would have their choice of what to see.

Twitchell noticed one movie that looked interesting among the options on the display board. The film was called *Quarantine* – a psychological thriller just like his *House of Cards* project. And although it was fiction, it was shot like a documentary from the point of view of the cameraman, making the film appear like a recording of a real incident. The film's creators had previously released *The Poughkeepsie Tapes,* a film about a theatrical, masked serial killer who documents his gruesome murders and dismemberments. *Quarantine* also starred Jennifer Carpenter, who Twitchell knew from her role as Dexter's adoptive sister. He rarely picked movies solely because of an actor or filmmaker, but this one piqued his interest and was looking very promising indeed. Traci was fine with it too.

Twitchell stood in line for popcorn, spending extra to have the big bag slathered in real butter, as Traci headed to the theatre to grab their seats. He walked down the hall a few minutes later and peeked his head around the corner to Theatre Eight. Traci was already sitting in the back row with nobody nearby. He usually liked to sit near the middle in the "audio sweet spot," but he didn't mind her choice at all. He sat down and the two of them made small talk.

The tension was palpable.

"I was an idiot in school," Twitchell blurted as the conversation lurched into the topic of their on-again-off-again romance. "I know I've said that before, but I've been learning lately how vital it is to can the bullshit and face yourself with brutal honesty."

And he was right. Traci had heard this speech before and she would likely hear it again. She had trouble trusting him. But he had caught her in a weak moment, separated from her husband and her current relationship souring in recent days. She was listening intently.

Twitchell was a magnet, and no matter how much Traci logically thought of the futility of a relationship with him, she found herself being drawn closer. Their relationship had always been intense and, at times, exciting. She tried to bring up the topic of his wife, but Twitchell didn't want to talk about it. Traci was left with the distinct impression that he was basically separated. He kept going over past mistakes, telling Traci he was just a teenager when they dated and how he had lied because he wanted to impress her. He thought she was his soul mate.

Their conversation was cut off as the theatre lights dimmed and the big screen came alive with sound and colour. Twitchell and Traci settled in and started watching.

Jennifer Carpenter appeared on screen as a bubbly TV reporter assigned to shadow a firefighting crew with her cameraman. They enter an apartment building infected with a virus similar to rabies, and the authorities lock them all inside to prevent the threat from escaping. It's not long before a police officer is bitten by a frenzied infected resident, her bite peeling off his skin. An old lady, foaming at the mouth, is shot multiple times. An infected rat rushes toward the cameraman and he stomps hard. The rat's guts spill out of its anus and mouth as if he's pressing down on a tube of toothpaste.

Twitchell took his eyes off the screen and looked to his left at Traci, the woman he had once loved so deeply. She liked to cover her eyes during the scary parts in a way he thought was so adorable. Her hair draped the sides of her face, and it took a moment before she finally sensed that he was staring at her.

She met his gaze. He felt a lump in his throat. She flirted back with a tiny smile. He took a chance and leaned in. She felt his hand on her arm and they began to kiss.

The beam of the projector cut above and over their heads. The light struck the screen and reflected back on their faces in a throbbing contrast of light and dark. The contours of her hips pressed against the stadium seat, edging closer to him. Blood sprayed across the screen as she shifted her weight near. He could feel her hot breath. His lips, once split and healed years ago in a soft line of pink tissue, pressed hard against Traci's.

The killing onscreen had continued at a steady pace. The cameraman was now fighting off a crazed, infected woman by smashing his camera into her head, the shot giving his direct viewpoint of the assault. She falls to the floor, but he doesn't stop, using a greater force with each strike. Blood pours down her face as she cowers from the attack. He delivers another blow, twisting her head, and a few more in quick succession. The cameraman finally calms down, his grunting easing, as he stares below at her lifeless body.

Twitchell barely paid attention as the slaying played out in the darkened theatre. In the back row, his kissing Traci had progressed to making out. He felt it was "real passion" and he was "really letting go." As the bodies piled up onscreen, their passion rose even higher. Whenever they heard a loud shrill or scream, they'd pause for a moment, smile, and then start kissing once more. He was on brink of falling in love all over again.

They put their passion on pause only to catch the end of the film, watching Jennifer Carpenter as she is dragged to her death. The screen fades to black. Traci thought the movie was "horrible" and hated watching such violence. Twitchell had hoped the movie would inspire his own filmmaking but hadn't seen enough to decide what he thought of it.

Traci wanted to leave. As they exited the theatre, Twitchell imagined she was torn up about her two relationships, being mistreated and needing reassurance that this time he was serious about her. She could have been thinking about all of this, but the real reason she was in such a rush was far closer to home: she had two little mouths to feed.

Traci loved her two dogs. They had to be fed and given their medicine between 5:00 p.m. and 6:00 p.m. each day, and with a long drive back to her home, she had to leave now.

As they reached their cars, Twitchell leaned in for a final kiss goodbye. There was no doubt in Traci's mind they had crossed a line in that theatre. She was confused and excited about what it meant. It lingered on her mind all afternoon.

Twitchell wasn't worried about getting caught. He realized his marriage to Jess was nearing its end, but he didn't want to face it just yet. He unlocked his car, swung the door open, and settled in, the old grey fabric hugging his body.

Traci drove south while Twitchell headed north. But instead of driving home to St. Albert, he decided to stop by his film set.

He had that big idea in his head again. Tonight, it was going to happen. He just needed a bite to eat first, then he could have some fun.

GETTING READY

AROUND 5:30 P.M., A message popped up on Johnny's computer screen from his work friend Willy: "Any plans for the evening?" Both were signed into MSN Messenger chat service.

Johnny boasted, telling him how he was getting lucky. He quickly sent Willy a link to his date's plentyoffish.com profile page.

Willy took a look and saw a photo of Jen in a bikini.

"7:00 p.m. tonight to meet at her place," Johnny typed in the chat screen. "But her instructions to her house were very weird."

Willy wanted to know what he meant.

"She won't give me her phone number and address, but I've got these directions to get to the house and I'm supposed to use the garage to enter."

Willy thought it all sounded strange. "When you get there, text-message me the address."

Johnny started getting ready for his date, leaving dirty dishes piled on the kitchen counter. In his hurry, he copied, then pasted Jen's directions into an email and fired it off to Willy at 6:00 p.m. At least his friend would have that information on hand.

Johnny gave his buddy Dale a quick call, telling him about his date and how he had to go through her garage to get to her house.

Dale had never been a part of Johnny's online dating scene and wasn't too happy to hear about this. "Call me when you get there with the address," he said.

"I will." Johnny hung up the phone.

Leaving the house, Johnny took one last look in the mirror before he headed out the door. He locked up his condo and walked down the stairs to the building's parkade. His Mazda 3 roared out of the underground as he shot across the city.

TRIPLE THREAT

IN JEANS AND HIS hoodie, a military blade secured to his hip, Twitchell checked his email while waiting in the garage. He was standing by the back door, his laptop placed on the little wooden table in front of him, as he anxiously flicked through his messages.

He had completed repairing sections of plastic sheeting that had fallen down since the previous Friday. Now the kill room was perfectly prepped. His mask lay nearby. Two steel pipes were beside his laptop. Both had been wrapped in black hockey tape. His fake handgun rested near the edge of the table. Twitchell's useless stun gun baton had been relegated to the back shelf. And a green bedsheet remained tacked to the ceiling, separating the plastic-wrapped section from the other side, where a bay door was opened slightly, inviting his visitor to enter.

He was going over in his head all the things he was going to say but found himself easily distracted. A beam of sunlight caught his eye. It streamed in through a hole in one of the bay doors, piercing the clear plastic, scattering rainbows like a prism across the room.

He heard traffic outside. His eyes darted under the partially opened door. A red Mazda 3 slowed as it passed the garage, then continued on.

Twitchell gulped. He checked his watch. Things were moving forward nearly a half-hour earlier than anticipated. His adrenaline soared.

He reached for the switch and flicked off the lights. Darkness fell. Twitchell lay waiting in silence. Blood rushed through his veins, his fingers quivering.

A moment passed. He could hear the car come back and pull into the driveway. Headlights beamed through the hole he had just noticed. A shaft of twirling light cut through the darkness. The engine stopped and the light vanished.

A man approached, ducking his head under the door, his clothes rustling from the movement. He took a few steps inside the darkened garage. Then, he stopped, seeming to notice the garage interior, the black plastic covering the windows. "Hello?" he called out.

Twitchell froze. Vibrating in anticipation, hidden from view behind his hanging bedsheet, Twitchell cringed, not sure what to do with the man refusing to move farther inside.

Seconds passed.

Twitchell held his breath. But his visitor remained still. He realized the man must have spotted him when he initially drove by. Twitchell had to think fast. "Hello?" he called back, cringing again. "Oh, hold on just a sec."

The lights returned and a yellow glow filled the room. Twitchell peered around his sheet and there he stood: Johnny Altinger, wearing glasses, thin and tall, staring right back at him.

Twitchell launched into an improvised routine. "Hey, I'm Mark," he said cheerfully. "I'm a filmmaker. I'm dressing this to look like a set." He motioned to the plastic sheeting covering his metal table, ceiling, floor, and walls.

Johnny just looked at him, a bit confused by what he was seeing.

Twitchell kept going, acting on the assumption that they both knew about the date. After all, Jen's email had mentioned that a man may be in the garage, using it as a workshop. He kept his jolly mood elevated as he tried to draw out the unexpected conversation. "You see this here?" Twitchell pointed to the wooden table and reached for the prop firearm. He pulled out the magazine and showed Johnny how it was full of plastic pebbles, a pellet gun.

Johnny took a closer look.

"I was the guy who made that *Star Wars* fan film," Twitchell blurted. He thought back to the television news coverage the project had received. "Have you heard of it?"

"No, I haven't," said Johnny, cautiously.

Seeing that the conversation was going nowhere, Twitchell tried to wrap it up. "Listen, Jen's not back yet. She's out on a short trip with her friends. She should be back in a bit, maybe ten minutes?"

Johnny nodded. "I'll come back," he said. He jumped in his car and drove off.

Twitchell took a deep breath, returning to his laptop as a distraction from his racing mind. He wasn't sure how he was going to do this. But before he could think of a clear plan, Johnny was already pulling into the driveway again, parking in the same spot and ducking under the door.

In a panic, Twitchell reached for his cell phone and pretended to be on a call. "Yeah? Okay. I'll let him know. Bye."

Johnny was standing in the garage again, looking at Twitchell.

"Oh, hey!" Twitchell smiled. "I just got off the phone with her. She said she's stuck in traffic and won't be back for at least a half-hour. Do you wanna stick around or come back or . . ."

Johnny was already turning for the door. "Nah, I'll leave." He pulled his own phone out and started dialling as he opened his car door. Twitchell watched him drive off.

He didn't know what to do next.

Johnny talked fast into his cell phone, his other hand juggling the steering wheel and the gear shift as he cruised along the freeway back to his condo. Dale listened in on the other end.

"Hey, I just left," Johnny said. "She wasn't there. But I met a *guy* in the garage."

"What?" Dale thought it sounded a little odd.

"Yeah, the guy was making a movie and he showed me a replica gun." Johnny wanted to keep it brief. He was using his pay-as-you-go cell phone, which had very little credit left on it. "I'll give you a shout a little later when I get home."

Back at his condo, Johnny collapsed on his couch, frustrated by the experience. He flipped open his laptop and typed out a message to his date. About twenty minutes later, Jen wrote him back, apologizing for the delay and saying she was now at her house, but it was up to him whether he wanted to come back tonight or postpone their date for another night. Johnny read it over, thought a moment, and decided he didn't want to waste any more of his evening, so he responded that he would head over soon.

He knew Dale would want to know about this so he fired off an email. "She's home now," he typed. "I'm heading over again! HEHE!" He hit send, slipped on his jacket, and headed for the door, ecstatic that after all this trouble his Friday-night date was finally going to happen.

—

FOR THE THIRD TIME that evening, the red Mazda crept slowly down the alley. A stillness drifted in the air. Rolling into the driveway, Johnny saw the garage door remained somewhat open for him to crawl under. He pulled a bag off the car seat, filled with things he'd need if he was spending the night, and stuck his keys in his pocket. A smile lit up across his face and he took a deep breath in, preparing to finally meet Jen.

As he rose from under the garage door, however, he noticed Twitchell was still standing nearby with a strange expression on his face. Johnny gave the filmmaker a bit of a nod, acknowledging that they had met before as he searched for words to explain his third visit to the property that evening. "I guess I'm just a glutton for punishment."

Twitchell looked at Johnny, thinking guys like him redefined what it means to put too much trust in a first impression. But he kept such callous thoughts to himself.

Instead, he just met his visitor's gaze, heart booming in his chest, and flashed him a wry smile.

Johnny had no idea.

AFTERMATH

JESS CHECKED THE CLOCK. It was nearly 10:00 p.m. Her husband should have been home from his Friday-night therapy session by now. The appointment had been written down in black pen on the cartoon bunny calendar she kept tacked up on the wall beside the kitchen table: "Mark appt." The usual start time was 7:00 p.m.

She picked up the phone and dialled his cell. Twitchell's phone was on vibrate and he pulled it out of his pocket after a moment or two.

"Hi, babe, what's up?" Twitchell had call display and was trying to sound cheerful.

"Not much. Where are you?"

"I'm just leaving the gym, hon."

"No, the gym is closed. The gym closes at nine."

"What are you talking about? It closes at ten."

"The big gym by our place?"

"No, my *old* gym, babe."

"I thought you cancelled that membership a month ago?"

He explained to Jess that his membership at the gym near their old rented townhouse was still active. "I procrastinated and changed over my membership a few weeks ago, but I still have a couple weeks this month that are paid for, so I figured I'd take advantage since it takes an hour to cross town anyway."

She thought for a moment. "Okay, well listen, on your way home can you pick up a case of ready-made baby formula at Shoppers?"

"Will do. Anything else?" Twitchell cringed and hoped she wouldn't ask him to get her a latte from Starbucks or some other inconvenient errand.

"No, but I'll probably be in bed by the time you get home." She yawned. "I'm *so* tired."

"I'll see you tomorrow then."

"'Kay, bye."

She hung up the phone and checked on Chloe. In the little room next to the main bedroom, her baby was asleep under her crescent moon nightlight. Her crib was sturdy oak. There were pictures of cartoon giraffes stuck beside it. Across the room, a stuffed tiger was perched on a dresser drawer. Below on the grey carpet a bright yellow plastic bucket was adorned with a smiley face, as if to say, "Don't worry, be happy." Chloe frequently slept through the night.

Jess crawled into her own bed in the adjacent room and pulled the covers around her. She kept a fan in the corner to blow air around the room and a baby monitor on the dresser next to her jewellery. Since Chloe sometimes slept next to her, she had put up a little gate on the side of the bed to prevent her from rolling onto the floor. On the other side of the bed, an Ernie doll from *Sesame Street* stood watch over a copy of the *Yellow Pages*, a box of tissue, and an alarm clock tucked in near the wall. Jess kept a pair of ear plugs on the floor, handy for days when she needed to block out the noise. She was a light sleeper.

DRIVING HOME IN A car that had become a mess of papers and bags, Twitchell was thinking about his evening as he pulled up to the store. The parking lot was nearly deserted and most of the store lights were off. He knew his wife was going to be pissed. He was too late. It was past midnight, the store was closed, and he had failed Jess yet again.

He decided he could avoid her wrath if he awoke early and rushed off to the store before Jess and the baby woke up. He cruised home in a long solo drive back north to St. Albert.

When he got out of the car, he felt a blast of frigid night air. He pulled his duffle bag out of the car and swung it over his shoulder. He opened the door to his house slowly and quietly, trying not to stir Jess or Chloe awake as he tiptoed down the flight of stairs into the basement. The room was littered with dirty clothes, boxes, and junk strewn over the blue carpet. In the corner, he had his own mattress and box spring set draped in red plaid sheets adjacent to his computer desk.

Twitchell was exhausted and decided to take a shower. The basement had its own ensuite, which he had been using since he started sleeping down there. He jumped in, showered, and dried himself off.

It had been a long day.

But before he went to sleep, he decided to do some laundry. He dumped out his clothes from his duffle bag into the washer. He washed his socks, pants, and shirt, as well as one of his newest purchases: a dark green hoodie. He threw his sneakers into the wash too.

All of the items were soaked in blood.

SILENCE

DALE RETURNED TO HIS computer later on Friday evening. He used it far less frequently than his friend Johnny, but he would fire off a short message in reply whenever he did get an email.

Checking his inbox, Dale noticed Johnny had sent him an email a few minutes after 7:00 p.m. Johnny had relayed how he was going back to the woman's place since she was finally at home. But why hadn't he sent on the address when he got there? He regretted not asking again for the woman's address during their brief phone call a few hours ago.

Dale headed to his house phone and dialled Johnny's number. It rang five or six times. Finally, the line was answered: "I listen to Joe! This is John. Altinger. I am not here right now, so leave a name, phone number, and I will get back to you soon."

Dale hung up. He tried again a few minutes later and at least once more before he went to bed. There was no answer each time, the silence adding to his heightened concerns.

THINKING OF THE WORKWEEK ahead, Hans wished Johnny a "Happy Thanksgiving" as he sent an email in anticipation of a new possibility. "On Tuesday I'm going to view two condos in your block," Hans wrote. "You know what that means: let's set up a car pool!"

ARRIVING BACK AT HOME from a Saturday-morning funeral, Dale dialled Johnny's number once more. Still nothing. Every call went to his voicemail. Dale called one of his friends and told him the strange news. His concerns were mounting.

By Sunday, he was even more worried. Johnny had failed to show up for their planned motorcycle lesson. He would never have cancelled without an explanation. Dale sent him emails and phoned him a few more times but received no reply. He phoned another friend with a feeling of dread. "I think Johnny is missing."

WILLY NOTICED JOHNNY HADN'T logged in to MSN Messenger all weekend. He could only imagine what his buddy had been up to instead. He began typing an offline message Johnny could read the next time he signed in. "How's it going? You still at the chick's place?"

DALE JOINED HIS FAMILY for Thanksgiving dinner on the evening of Sunday, October 12, but he found himself in the lowest of spirits. His mind kept drifting back to Johnny. Where was he? What could possibly be preventing him from returning his calls? Who was the filmmaker in the garage Johnny had mentioned? It had been two days since their last phone call. His anxiety increasing, Dale abruptly cancelled plans to visit with a few friends after dinner. Instead, he called another friend and his wife for support. He was determined to begin searching for Johnny.

Under an autumn sunset, the three of them parked at Johnny's condo tower and headed for the main door. The metal door latch popped open with a big tug. Dale hurried down the hallway and arrived at Johnny's front door. He knocked. He waited. There was no response.

They took the staircase to the underground parkade, treading over an expanse of concrete and oil stains. In Johnny's parking stall, his car was gone but his two motorbikes were still sitting there, uncovered and gathering dust.

Feeling defeated, Dale and his friends tried Johnny's patio door. It was locked too. Dale leaned in for a look through the window. He pressed his hands to the glass, staring into the nothingness; not even the moonlight offered him hope of seeing movement inside.

His friend Johnny had disappeared.

DARK COMEDY

TWITCHELL LET OUT A big yawn as he stirred awake on Saturday morning. He had overslept. Jess and Chloe had already started their day by the time he finally awoke from his deep slumber.

Jess spotted her husband as he trudged up the stairs. "Where's the baby formula?"

"Oh, sorry," he said, trying to wake up. "When I went there last night they were all out of stock." He told her he didn't mind jumping in the car now and getting some. He could tell she wasn't impressed.

He drove to the store, returned, and the three of them had noodles for lunch. Jess was then free to run a few errands before they dropped off the baby at Twitchell's parents' house. Finally, there was some free time for the two of them to spend together without the responsibility of caring for a baby.

That evening, Jess and Twitchell decided to drive to Bourbon Street, a wing of West Edmonton Mall decorated to look like the famous French Quarter in New Orleans. After dinner at one of the strip's loud restaurants, the couple headed to a comedy show a few doors down. They settled in at one of the black-top tables, staring at a stage with a fake city skyline.

Twitchell found himself in a flurry of conflicting thoughts. But as he sat there, looking at the main act rip one-liners and get the crowd going, he saw his wife experience a moment of happiness. She had no idea what was going on in his life, not a clue about what he had been doing with his Fridays. He wanted that facade to continue.

So he began to join in the merriment, first with snickers and soon with howls of laughter. With every joke the comedian told, Twitchell laughed a bit louder. Soon he was roaring, his mouth wide open as his tongue leapt back from his teeth.

The couple shared a lot of laughs that night, actually. In fact, Jess looked at her husband in amusement and assumed he was having a blast. For the first time in a long while, he seemed to be in good spirits and his easygoing self again. Over the weekend, she saw how her husband had even worn his green hoodie, fresh out of the dryer and smelling great, still looking new.

———

ON SUNDAY AFTERNOON, TWITCHELL and Jess picked up Chloe while dropping by to have Thanksgiving dinner with his parents, Norm and Mary, at their home. They arrived around 4:00 p.m. and enjoyed plates of wonderful food. He would get a second big meal the following day when they went to his in-laws. But Twitchell wasn't a fan of the traditional turkey. He found the meat too dry and stringy.

When he and Jess returned to St. Albert with Chloe three hours later, the jovial mood had disappeared. Twitchell suddenly became spooked and jumpy when they arrived at the front door.

"It's not locked," he said, pushing it open.

Twitchell looked at Jess, who was usually quite good at remembering to lock it. She thought she could have forgotten but was pretty sure she didn't.

"Maybe someone tried to break in," he said. He entered the house first and took a look around as quietly as possible. Jess and Chloe waited outside. He quickly scanned each room, looking for any signs of an intruder. Seeing none, he made sure nothing had been stolen. Everything seemed fine. He walked back to the door and the incident was passed off as nothing but a sudden rush of paranoia.

When he finally had a chance to relax, Twitchell reflected on the past few days of his life – his Friday afternoon movie date with Traci, followed by the experience in the garage, his weekend of suburban get-togethers – and he couldn't resist returning to the Internet and dropping major clues about what he had been up to. Renee found herself treated to an ambiguous message describing how busy his weekend had been with a double helping of Thanksgiving meals. "I've also had something else keeping me busy," he wrote, "but I'm really concerned about telling anyone because of the implications. Suffice it to say I crossed the line on Friday . . . and I liked it."

She was struck by his odd choice of words and demanded an explanation. "You wouldn't have brought it up unless you needed someone to confide in," she wrote. "So spill it, Mark."

He asked for her phone number and she passed it along.

It was as if Twitchell was looking for someone to unload on. Over the course of late September and the first few weeks of October, he had also returned to S. K. Confessions and written about how having a child could be a source of great comfort in this area:

> The cool thing about a seven-month-old is that you can openly tell them anything, and they can't rat you out. I needed that from my daughter, since anyone else I could spill to would be dialing 9-1-1 before I finished. I knew I only had a limited amount of time before Zoe's comprehension got to the level where that wouldn't fly, so I got in as much talk time as possible in her early development when the words were just soothing sounds to get her used to the English language.

What he was up to required discretion, a level of privacy to block unwanted attention. Renee was a stranger on the other side of North America and he thought talking to her could be comforting. "Cheers and good health to all you care about," he replied to the message she sent with her phone number. He settled on plans to finally reveal to her what he'd been up to in a matter of days.

CHANGING STATUS

FOR JOHNNY'S FRIENDS, THANKSGIVING Monday had begun with hope under threat. He had been missing for almost three days, but as if hearing their growing calls of concern, he finally reached out during a morning binge of Internet activity.

Willy was the first to hear from him. At 8:42 a.m., his friend and co-worker had finally replied to his offline MSN message. "Hey man," Johnny wrote in an email. "No worries on my end. . . . The girl and I hit it off big time. I know it's only been a few days but I think I'm falling hard and she feels the same way." Johnny explained how he was planning to leave on a tropical vacation and his new girlfriend was footing the bill. "Never done anything so spontaneous and it would be a great experience to get in before I die."

Ten minutes later, Johnny created an out-of-office message that automatically sent emails to his friends, bragging about the "extraordinary woman named Jen" he had met who was taking him to Costa Rica for a few months. An email of resignation was quickly sent to his boss. "I thank you for the opportunity," Johnny wrote in conclusion, "and rest assured I would not be leaving unless the new path I've chosen was truly life-altering."

His Facebook page also lit up with activity. In his first post in nearly a month, he wrote: "John Altinger is taking off to the Caribbean for a few months. See you all when I get back!" He changed his relationship status to "in a relationship." Some of his friends were thrilled to hear it. "Have fun! Take lots of pictures," replied one friend. "For a couple of months?" another asked. "Tough life!" And as if to prove that he was finished with online dating now that he had found this amazing woman, Johnny's plentyoffish.com account was deleted that same morning.

DALE RECEIVED THE SAME email as everyone else, which added to his suspicions. He doubted Johnny would leave the country without calling his best friend to at least make arrangements for his motorbikes to be covered and looked after. Besides, Johnny was more likely to go to Germany and visit a car factory than take a Caribbean holiday. He hated the heat. Dale typed a reply: "Who's going to pick your brother up at the airport?" It was a lie to test what Johnny's response would be, but the question remained unanswered.

Dale finally had enough of the continuing strange activity. But when he tried to file a missing persons report, an officer told him to go away. A middle-aged single man running off on a wild romantic getaway with some woman? The officer didn't think it sounded like a crime had been committed at all – some would call the guy damn lucky, actually – and it would be a waste of police resources to launch an investigation.

DEBRA TEICHROEB HADN'T THOUGHT of Johnny in a while, but reading over his email about a tropical vacation brought back memories of how she had rejected his romantic intentions. The Johnny she knew and cared about didn't do things on a whim. He planned trips months in advance. Running off on a whirlwind romance took her by surprise. But maybe he had changed.

Sitting at her computer, Debra thought about responding but didn't know what to tell him. She found it odd that he had not called her "Sunshine" the way he did when he had written to her so many times before. The tone of his email was so formal, as if all his personality had been stripped away. She considered telling him to be careful on his trip, but then she turned away from her keyboard and decided to let it be. With their history, she knew it was not her place to question his relationship decisions.

Later on, Debra noticed Johnny signed in to MSN Messenger. His new status update on the chat service confirmed how happy he had become. Words displayed beside a little icon and his name told of a life on holiday, a life of pure bliss. She could almost imagine the palm trees he was seeing, nearly taste the cocktails of coconut and lime. "I've got a one way ticket to heaven," Johnny had written of his trip, "and I'm never coming back."

A BLAZE IN THE SUBURBS

THE LIT MATCH TUMBLED out of Twitchell's hand and dropped in a free fall into the oil drum. The flame ignited an explosion that flashed in a burst of orange and yellow, shooting flames up into the sky. The air smelled of burning gasoline as light smoke billowed, carried by the wind.

Twitchell did not detect this expanding odour. He had no sense of smell. He simply stood back, watching the contents of the barrel slowly burn. He had spent a few hours loading up the barrel from his garage film studio into the back of his car. He then drove it across town to his parents' house, where he planted it in the middle of their backyard. Nearby, a grouping of full garbage bags had been piled up, each one twisted tight and sealed with duct tape. Twitchell had soaked everything in the barrel in a splashing of gas from his jerry can. As he had hoped, his parents weren't home, so he had the whole place to himself.

The yard had a single sidewalk leading from the house to a detached garage and a parked RV. Sandwiched in between was a large pad of grass, now dying as winter approached, with a blue spruce tree off in the corner and a clothesline cutting across the open expanse. Neighbours had built high fences on both sides, closing off his parents' yard from any prying eyes.

The burn lasted only a few minutes and died down as the fuel disappeared. Twitchell might have been smarter to mix some oil with the gasoline to make it burn longer, but he was a city boy and some things can't be learned on the Internet. He peeked his head over the lip of the drum to look inside. Most of the plastic from a garbage bag had melted away, but their contents were still smoldering. The fire was giving off such little heat that he couldn't have cooked a hot dog if he tried. He reached for the jerry can and poured a bit more gas into a coffee cup, then poured out the cup with his arm outstretched, twisting his face away from the drum. A whoosh of flames erupted as the cup was emptied, but again the blaze died out quickly. He tried two more times with the same result. The barrel contents weren't continuing to burn once the fuel was spent.

A siren whined in the distance. Twitchell froze. He scanned for signs of nosy neighbours, but he couldn't see a single window that had a view of the backyard. Then he spotted the dead giveaway drifting skywards. Someone must have seen the clouds of black and grey and called the fire department. The truck's siren howled as it approached, bearing down closer on his parents' home.

Twitchell ran over to the house and grabbed the garden hose rolled up near the barbeque. He turned the tap and doused the barrel down in cold water. The steel drum hissed as steam spat off the hot surface. The paint had peeled off the bottom of the drum and exposed the raw metal. The rest of the drum had turned a very light pink, the enamelled paint transformed by the fire.

But the wail of the fire truck's siren stopped as the blaze was extinguished. The truck never appeared. Twitchell thought it could have been a massive coincidence, but it turned out the fire truck had actually been heading to a call a few blocks away.

It was a sufficient scare to put Twitchell off his mission. At this pace it would take all week to burn everything he wanted destroyed. So he pulled out a roll of garbage bags, rebagged the charred barrel contents, and loaded everything into his car to drive it back to the film studio for another day, another plan.

As Twitchell's dealings with the barrel continued, his messy car became an issue. One day, when Jess was running late for an appointment, she jumped into her husband's Grand Am to move it out of the driveway so she could get her own car out.

She was overcome by the strong odour of gasoline and saw the car was messier than usual. In the backseat was a pair of overalls, similar to what someone would wear to cover their whole body when spray-painting. She was about to start the engine when her husband came flying out of the house, hustling toward her, looking quite concerned. She knew that he didn't like her touching his car, but his reaction this time was certainly on a heightened level.

"What are you doing?" he asked excitedly.

"I need to move your car to get out," she said, motioning to her own car blocked in front. "Why does it smell like gas?"

"Oh. I was filling up a jerry can to put in the trunk as a precaution, but I spilled some."

"But we already have a can of gas," Jess said, reminding him that they had bought one recently for the new lawn mower.

"Well, this is another one."

She was late and it was turning into one of their old fights that began with them bickering over nothing, so she dropped it. "Well, okay," she sighed and took off down the road.

It was probably for the best that Twitchell had no sense of smell. Anyone close to the burning oil drum would have noticed a very distinct scent, strong enough to curl their noses.

When the police discovered the burning barrel in the garage weeks later, it offered solid clues as to what Twitchell had been doing in his parents' backyard. Opening the barrel revealed a wet paper towel and pieces of duct tape all stuck together. Black ash was scattered throughout. When the barrel was tipped over, the contents spilled out in clumps, like nuggets of coal. There were bits of a burnt cleaning sponge, metal rivets, and a round piece of metal, possibly a ring.

The last piece of ash held a thin metal strip as long as a pencil before curving at one end. Police officers took a closer look and they all reached the same conclusion: it looked like the arm off a pair of someone's eyeglasses.

SLEEPLESS

HANS STROLLED INTO WORK on Tuesday afternoon to hear Johnny had quit his job via email, yet nobody seemed to know where he had gone. Hans thought back to the last email he had received from his friend – a response to his interest in car-pooling. "No car pool for me," Johnny had written him on the weekend. "I'm taking an extended vacation. Good luck."

Everyone at work was talking about Johnny's sudden departure. Their boss emailed him to find out where to send his final paycheque but was greeted by silence. It bothered Hans.

As the week rolled on, Hans drove past Johnny's place, parked, and walked up to his patio door. He tried to look through the glass. He could see the computer desk but little else. He was puzzled. His closest friend at work had just up and left with no explanation.

BY WEDNESDAY, OCTOBER 15, Dale and his friends had bothered the police enough to finally get their attention. An officer relented, agreeing to send someone down to at least take a statement. After dinner, Dale, his friend, and his friend's wife waited for the cop's arrival at the couple's house. They sat on the couch. They chatted. They discussed the strange emails and how they could never get Johnny on the phone. There had been odd moments during their search. Dale's friend had received a Facebook message from Johnny after demanding he phone Dale immediately. In reply, Johnny's excuse for not calling was that there was "terrible reception" where he was staying but not to worry. "I'll try to get in touch with Dale as soon as possible," he had written. "But in the meantime, let him know I'm having the time of my life."

The evening passed slowly as they waited for the police. Everyone turned sleepy. The clock ticked past midnight. The three of them checked the time more frequently, but the hours slipped away. Dale awoke at four in the morning to go to work. He realized the police had brushed him off again. It was as if Johnny's disappearance couldn't have mattered less.

FEELING A RUSH

RACING DOWN THE FREEWAY, Twitchell had romance on his mind. Back at home his wife and child were drifting off to sleep. It was ticking past 10:00 p.m., closing in on half past the hour, but all he could think about was Traci again, not his family.

He knew this was wrong, but with everything going on in his life, he couldn't stop himself. His marriage was on the rocks anyway, he reasoned, and his activities on Friday, October 10, had lit a fire in his belly that he couldn't ignore. Traci had just invited him over to her place during an online chat. It was clear what she had in mind. Traci was a perfect escape for him and the thought that he could have her again tonight was thrilling, exhilarating.

Traci lived in a trailer in a farming town an hour's drive south of the city. Having looked up directions on his computer, Twitchell decided to take the ring road, the most direct route, which curves around the west end and joins up with the highways that lead all the way to Wetaskiwin: home of the auto mile, where "Cars Cost Less." All of his life he had been terrible at directions so he scribbled down a few maps in black pen on sticky notes to help him get there. He stuck them in his car. The first neon-yellow Post-It led from his home in St. Albert to the highway. The second detailed what to do when he arrived in Wetaskiwin, and on the third he had written down Traci's street address and the town's strange name.

Twenty minutes into this road trip, his impatience and excitement were taking over. He hit the gas. The engine purred and his car shot forward as he veered down a hill. Other drivers were holding him back so he weaved in and out of the two southbound lanes to get ahead of them. His speed climbed in to the 100 km/h zone as he pushed his car harder, closing in rapidly on a vehicle up ahead. He was about to switch lanes again when the vehicle pulled out of the way and moved in to the right lane. Twitchell blew past it at 128 km/h. The road ahead was straight and flat. He had just crossed the river when he saw blue and red lights flashing in his rear-view mirror.

Shit. It's a cop.

Twitchell's beat-up car crawled to a stop near an overpass. A tall and well-built man with a crew cut in a dark uniform walked up to his car. Twitchell rolled down the window.

"Licence, registration, and insurance, please," the cop said.

Twitchell opened his messy glove box and handed him the papers, pulled out his wallet, and passed him his licence. The cop returned to his patrol car to check everything out.

His name was Bob Reiche. He was on duty as a peace officer for the Alberta Sheriffs, running patrols along the southern leg of Anthony Henday Drive, the city's ring road. And as he entered the details on his computer, he noticed Twitchell's licence plate: DRKJEDI. He walked back to the car and couldn't resist.

"Well the force wasn't very strong with you tonight, now was it?" Reiche said with a big grin. "Because you just blew past a fully marked patrol car." He pointed behind him. His cruiser was all white, with "SHERIFF" and "Highway Patrol" in big blue letters on the back bumper.

Twitchell tried to see the humour in it and joined in on the joke, telling him of his *Star Wars* fan film in post-production. He smiled.

When Reiche asked why he was speeding, Twitchell whined and lied, hoping to talk his way out of a ticket. "Can't you give a guy a break?" he pleaded. "I'm a film producer. I'm making a movie and I'm on my way to the airport right now." He told Reiche he had to pick up a big-name celebrity. "He's annoyed that I'm not already there."

Reiche headed back to his patrol car to write up the ticket. But he couldn't stop thinking about the novelty car plate. He signed and dated the ticket, and with a smile, he returned with good news. "Hey, are you Darth Vader?" the cop chuckled. ·

Twitchell tried not to show his frustration and impatience. The sheriff noticed his change in demeanour and stopped cracking jokes. He handed Twitchell his yellow ticket for $89.

"I gave you a break," Reiche said. "The ticket is about half of what you should have paid."

Twitchell thanked him for knocking down the amount. When he had time later, he would pull out his computer and write in S. K. Confessions about how the cop had "no clue" about who he had just pulled over. If only the officer had taken a closer look at his car, peered inside, or examined his trunk. "He just did his duty and took off," he wrote. "Now every time I pass a police car on the road, I chuckle to myself."

Twitchell stuffed the speeding ticket into his white and black backpack, next to where he usually kept his laptop. He dropped the bag on the floor of the passenger side of the vehicle. There the ticket would sit, forgotten, never to be paid.

He had more pressing concerns on his mind, after all. A Post-It note was nearby, stating his chosen desires. And in his backpack, he had stashed a few condoms and a bottle of cologne.

Traci was less than forty minutes away.

DAWN BROKE. TRACI WAS already awake. She was getting dressed for work in the early morning of Tuesday, October 14. It was her first day back since the long weekend and she had to leave soon to drive to Nisku, on the highway just outside of Edmonton. Still a bit groggy, Twitchell rubbed his eyes and looked up at her from the covers of her bed. While he had been putting on weight from his diet of junk food, Traci was in terrific shape. She had a tattoo on her left shoulder that he had helped design when they were dating back in college. He remembered the Celtic cross tattoo quite well. It had been his idea to add intertwining vines to it, which Traci agreed looked really cool. She had been inked up with another tattoo since then. On the back of her neck was a Celtic knot of interwoven lines joining into a circle, symbolizing everlasting love.

The night had been everything Twitchell had wanted, but Traci was still not convinced it had been a good idea. In the sobriety of the harsh daylight, she didn't know what to make of it. Twitchell had re-emerged in her life while she was still seeking a divorce and stuck in the middle of another tumultuous relationship that seemed to start and end on a regular rotation. It didn't make her feel any better to see that while she was frantically trying to get ready for work, it seemed like Twitchell, lying back and looking comfortable, had nowhere to be.

Despite her misgivings, she decided to trust him with a key. It was around 5:30 a.m. and they had been up all night. She told him to lock up when he left. "Just leave it under the barbeque," she said before heading out the door.

Twitchell drifted back to sleep and awoke hours later. When he opened the bedroom door, her two little dogs went nuts. He looked down, annoyed as the pug and Boston terrier mixes yipped and barked, nipping at his feet. He brushed past the pair into the main room of the trailer. The television had been left on and it was broadcasting an episode of *The View*. Twitchell shut it off, packed up his things, and walked out the door. He then stuck Traci's spare key under a lawn ornament, ignoring her instructions, and jumped in his car.

Twitchell drove across the railway tracks, cruising through the sleepy town – a mix of suburbia, pawn shops, liquor stores, and bingo halls. He reached the highway and drove past a huge water tower surrounded by a cemetery. One of the last things he saw of Wetaskiwin was row upon row of tombstones.

As he approached Edmonton nearly an hour later, Twitchell felt his stomach rumble so he detoured for breakfast. A bit later, with a belly full of eggs and chocolate milk, he parked at his rented garage and opened the back door. It had been just over three days since his Friday-night experience. The air was stuffy and stale. He flicked on the light. A bulb glowed above, light reflecting off dozens of staples that remained stuck in the ceiling.

He paused a moment to admire his special room. Half the space was taken up by a red Mazda 3 while his metal table, metal chair, and oil drum cluttered the other side.

It was chilly in the garage. There was no heating system to ward off the biting autumn air. Twitchell could nearly see his breath as he grabbed a pair of scissors and rolled out clear plastic sheeting over the concrete floor. He then cut two layers of plastic sheets and draped them on top of his metal table, like an oversized tablecloth. On one side of the table, he placed a metal pipe with hockey tape wrapped around one end; on the other side, he placed a bottle of ammonia and a roll of paper towels.

He duct-taped two grocery bags around his ankles to seal them shut around his shoes. Twitchell took several minutes to fashion a make-shift apron out of plastic sheeting and duct tape, which he then hung around his neck. He pulled on a pair of plastic gloves and pushed a painter's mask over his face. He knew the ammonia could burn his lungs.

Twitchell opened the trunk of the Mazda and withdrew the large garbage bags he had salvaged from his unsuccessful fire. He lifted each one, dropping them on the plastic-covered concrete beside his metal table. He hoisted one of the bigger bags onto the tabletop.

At last, he retrieved an emerald green plastic case off the back shelf and placed it on his table. It was no bigger than a briefcase and had a bit of heft to it. Embedded into the hard plastic were the words "Outdoor Edge Game Processor."

He flicked the case open.

Inside, four knives were stacked nicely on the left. Each blade was contained within its own compartment, the knife sharpener stored directly above. On the right, a meat cleaver that didn't match the others was resting within. Beneath it were a carving fork, cutting shears, a long big-toothed saw, and a pair of rib spreaders.

Twitchell's fingers dangled over the instruments as he decided which one to choose. He finally reached in for the butcher knife. Twitchell grabbed the handle tightly and raised the knife near his face, admiring the heavy sharp blade.

A WINDOW OPENS

JOHNNY'S BEHAVIOUR CONTINUED TO frustrate his friends. He seemed totally preoccupied with his new life with this rich woman in the Caribbean. Six days after his date with Jen, he signed in to Facebook again. Johnny's updated status showed his new path was having an even greater hold on him: "Wondering why anyone would leave sun and surf to come back to snow and stress." A friend demanded to see his vacation pictures, but Johnny ignored him.

Facebook had become a pivot point for those who cared about Johnny Altinger. Friends who knew him, but didn't know each other, began connecting through the site. Messages were shared as they asked questions, searched for answers. Dale continued to lead the pack. The police had told him they would need more evidence if an investigation was to occur. When Dale finished work on Friday, October 17, he discovered his friends – the married couple who had spent a long night with him waiting for the police – had stopped by Johnny's place that day and found a window ajar. He rushed over to the condo and the couple joined him for Dale's first peek inside.

His friend's wife crawled through the window, tiptoeing across Johnny's condo to unlock the front door for Dale and her husband. The three of them scoured the place for any clue of Johnny's whereabouts. Dale headed for the bedroom while his friends searched the kitchen. They saw dirty pots on the stove, a hot dog unwrapped in the fridge. Trash cans were emptied, receipts gathered. If Johnny had gone on vacation with his date, he clearly hadn't returned to his condo to pick up a few essentials: his luggage was still in the closet, and he had left behind his beach towel and shaving kit. But Johnny's laptop was missing, as well as his printer.

Dale searched the bedroom dresser. He thumbed through clothes until he stumbled upon some of Johnny's documents.

Among them, his passport.

INCONVENIENT ERRANDS

It was Friday, October 17, when Twitchell returned to his garage once again. He had run out of ideas on how to solve a remaining problem that had emerged exactly one week earlier. In a sigh, he pulled out his cell phone and called Joss.

His friend picked up after a few rings, taking a break from pulling security system wiring through an under-construction electronics store. Twitchell tried to sound upbeat as he shared the exciting news: he had been at a gas station recently and randomly met a guy who was moving to the Caribbean with his sugar momma and trying to get rid of his stuff for whatever he could get. Twitchell explained with glee how he had bought the man's red Mazda 3 for only forty dollars.

"Wow!" Joss said. "Sounds like one of those deals that's too good to be true."

"Yeah, I thought so too," Twitchell replied, "but I have all of the papers for it and I got a bill of sale." He asked him if he knew where the nearest registry office was located so he could fill out the ownership paperwork and sell it right away.

"Why not keep it?" Joss offered. "It's a nice car."

"It's a standard. I can't drive it." Twitchell asked Joss for a favour: would he come over to the garage right away and drive the Mazda 3 for him to his home in St. Albert?

Joss looked at the clock. It was shortly after 3:30 p.m. He told Twitchell he didn't have time to drive to St. Albert that day because he had to meet someone at 4:00 p.m. "How 'bout I park it in the driveway at my house?" The garage was only a few blocks away from where Joss lived with his parents. Joss would just have to check with his dad, but he didn't think it would be a problem.

Twitchell accepted the compromise but didn't explain to his friend why he had to move a car that was already parked in a garage. Joss didn't think to ask.

They met at the rental property a few minutes later. Twitchell watched as Joss examined the car in astonishment. It looked to be in such great condition for only forty dollars. Joss drove it over to his parents' house and Twitchell followed, collecting the licence plate and keys.

Over the weekend, Twitchell received several phone calls from Joss about the car, offering to buy it for much more than he had spent. But Twitchell always politely declined, saying he'd have to think about it. Joss thought his friend had all the luck. Talking about the car purchase with his own family, Joss kept shaking his head, thinking it was like Twitchell was born with a horseshoe up his ass.

If only Joss had examined the car's exterior more closely, he would have noticed a strange stain that blended into the glossy red paint on the Mazda 3's back bumper. The red liquid had dried in a flow pattern, pointing from the bumper back into the trunk. Opening the trunk would have revealed further stains soaked into the trunk carpet and dripping into the spare tire below.

At a glance, anyone passing by might have just assumed that someone had been loading and unloading leaky garbage bags into the trunk of the car, spilling some of their contents with every messy trip.

INVESTIGATION

THE DISCOVERY OF JOHNNY'S passport was a vindication of Dale Smith's concerns. He knew the police couldn't ignore him now. And the back-and-forth of messages between Johnny's Facebook friends had uncovered that he had emailed one of his co-workers, Willy, the directions he had received from his Friday-night date. Everything was coming together.

With this newly gathered information, a phone call to the police finally resulted in action. Officers acknowledged there was a potential crime worth investigating, especially with a passport located for a man supposedly on vacation overseas.

A missing persons report was filed and a case number assigned. Two constables coming on night shift were handed the file. Exactly one week since he was last seen, a patrol car started driving to a rented garage, following the very same path Johnny had taken.

JOHNNY'S FRIENDS CONTINUED TO expand their search for the latest information, even after the police became involved. The creation of the "Find Johnny Altinger" group page on Facebook allowed them to share stories and photos, as well as theories on his whereabouts. In Vancouver, Marie was startled to receive an invitation to join such a group and to discover that the old friend she had just visited in the summer had vanished. "I hope this isn't true," she wrote.

Dozens of people, in fact, had been caught off guard when they received the same invites to join the group. Johnny's closest friends had never stopped spreading the word of their suspicions behind Johnny's Caribbean vacation, which surprised many who had assumed his status updates were legitimate. Family members across the world were soon told the news.

Johnny's mother, Elfriede, called his phone while she was in Mexico on vacation, but her calls were always diverted to his voicemail. In her sadness and confusion, she found she started calling just to hear the comforting recorded voice of her son on the other end.

It was a habit that would consume her for years.

EARLY TROUBLE

On the night of Saturday, October 18, Twitchell's cell phone rang as he sat at home with Jess and the baby. He had been fiddling on his laptop earlier and wasn't expecting any calls. He picked up and to his surprise, a police officer was on the other end.

Constable Christopher Maxwell was sitting in his police cruiser, parked on a road not far from his southwest division station. Talking into his cell phone, Maxwell wanted to confirm Twitchell was the rental tenant occupying a garage on the south side of the city. He had been given Twitchell's name by the property manager, who had a signed lease at the ready with his contact details.

"Yes, I am," Twitchell replied, feeling his anxiety rise.

Maxwell began running through a series of questions. "When was the last time that you were at the garage?"

"It would have been Friday on the 10th of October."

"Do you remember someone showing up there on Friday, around 6:00 p.m.?"

"No."

"Okay," Maxwell continued. "Do you remember a red car being at your garage?"

"No."

"Did you know of any women meeting a guy at the garage?"

"No."

Maxwell noted how Twitchell's answers were all very short. He had driven to the garage the night before with another officer, but it was locked up and the house tenants knew nothing. "Listen, would you mind coming down to the garage? We're dealing with a missing person and we just want to have a quick look."

Twitchell sounded surprised. "That's fine," he said.

Hanging up the phone, Twitchell headed out the door without giving Jess much of an explanation about what was going on. He was quick to phone Joss, however, to let him know the police had just called. "It sounds like there's been a break-in at the garage," he said. "I'm on my way down."

TWITCHELL'S GRAND AM RUMBLED down the alley, headlights cutting through the darkness. As he pulled in near the garage he could see the outline of two uniformed officers. Their patrol cars were parked nearby. He shut the engine off and got out of the car.

He was met by Constable Maxwell, who had a shaved head and a soft voice. He was standing beside a taller officer, a young woman with high cheekbones who Twitchell didn't realize was Maxwell's superior, a temporary acting sergeant brought down to help the constable follow up on the missing persons complaint.

Maxwell did all the talking. "I'm the guy you just talked to on the phone," he said to Twitchell. "We just want to make sure everything is okay and just rule out that the missing man isn't inside."

Twitchell appeared happy to help. "Sure. Okay."

The trio walked together, squeezing in beside the garage and the fence shared with the next-door neighbour. As they rounded the corner and reached the back door, Twitchell stopped in his tracks. "That's not my lock." He scratched his head, looking at the door to the garage in disbelief. "Mine's silver with black."

Maxwell took a closer look. Whoever installed the metal latch had drilled the screws in from the outside. Anyone with a screwdriver could easily remove it, defeating the purpose of the padlock. He grabbed a utility knife from his belt and started undoing the screws.

"I haven't been back here since October 10," Twitchell repeated. "Maybe somebody changed the lock when I wasn't here?"

The padlock popped off. Twitchell used his key to open the deadbolt and Maxwell stepped forward. "Here, let me go in first." The back door creaked open. As Maxwell entered, his sergeant right behind him, both caught a whiff of gasoline and the escaping smells of burnt materials. A dim light was glowing inside.

Twitchell stepped through the doorway to join them.

"Just stay where you are," Maxwell urged. The officer scanned the room, stepping forward slowly. The space was fairly empty. The air hung thick with a burning smell. He saw an oil drum placed to the side, near a large metal table and chair. Used cleaning supplies were piled up on a small wooden table by the door. Maxwell leaned in to his sergeant's ear. "Take a look at that." Her eyes dropped to the wooden table, where there was a receipt from a hardware store. The customer had paid with a MasterCard for plastic sheeting, rubber gloves, paper towels, and a bottle of heavy-duty cleaner. The purchase was dated October 15. She noted the last four digits of the credit card, which hadn't been blacked out.

The officers whispered again, then slowly backed out of the garage, closing the door behind them. The sergeant walked to her patrol car and called the station while Maxwell took Twitchell back to his cruiser.

Sitting inside the vehicle, they made small talk as Twitchell filled out a written witness statement. Maxwell continued the conversation with a question his sergeant had wanted him to ask. "Mr. Twitchell, would you mind showing me your MasterCard?"

Twitchell lifted his eyes off the statement he was writing, looking puzzled, hesitating.

"Can I please see your MasterCard?"

Twitchell didn't move.

"Sir, can I see your MasterCard?"

Twitchell finally pulled out his wallet and lightly fanned the cards inside like there was nothing of interest to see. Maxwell leaned over from the driver's seat and pointed to the wallet's pouches. "No, in there." Twitchell gave up and slid out a MasterCard from one pouch and handed it to Maxwell, who checked the number. The last four digits were the same as those on the receipt found in the garage.

The officers had discovered that Twitchell had lied about the last time he was at the property. The receipt easily proved he had been inside the garage with cleaning supplies five days later than he had claimed. But why?

Thinking of this new development, Maxwell felt a bad feeling take hold as he sat in his patrol car next to Twitchell. He feared there was something suspicious behind the man's lie. Maxwell knew a detective would have to be called in to help sort this mess out – and he'd have no problem sharing his suspicions with detectives if the case ever took on a more sinister dimension.

STICKY SCENARIOS

BOBBING HIS HEAD, TWITCHELL could not stop talking as his laughs and smiles spilled sideways from his mouth. The fact that he was sitting across from a detective at the southwest police station at three in the morning seemed to have little impact on his elevated mood. He let his wife's calls go straight to his cell phone voicemail, motoring through a rundown of his search for investors, securing A-list acting talent and his history in film and sales jobs. "Don't get me started on this stuff," he chuckled, settling into the round table crammed into the corner of a police interview room. "I could go for hours."

For the moment, Detective Mike Tabler sat quietly across the table from him, resting his head into his palm, listening to Twitchell babble on. The banter was clearly one-sided. The veteran cop with grey-blond hair let Twitchell keep going until the steam ran out and he sputtered and coughed. That's when he'd reach in and slowly direct him back to the basics of why he was there.

The detective's tall and thin stature was largely hidden as he listened in his chair, a pen resting unused beside his notepad on the white table. Tabler's silence also hid his booming baritone voice, which, when projected, could rumble until it filled the room. Years of smoking had given him a raspy bass undertone.

Tabler asked about the last time Twitchell was at the garage, which prompted the filmmaker to start talking about his cleaning supplies, clarifying that he actually meant October 15 was the last day he was at the property. He leaned back in his chair. "When you do anything that's this involving, like suspense thrillers or anything like that, you want to have something that looks like blood on the screen."

Tabler feigned enthusiasm as Twitchell described how to make and clean up a fake blood mix of corn syrup and food colouring.

"It looks really good on camera," said Twitchell. "But it's sticky as hell. It gets everywhere and it's a nightmare." He swallowed, catching his breath.

"And last time? It got all over the chair, got all over the floor." He chuckled again. "It's like . . . *ridiculous.*"

"Sounds kinda unique," Tabler offered.

"But it's a huge mess too, like dripping stuff everywhere." Twitchell explained how one scene involved thrusting a sword through a fake torso, fake blood pouring out of its back.

Tabler finally interjected, shifting his weight as he raised his low-pitched voice. "I'm just thinking about this." He waved his hand as his thoughts came to him. "I mean, it's kinda odd that you're filming that kind of thing and we end up going to that garage because of a missing person, who supposedly went there."

Twitchell jumped in quickly. "Yeah, that's really freaky too. As soon as they called me on the phone and said this is what's going on, I got this weird chill." He expressed concerns about who else knew about the garage, pointing out that Mike and Jay also had a key.

But Tabler knew it wasn't adding up. The story about the mystery padlock was suspicious. For one, it didn't explain how someone else could gain entry because the door deadbolt was still locked. The detective finally swung the conversation to the main point of the case. "So, now you've been told that we're looking for a missing man."

"Uh-huh." Twitchell nodded.

"Have you been told his name?"

"No."

"The name is John." Tabler paused, looking at the filmmaker. "Altinger."

"Okay," Twitchell said, his smile fading.

"Does that name ring a bell for you?"

"No."

"Never heard it before?"

"No," he repeated, shaking his head.

"He's nobody who you'd been using as an actor?"

"No, I don't think so." Twitchell frowned, shrugging it off. "I don't know if Mike or Jay know him, but nothing in terms of casting or production crew or anything like that."

Tabler looked down at his notes, figuring out what to cover off next. He went over how the police already knew Johnny had driven to the garage.

"But the girl wasn't there." He raised his hand up. "Met a *guy* in the garage."

"*In* the garage!?"

"Apparently." Tabler slapped his palm on his notes. "And that's where the trail goes cold."

Twitchell slid back in his seat. Hands clasped on the table in front of him, he looked as baffled as can be. "Okay, let me get this straight." Twitchell went over the story of the missing man Tabler had just told him. The detective asked again: "Now does that sound like anything that you know about?"

"Not at all," said Twitchell, expressionless.

"Does it sound like anything that could be related in any way to any movie sort of stuff you're doing?"

"Not that I'm aware of."

Tabler kept prodding. Twitchell insisted he had never heard of a woman named Jen and descended into a long rant about distrusting the garage deadbolt, leading to his padlock purchase, as if to repair this hole in his story. As the detective was about to wind up the ninety-minute interview, Twitchell explained he had been writing an article about online dating, but that was the full extent of his knowledge about such websites. He did not frequent them otherwise.

Tabler thanked him for his insight and allowed him to leave. He thought they had developed a good rapport. Twitchell had been cool, calm, and confident. No stammering. But what the detective had just witnessed had also been incredibly strange. Could it just be a coincidence that a missing man's last known location happened to be the site of a blood-soaked horror film? There was really no other choice but to take it up the chain, to the division's staff sergeant. The homicide unit would likely have to be consulted, maybe a couple of detectives brought in to make the call on what to do next – and to sort out fact from fiction.

But it was now early Sunday morning, nearing five, and Tabler was heading home from his extended late shift. This was someone else's battle, not his.

TWITCHELL FLIPPED OUT HIS cell phone and dialled Joss again as he hurried from the police station. His friend jolted awake, a ring tone blaring through his bedroom at 5:00 a.m., and he picked up to hear Twitchell speaking in a slight panic. "I'm really stressed out."

Joss tried to wake up, rubbing his face, breathing in deeply as Twitchell complained of being at the garage all night and facing questions from police.

"It was *weird* in the garage," he continued quickly. "Stuff had been moved around. The police had to unscrew a bolt to get in. They kept asking me questions accounting for all my time at the garage. And they had questions about a missing person."

Joss tried to be reassuring. "Well, if the garage has been broken into, it's a good thing we moved that car the other day and it wasn't stolen too."

"Oh. I forgot about the car."

"Wait a second," said Joss in confusion. "The police are asking about the garage and you forgot about what could potentially be a stolen car that was just there a day or two ago?"

"I must have just blanked," he sighed, starting to ramble again. "You don't think the car and the missing person could have any connection, do you? This could have been a setup. If it was setup, I must have been followed to the garage. And if they followed me, what about my wife and daughter? Oh God!"

"Calm down," Joss replied. "Just calm down. Thinking about a setup is, it's just silly and time-consuming. Don't worry. Just call the police first thing in the morning and tell them about the car. They deal with stressed people all the time."

"Listen. I gotta go," Twitchell said. "Jess is calling."

Joss fell back asleep, the sunrise still an hour away or more. When he awoke later, his thoughts returned to Twitchell. He was worried there could be a connection between the car parked in his parents' driveway and this police investigation. If the car was stolen, Joss wanted it off his parents' property immediately. He dialled Twitchell's number. "Any news?" he asked over the phone.

Twitchell sounded groggy. "Nah, I just woke up. I haven't called them yet."

Joss checked the clock – it was around noon – and became frustrated with the delay. "You better call them about the car right away," he warned. "If you don't call them, I will."

CRASHING

THE ROAR OF A homicide investigation thundered in Twitchell's ears as detectives picked apart his life, one piece at a time. Within twenty-four hours, his car and house had been seized, his garage film studio wrapped in crime scene tape, and a defence lawyer consulted. Twitchell had nowhere to go but his parents' bungalow, so he retreated to the cover of his childhood home, nestled in the suburbs north of the city centre.

His wife found him quickly, beating a police surveillance team that was still trying to locate him. On Monday, October 20, Jess stormed into her in-laws' basement, hours after losing her own home, to find her husband hiding from the world. A futon with one pillow was pulled out as his makeshift bed. Among the wood-panelled walls and discarded furniture, she demanded answers after months of suspicion. He easily crumbled in his weakened state, but used no tact in these cleansing efforts, dumping the truth on her lap like a shovel to the face.

As she listened in disbelief, Twitchell admitted to his secret life of unemployment.

His film career was in shambles.

And they were broke. All his money was gone.

The disclosure drew tears and screams. She demanded to know why the police were rummaging through their lives, but on that point, he refused to talk. Jess could not accept it.

Devastated by his startling admissions, she turned to ask one final question, as if grasping for something, anything, to salvage from the ruins of their marriage.

"Is Phil Porter real?" she pleaded.

"No," he finally admitted coldly. "He's not."

Jess stared at her husband, stunned by what he had just said. Her voice started to crack and waver. "Well then, who *was* that man?"

"An actor I hired."

Twitchell watched as his wife's face lost all its vibrancy. The light dimmed in her eyes, a look of despair contorting her face in a way he had never seen before. Her tears flowed, her throat closing in as she heaved in wailing sobs that echoed through the house. Her weeping came crashing in waves, each one more overwhelming than the last.

She had been deceived in every possible way. Her husband was a liar. He had been cheating on her. Worse still, he was now a murder suspect.

Jess fled the home that night with an ache that would not leave her, racing to be freed of a terror that had gripped her so tightly.

Alone in the basement, Twitchell fell to the carpet. "I've destroyed us," he mumbled, curling in a fetal position, as if a level of insight had finally come to pass.

———

IN THE FOLLOWING WEEK, while under siege, Twitchell found comfort in building a suit of armour, an effort that gave meaning to days that were now clicking by with little significance. Upon completion, the make-work costume could be strapped around his entire body, from head to toe. Like many of his previous designs, it also had the potential to earn him some money. He certainly needed it. Despite his mounting problems, he was still dreaming of his future, thinking of the Halloween Howler again and believing he could win the grand prize as he did the year before. This was no *Transformers* outfit. The same techniques of foam board and spray paint were being used, but, this year, he would be stepping into the main hall as the billionaire playboy and superhero Iron Man. He set to work in his father's garage workshop, hoping to finish a spectacular creation.

Much had changed since last Halloween. Back then he wasn't a father, he still had a day job, and he had kept his dabbling in darker fiction to a minimum. He was heavier now too and had recently started growing a little goatee. A posting to his Dexter Morgan account read: "Dexter is looking forward to increasing the strength of his disguise."

He rarely left the house, but he took up residence at his parents' computer, set on a desk in a converted dining room beside the kitchen. The Internet gave him full access to his friends. On Thursday, October 23, just past 10:00 p.m., he was browsing Facebook again when he noticed that his wedding photographer had sent him a message, asking how things were. He had to confess that his marriage was falling apart. "I don't know how to explain this," he typed. "I rarely think about long-term consequences before I act."

He was emotional. Thinking of the police, his marriage, the film shoot, and the past few weeks, he became desperate. He typed out a long angry email to his film crew that evening, furious at the detectives who were taking everything away. The message was sent from one of his secret email accounts, with the username "Tyler Durden's Hero," a reference to the disturbed main character in the film *Fight Club*. He sent his email to Joss, Mike, and Jay, his cameraman David, and set builder Scott. His email urged them to distrust the police:

> *You all have a right to silence and you should exercise that right. . . . I've been screwed around with and I don't appreciate it, so it's time to stop this and make them do their own jobs. I'm serious. The time for dry sarcastic humour and flaky jokes is over and this is no prank. Sometimes what we see on TV is in fact a true representation of how they work. Sometimes they do lie and make things up in order to get people to say things they otherwise would not. . . . If they ask you questions, just tell them you don't know anything.*

The email worried his crew. Scott had called Twitchell earlier in the week to ask if it was okay to accept a job offer. He was concerned that by doing so he would give up his chance to work full-time on *Day Players*. Now cops were circling and Twitchell was furious. The bigger issue remained that his demands had come far too late. Everyone had already been interviewed by detectives or given statements. The noose was tightening around his neck.

That evening, while Twitchell was sitting at his parents' computer and sending out these messages, someone logged in to Johnny's Facebook account and added a friend. The activity came just after one of his friends had posted a message on Johnny's Facebook wall stating that the police department's homicide unit was for looking for him. For the police, who did not believe the missing man was behind such activity, the suspicious timing said everything.

RENEE HAD IGNORED TWITCHELL'S attempts to call her. Although she had given him her number, she told him she didn't pick up because she thought it was a U.S. election campaigner. But the truth was that, while she wanted to know how he had "crossed the line," she simply wasn't ready to find out. She realized her communication with him had drastically altered. He was no longer the hotshot filmmaker who had offered her a chance to break into the industry, but a man in crisis. She prodded for information in emails and saw he clearly wanted to hide something. "I can't even begin to go into the details," he wrote. "So don't ask." Instead, he was cleaning out his Facebook account, getting rid of messages: "Me and my manic deleting." Renee wondered what was so important that he had to delete it. A tiny alarm bell started ringing in her head.

Twitchell asked if she'd be willing to go away to a tropical island with him. While the fantasy seemed amazing, in reality, she told him she would have to politely decline. "Just the fact that you actually gave my offer any thought of actual consideration makes me smile," he replied. He then confessed to lying to his wife for months, offering Renee a brief glimpse into what was transpiring in his life. "The impounding of my car and the searching of my house brought everything out in the open and my own *House of Cards* came crashing down. I can certainly appreciate the irony of that title now more than ever."

As Halloween drew closer, his mood soured. He was "blah" on Facebook and coming up with ominous and sinister messages on his Dexter Morgan page again. "Dexter feels the dark passenger getting restless again," he wrote.

THEN, HOPE ARRIVED. A potential new investor had seen Twitchell's website and emailed him, asking about his *Star Wars* fan film and how he could help. Twitchell directed him toward *Day Players* and explained in great detail how he was raising money for the comedy film and how investing came with virtually "no risk" and a profitable windfall.

"You certainly got my attention," the businessman wrote back. "I have a busy week coming up but I might be able to open up a slot for a meeting."

Twitchell started thinking he really could get his project off the ground. *House of Cards* actor Chris Heward had already called to say he was still interested in investing and wanted to find out more. His crew was thinking about investing. And then John Pinsent from Venture Alberta had finally sent him a cheque. When it arrived in the mail, Twitchell's dad gave him a lift to the bank to deposit it. Twitchell then headed to the mall and spent some of the newly acquired funds that were meant to be "held in trust."

A day later, his potential new investor emailed again with good news: he wanted to meet with Twitchell and would be bringing an interested friend. Twitchell suggested they meet quickly, even on the weekend if possible. "I'm free all day Saturday and Sunday," he wrote. "Just let me know."

He was pushing everyone hard. Other investors at Venture Alberta were receiving emails as Twitchell talked of having just secured a home-video distribution deal through Warner Bros. and a U.S. financier who was backing his movie's entire budget. All he needed was to sell ten units, or points, of $35,000 investments to unlock the funds. "To give you a feeling for the landscape," Twitchell wrote to one potential investor, "my co-producer has one investor ready to drop on three units at once and has almost done his due diligence with no hiccups."

The truth was, however, that these pitches were, at best, the exaggerated vernacular of extreme salesmanship and, at worst, a string of blatant lies. His co-producer was quite surprised to discover his track record was being used as leverage with investors because he had none. The Producers Guild of America, an agency representing the vast majority of film producers, had never heard of him. He had never even worked on a Hollywood production, as Twitchell had claimed. The Californian was actually a friend of a friend, a man who had dabbled in low-budget independent film for years and shared Twitchell's dream of striking it big. His only connection to Warner Bros. was a contact who could possibly get a script read by a studio executive – if they had a major star attached. There was no distribution deal, no studio lot access, and certainly no U.S. investors lined up and ready to sign. The man had not yet sent Twitchell's proposal to his own lawyer for a review of its legitimacy.

The talent agency representing Alec Baldwin was also surprised to hear the star had been linked to Mark Twitchell's project. His agent had received a letter from the unknown Canadian director, but with no secured money attached, it was just another proposal gathering dust on the desk of a big star.

But of course, Twitchell's potential new investor – and anyone else who had given him money for the project – would not have known any of this. On paper, the project looked quite promising. Twitchell could write anything he wanted as he crafted his proposal, twisting reality until it transformed into a viable business opportunity. A part of him honestly believed he was going to make it, that stardom was only a cheque or two away. With so many people ready to hand over their money, he saw no reason to doubt his ability to get the film off the ground and into production.

Twitchell suggested meeting on Saturday, at a coffee shop in the north end, not far from his parents' house. The investor was busy on the weekend, but told him he could meet the day before for a brief meeting. His friend would be coming too. "I think that once he sees the data in black and white he will be just as excited as I am," the businessman wrote.

They confirmed their plans to meet on Friday, October 31, 2008.

Twitchell could not wait.

THE MEETING

TWITCHELL ROSE EARLY FOR his favourite day of the year. Carved pumpkins decorated front doorsteps. Children had their spooky costumes ready for trick-or-treating after school. Twitchell was checking his email at his parents' computer desk, seeing that the novelty of the day wasn't forgotten by someone his own age. "Happy Halloween," Renee had written in an ecard. "And hope everything is going better for you!" Her card included a picture of Dexter Morgan with a simple caption: "Thinking of you." He was touched. "You're so sweet you're giving me cavities," he wrote. "Thank you for this."

He headed for the kitchen, grabbed a notepad, and started scribbling down his list of things to do for the day. He still had to put the final touches on his Iron Man suit. He spent the rest of the morning spray-painting a red coat over the chest plate and helmet. All of the body armour would need another coat and he still had to make the neck guard and glue Velcro to the skin-tight black body suit he would wear underneath. But seeing the time, he knew it would have to wait until later that afternoon. He went back to the computer, dropped the names of his new business associates into his investment contracts, and printed them off. He slipped on his sneakers and zipped up his fleece jacket, two tickets to the evening's Halloween Howler tucked into one of the pockets, his keys in another.

He had a brisk twenty-minute walk ahead of him to reach the coffee shop on time. He hurried along his street, passing the park where he played basketball as a kid, his shoulders up high to shield him from the chilly weather. Thick clouds were covering the afternoon sun. At the end of his street he turned north and noticed a white van racing at an incredible speed, looking like it was out of control. The tires were screeching as it tore around the corner and skidded to a stop not far from where Twitchell was walking. The driver honked, just once, catching his eye.

An army of police officers in tactical gear spilled out from all sides of the van. Black helmets bobbed in a march, then scattered as their assault rifles were held at the ready. The squad was shouting, their voices blending overtop of one another.

Twitchell stood in amazement at the drama unfolding around him, not comprehending at first what was being yelled in his direction.

"Get on the ground! Get on the ground!"

The police demands finally registered and he dropped to his knees. The tactical team swarmed. He lay on his belly in the dry grass of a neighbour's front lawn. His arms were pulled back and he felt the cold click of hand-cuffs closing in around his wrists.

A detective with glasses appeared and leaned over, his badge dangling from his neck. The man confirmed the team had caught the right suspect. Then he inched closer so Twitchell could hear him: "You're under arrest for first-degree murder."

Twitchell was yanked up to his feet, hands cuffed behind him. Feeling wobbly, he nearly fell as one leg collapsed under his weight, twisting to the side. The cop steadied him and he was paraded over to an unmarked police car. The tactical team watched closely.

Standing there in disbelief that this was really happening, Twitchell kept his head low as the detective emptied his pockets, finding a handcuff key that appeared to match the cuffs used in the failed attack on Gilles Tetreault.

Twitchell had fallen for their trap. The excited investors he was supposed to be meeting were a con job, but he wouldn't be told for months that it was an officer in the hate crimes unit who had orchestrated the entire week-long conversation with him. Getting Twitchell to leave his parents' house on his own had prevented a potential standoff and eliminated the chance that any remaining evidence inside could be destroyed. And there was something simply satisfying for the investigators in having lured a suspect through the Internet when he had done the same. When they realized the timing of the arrest had also denied Twitchell his chance at winning the Halloween Howler costume competition, their satisfaction deepened.

Twitchell was tossed into the back of the police car, where he stewed as the detective climbed in the front, joining another detective, and read him his rights.

The cops were confident they knew what had happened, where his life had morphed into real-life crime. But Twitchell saw things entirely differently: they didn't know the real story and there was so much more to tell. He furrowed his brow, hiding what was really on his mind.

As the car rolled toward police headquarters, Twitchell could only stare out the window, convinced deep inside that despite his sudden predicament, he still held the upper hand.

PART THREE

THE PRESTIGE

COSTUMES UNRAVELLED

IN A HOLDING TANK in the homicide section of police headquarters, Twitchell stuck his hands in his pockets and stared straight ahead. The shutter on a camera clicked. Constable Gary Short from the police forensics team took photos of Twitchell's face, his hands, his little goatee. Twitchell slipped off his T-shirt, exposing his hairy belly and a jagged appendix scar. He had a *Star Wars* tattoo on his shoulder of the rebel alliance's insignia. More photos were taken. He turned around, revealing his naked back, another tattoo, and a cluster of pimples. He removed his jeans and stood on the cold and freckled linoleum, wearing nothing but his striped jockey underwear. The man was a spectacle. Constable Short had him turn again so he could take a picture from each angle and complete his routine booking and arrest photographs. One of the last photos captured a solid black tattoo burned into Twitchell's right ankle – the helmet of Achilles. He barely said a word as he was photographed, the camera flash flooding his skin with bursts of white light.

Twitchell slipped on a new pair of street clothes provided to him just as Detective Bill Clark walked in. He smiled at his murder suspect and offered his hand. "Do you remember me?"

Twitchell hesitated. "Yeah, I do." He didn't like Clark, but he still grabbed his palm and shook as the pair met in person for the first time since their overnight police interview.

"Listen, sorry, I wanted to call you, so you could turn yourself in, but you left the house and tactical jumped the gun." Clark was lying, but he wanted to get Twitchell settled and in the right frame of mind.

"Oh, okay."

"You talked to your lawyer yet?"

"Yeah."

"Okay, well, follow me."

For Twitchell's arrest interview, Clark had spent hours preparing a PowerPoint presentation of all the gathered evidence in the hopes of overwhelming him. Clark knew he had messed up his first interrogation. Back then he thought he could prey on Twitchell's emotions to elicit a confession. But the investigation had revealed much about Twitchell. Clark thought his suspect was intelligent, but heartless, lacking the typical feelings of remorse some killers express. The detective imagined a laptop loaded with the facts would be far more effective against such an emotionless opponent.

Clark sat Twitchell down and explained how the police team had come to its conclusions. One of the latest pieces of evidence was from the crime lab. Only hours earlier, preliminary results had come back, triggering the afternoon arrest: a DNA match had finally linked Johnny Altinger to a blood stain found in the trunk of Twitchell's car. It was only a matter of time until all of the results came back with the same conclusion.

Clark moved the laptop closer to Twitchell's face as he went through the pile of evidence, but his suspect hung his head low; Clark grabbed a paper copy of his presentation and placed it in Twitchell's lap, where he couldn't avoid seeing it.

"I won't be saying anything." It was Twitchell's standard reply for hours.

Clark got him talking a bit about *Dexter,* but the arrest interview was achieving only short answers. He finally asked Twitchell bluntly: "Did you film it?"

Twitchell shook his head.

The detective watched him closely. His answer appeared unrehearsed and truthful, but he couldn't be sure. Clark dug deeper and asked if the entire case was a hoax.

Twitchell finally responded with a question: "Just out of curiosity, does a person not get into trouble for the hoax as well?"

Meanwhile, a forensic examination of the clothes Twitchell had been wearing upon his arrest determined that his belt and sneakers were soaked or spattered in blood.

LEGS CROSSED AND FEELING anxious, Traci sat crying on a couch in one of the soft rooms down the hall from Twitchell's interrogation. She was devastated that she had not only fallen for her old flame once again but had now been dragged into a homicide investigation.

A detective seated across from her read out a few passages from S. K. Confessions that mentioned "Laci." Twitchell had written about their volatile relationship in great detail, from their meeting in college to the rekindling of their passion at the movies. Some of his words cut deep. Every flaw about Traci was exposed and criticized in the document, whether her religious beliefs, her past relationship decisions, or her personal health issues. It was deeply personal, brutally cruel.

Traci shook her head. "He's such a conceited asshole." She tugged on her hair and sighed in frustration. "I'm sorry, I've just, really, in the last three weeks, I've grown to hate him. I've never hated him until now." She tugged again at the hair on the back of her head.

The detective looked up from his notes. He told her that for a man who had lied, it certainly seemed like he was being truthful in his writings. Traci had just confirmed it.

"But he's *not* the same guy," she said. She thought back to when they were first dating and compared it to his demeanour during their affair. "I don't know how it's different, but he's just not the same guy I used to know."

"What do you mean?"

"Like, he seems less connected with the world. He just seems . . . meaner." Traci didn't know how to describe it. "I know what he's doing to his wife, I know that I'm a part of that. And I know that's *mean*. It's cruel. And the fact that I'm a part of it . . . it's just disgusting." She raised a tissue to her eyes, tears streaming freely. "That's how I feel," she said. Her voice trembled. "I'm angry. I just *hate* him."

CLARK SQUINTED AT TWITCHELL, who was still sulking and refusing comment. After more than two hours of interrogation, Clark had finally given up on his presentation. All that work for nothing. It was time to bring in Detective Paul Link. Clark introduced him as the big-shot "Inspector" as they had planned. But the impact was minimal.

It would take Link several hours before he achieved even a small victory in the interview room. He asked Twitchell how he thought it would look if he continued refusing to speak, considering everything he did could be used in court as evidence.

Twitchell thought back to Clark's PowerPoint presentation and turned to Link. "I'm not denying what he just showed me," he said plainly. "Just . . . not able to talk about it."

About an hour and a half later, as late evening approached, Link was giving up too. He was running out of questions. He decided to give Twitchell two options. He shoved a piece of paper in the suspect's hands that laid them out clearly:

OPTION ONE:
- Say nothing
- Look like a fool
- Put your family through continued aggravation
- Show no remorse
- How will others view that?

OPTION TWO:
- Explain
- Not look like a fool
- Closure for your family
- Being accountable
- Salvage your own dignity

Twitchell was tired. The interrogation was draining. He started to beg for a night to sleep on it. "Option two is what I'm leaning to, but I just can't do anything 'til tomorrow."

It was late anyway. He was led out of the room and taken to the holding cells in the basement of police headquarters. He'd spend the night in isolation. Detectives were left to contemplate how best to crack his hardened exterior.

BACK AT THE HOME of Twitchell's parents, the forensics team was photographing every room and gathering potential exhibits. In the basement, scraps of foam plastic Twitchell had used to build his Iron Man costume were scattered about, stuck into the shag carpet. In their search, police found a pair of black leather gloves; blood was caked into the stitching around the wrist of one of them. Outside, they spotted a curved mark of scorched grass in the middle of the backyard. It was the same dimensions as Twitchell's oil drum. Above, a clothesline was coated in black soot.

Twitchell's parents were waiting at his sister's place while the police made these discoveries. They had been driven there earlier by a detective tasked with executing the search warrant, which included their vehicles, as soon as they arrived home from work.

The sight of forensic investigators descending on the normally quiet neighbourhood had enraged Twitchell's mother. But Twitchell's father was far more subdued, even pausing to express his sympathies for the victim's family as the pair were escorted from the property. Then, later that night, he made a rare unsolicited comment, catching the detective completely off-guard. "Officer, can I offer you some advice?" Twitchell's father had said. "Have a vasectomy."

A DRIVE INTO THE STORM

THE MORNING AFTER THE interrogation, Twitchell sat in an office chair at police headquarters once again, digging his fingers into a fast-food paper bag. He pulled out a warm Egg McMuffin, peeled back the greasy yellow wrapper, and took a big bite, breathing in through his nose as he chewed. His leg started bouncing as he sucked back on a drink.

Detective Link walked in, closed the door, and took a seat across from him. It was a different interview room from the night before, in the polygraph wing down the hall from homicide. There was a particle-board wood desk crushed into the corner. Link gave Twitchell a moment to finish eating and then stuffed back into his hands the piece of paper with his two options written on it.

Twitchell sat in silence for nearly an hour, pulling his head deeper between his shoulders, thumbing the paper between his fingertips. A grey long-sleeved shirt the cops had given him stretched tight, his belly spilling over his pants, and he pulled a neon pink and blue ski jacket closer around his chest. When he finally opened his mouth to speak, he told Link that nothing had changed.

"And why is that?" Link was hunched low across his knees, looking at Twitchell.

"Because I just need to see the lawyer first and then I'm sure the statement will come after."

It was like Link had made a breakthrough. "Have I got your word on that?" He shot out his hand, but Twitchell just stared at him. "Give me your word on that," Link repeated. "That's all you've got left is your word, Mark."

"Well . . ." He lifted his fingers a moment, hesitated, then curled them back into his palm.

Link kept his hand held out. "Give me your word. And we'll make that happen. We're trying right now. We've left messages. We're trying to get him down here."

"I know. I know. I'm just saying the last step is to talk to him, so . . ."

Link took a gamble and left the room to track down Twitchell's lawyer. Twitchell had already been given his one phone call, but Link felt the goodwill could be returned as promised with a formal statement, handshake or not.

Twitchell had ten minutes on the phone with his legal counsel. Link returned to the interview room, sat down, and asked for the promised statement. But Twitchell stayed silent and barely moved from his chair, ignoring his presence in the room.

Link started shouting. "You went back on your word! I actually gave you, that's the sad, despicable part of it, is I *actually* gave you the benefit of the doubt. And I actually *believed* you."

Twitchell didn't move.

"And I thought possibly this whole thing could be a hoax." Link sounded defeated, like he was embarrassed about what he had confessed. "I was trying to take your side there, to write it off as just a bad, bad mistake and just a hoax. But it's not even that."

Twitchell continued to look down and away from Link.

"Do you have the energy to look me in the eye? Have you got it, Mark, or are you just going to cower some more? . . . Mark?"

Twitchell kept his chin down and never met his gaze. Link stared at him for minutes, but he eventually gave up and stormed out of the room. Throughout nearly fourteen hours of interrogation spread out over two days, not once had Twitchell denied killing Johnny. But he had also become a near-mute ever since being granted that second call with his lawyer.

Detective Clark walked in and threw some Halloween candy on the desk beside Twitchell's chair. It would be his last meal before eating prison food for months. "Okay, Mark," Clark said. "Grab your snacks. Let's go."

CLARK HIT THE GAS and pulled his sedan out of the parkade beneath headquarters. Twitchell sat in the backseat in handcuffs next to Link. Acting Detective Dale Johnson joined the three of them, riding up front with Clark. Twitchell had to be placed before a Justice of the Peace within twenty-four hours of his arrest. The four of them were going to drive around the city for the next three hours, the cops trying to pressure Twitchell into talking, until they ran out of time.

"I see it rained last night," said Clark, wearing sunglasses, looking up at the sky from behind the wheel as they drove over the wet pavement. "Didn't snow, eh? We're lucky." He flicked on the radio. "We'll see if we're on the news yet." The radio buzzed low in the background. Clark tilted his head to see Twitchell in the rear-view mirror. "We'll go where you took the oil drum and tried to burn the body. In your parents' backyard."

Twitchell peered down at his hands in cuffs.

They reached the house and Clark pulled over, turning up the radio as the sounds of trumpets signalled the start of the news hour. *Good afternoon. It is twelve noon.* The broadcaster's voice was deep and campy.

> *From the 630 CHED twenty-four-hour news centre . . . A twenty-nine-year-old man is being charged with first-degree murder in the disappearance of another city man. Police say they will release more details this afternoon following the arrest of Mark Twitchell. He was taken into custody yesterday on the north side of town and charged in connection with the disappearance of John Brian Altinger. He has not been seen since October the 10th. Once again, news conference scheduled for three this afternoon. 630 CHED will be there.*

Twitchell alternated his gaze between staring at the back of the driver's seat and out the window, ignoring the radio. But then something caught his eye. A man was approaching the car from the passenger side with a big camera slung over his shoulder. Twitchell turned white and his eyes flared wide open.

Johnson turned to look. "Who is it? Is that the media?"

"Yeah!" Clark said, climbing out of the car. "I'll go talk to them."

Twitchell, stuck in the backseat, pulled his head way back and to the side, trying to hide his face. "Let's go back to HQ," he pleaded. He dropped his head down as the cameraman spun around to the other side. He hid his face with his hands. "Seriously, let's just go back to the station."

Clark shooed the cameraman away and jumped back into the car. "Where do you want us to head to, Mark?"

"Station."

"Station? The body's not at the station."

Twitchell frowned. The detectives explained what was about to occur. Link jumped in first. "This is just a sign of what's gonna happen. You'll be all over the media. This is the first taste of it. How do you feel about that? . . . You're infamous now."

"It doesn't matter."

"It's just the start of the frenzy," Clark added. "It's going to continue on until the body surfaces."

The four of them drove next to Twitchell's sister's place. Clark tried Susan's apartment. Through her tears, she was in no condition to help the detective convince her brother to talk, even if she wanted to. The cops decided to head south instead, toward Twitchell's rented garage. Everyone got out of the car and showed Twitchell the property, still surrounded with police tape. Another television camera crew was already there, waiting. Twitchell was led to the back door of the garage. Clark knew crime scene visits sometimes prompted murder suspects to finally open up, the heightened emotions tied to the place bringing back vivid memories. But Twitchell just stood there, looking bored, as he again turned his head away from the watching media.

Twitchell's reaction was confusing for many of the detectives. They thought he would have been thrilled to see the cameras, considering how his filmmaking career depended on gaining publicity. He was rejecting the limelight after creating what detectives considered to be an elaborate crime designed, in part, with the objective of attracting attention. It didn't make sense.

As detectives continued driving him around town, looking for the body, Twitchell would sometimes yawn. Other times, he appeared catatonic as they repeated the same questions. *Which sewer? Where? Go ahead, Mark. End it now.* He sucked his teeth, chewed on his lip, and closed his eyes when the sun struck his face. He refused to talk, no matter who was asking.

Driving back to headquarters, Clark knew they were running out of time. But he had one last trick – a prearranged call on his cell phone. Clark spoke to the caller for a moment, then passed the phone to the backseat. "Traci Higgins for you, Mark."

Twitchell's expression went blank as he clasped the phone between cuffed hands. They spoke for ten minutes, but Traci did all of the talking.

She begged him to give up the body, telling him she didn't understand why he wouldn't cooperate.

"There's a time and place for everything," he replied. "I know what's going on, but you need to understand that I can't talk." Twitchell was infuriated. He thought the cops had gotten to her and fed her lies to get her on their side. "I wanna say something, but I just can't. I'm sorry." It was all Twitchell was willing to offer. His eyes started to tear up, but he fought hard and pushed his emotions down. He remained cold and distant until the phone call with the woman he would always love came to an end. It was the last time he would ever speak with Traci.

When they reached the station, Clark stopped the car for a second to lay down some harsh facts. "Tell your lawyer, when he decides – and it will come up – that if he wants to make the body deal for second degree? *No deal.*"

Clark knew that in light of the evidence they had, they probably only needed the body to bring closure for the family, not to prosecute for first-degree murder. And he was fed up after two days of dealing with Twitchell's attitude. "I think he's going to come up with that one. So, shut him down," he spat. "No sense even making the call. No. Deal."

THE BIG REVEAL

SQUINTING IN THE THREE o'clock sun, Detective Mark Anstey stood outside headquarters in a suit, burgundy shirt, and silver tie, announcing Twitchell's arrest to a semicircle of reporters. But more to the point, he was using the media to help find the surviving victim. He was never much of a media performer, but he endured posing for cameras and holding up one of Short's photos of the hockey mask in the hopes that the man would see it on the news and finally come forward. Anstey didn't dare utter a word about S. K. Confessions, the blood trail, or any forensic evidence. But in explaining the first attack and how the police could charge someone with first-degree murder without a body, he had to reveal the basics of the case. It was a killing that mirrored Twitchell's movie script, he explained. Both included luring a man through online dating, a vicious killing and dismemberment, and the use of the victim's personal information to convince loved ones that he was still alive. And there was more: "We have a lot of information to suggest that he definitely idolizes *Dexter*." Anstey paused, swallowed, and bobbed his head, making sure he didn't blurt out the "hold-back" details to the press. "And a lot of information that he tried to emulate him during this incident."

And so it began.

The initial trickle of radio bulletins and website briefs burst into a flood of the bizarre and sensational. Twitchell had left a digital trail of his life all over the Internet. Even his personal Facebook profile was open to the public, feeding the media's hunger for details. Suddenly he was the lead item on the six o'clock newscasts.

No one warned his friends. Most found out through the media. Twitchell's old roommate, Jason Fritz, was at home as he caught his friend's name on television. Joss and Mike had already been called by reporters. They were beginning to panic as the story went viral and sensational newspaper headlines emerged:

DEATH MASK?

DID LIFE IMITATE SLASHER FILM?

And later, as journalists continued chasing the story:

TERROR IN THE 'KILL CHAIR'

It seemed unbelievable. But with no body, Twitchell's friends wondered, surely this must be some kind of mistake?

The world took notice. A producer with ABC's *20/20* flew to Edmonton and started interviewing a slew of locals about the bizarre slaying. CNN's legal affairs program *Nancy Grace* had a producer call around, as did television news magazines *Inside Edition* and *Dateline NBC*. Detectives checking online found stories about the case had reached as far as the Philippines, Europe, Argentina, and Australia.

It even attracted the attention of Hollywood. Errol Morris, an Academy Award–winning director acclaimed for his documentaries *The Thin Blue Line* and *The Fog of War*, was blown away by the outrageous details. His production team researched the case for months. Twitchell was the perfect subject for an episode of *Tabloid*, a half-hour television documentary series Morris was creating.

Of course, the Twitchell story also dominated the city newspapers.

But it wasn't the first time he had grabbed the front page – a fact later republished as reporters discovered images of the newly arrested Twitchell had already been captured in their local newspaper archives.

Back in 1999, Twitchell and his sister were teenagers wanting to share in the thrill of *Star Wars: The Phantom Menace*. They headed to West Edmonton Mall's movie theatre in costume to celebrate the premiere of the long-awaited motion picture.

Their outfits attracted newspaper photographers who were looking for a colourful *Star Wars* photo for the next day's edition. Susan had come dressed as one of Jabba the Hutt's dancers, but Twitchell's effort was far more elaborate. His face was painted red and black and it looked like he had a shaved head.

Twitchell was dressed as Darth Maul, an evil Dark Lord of the Sith. He had a crown of horns, a black cloak, and a sinister grin. As the photo was taken, he stared directly into the camera lens, his eyes shimmering like the devil himself.

—

THE XPRESS ENTERTAINMENT WEBSITE was shut down quickly. Twitchell's closest friends stopped answering their phones. Others, like Rebecca, who had expected to meet Twitchell at the Halloween Howler the night he was arrested, thought it was some kind of sick joke when she began to receive Facebook messages from people she didn't realize were journalists, asking about a murder.

As the news sunk in, these same friends severed their digital connections with him. Twitchell's personal Facebook profile was being emptied of contacts. The Internet was being scrubbed clean as those who knew him tried to remove any mention of the man from their personal lives.

JOHN PINSENT PULLED THE newspaper off his front porch. He walked into the kitchen, flattened out the front page, and took a sip of his morning coffee. LOCAL FILMMAKER CHARGED; SCRIPT SEIZED BY POLICE. He grabbed his chest and read the headline a few more times. He had just given $35,000 to a man charged with first-degree murder. He reached for the phone. "Has that cheque cleared? Has it cleared?"

At the Venture Alberta group, investors had to be reassured that they had considered funding a different movie pitched by the filmmaker, not the short film the police were saying had been replicated to some degree as a real-life murder. Phones rang across North America as news spread of Twitchell's arrest.

"Have you read the papers? Have you seen the story about Twitchell?" The voice was talking excitedly from investor Randy Lennon's cell phone.

"What are you talking about?" he replied.

"Twitchell murdered a guy!"

In a strange twist, Randy was in Florida helping a businessman secure ownership of the Tampa Bay Lightning hockey team. His contact, Oren Koules, was one of the original producers of a serial killer movie franchise that hinged on elaborate storylines not unlike Twitchell's own *House of Cards*. The series had a simple title: *Saw*.

A THREAD OF DISBELIEF spread through the *Star Wars* fan community. Many hard-core fans had either met Twitchell at sci-fi conventions or spoken with him over online message boards. Volunteers from the local *Star Wars*

Fan Force and 501st communities had helped Twitchell during filming of *Secrets of the Rebellion*. Some were terrified they had met such a man. Their instinct was to protect their own – out of fear their hobby was going to be associated with a horrific killing. "This definitely puts the wrong kind of spotlight on our community," one frightened fan wrote on theforce.net message boards. "Great, just what we need, another stigma," added a second worried *Star Wars* enthusiast. "Hopefully this won't have a lasting effect on the public's already so-so impression of fan filmmakers," another stated.

Their conclusions were based upon pure denial. They decided the forensic evidence must have been faked to draw out this very reaction, like some kind of sick joke used to gain media exposure. One of the forum moderators agreed, writing that the story was screaming "viral publicity stunt." He noted the arrest occurred on Halloween. "Just sets off alarm bells in my head," he wrote.

It was new territory for fans used to heated debates about trivial details within a fictional universe. Now moderators had to consult theforce.net's terms of service to determine what should be done with Twitchell's own account, Achilles of Edmonton. The moderators made the announcement: "We have not banned his account. Murder is not a bannable offence here on TFN. . . . Well, it isn't. I do not expect he will be dropping by the forum anytime soon, however."

JOHNNY'S FRIENDS POURED OUT their raw emotions online as well. As the shocking news trickled out onto Facebook, condolences overtook the initial purpose for the group "Find Johnny Altinger." Everyone had been dreading the worst, but this was beyond anyone's most fearsome nightmare.

Marie was hit hard. "Oh my God. Johnny was like a brother to me," she wrote on his group page. "I will miss him terribly."

Hans was speechless, only able to post a link to the latest news story. Others were bewildered. "I catch myself wondering if this is just a dream as I'm reading the articles, thinking it can't possibly be reality," wrote a relative who had helped set up the Facebook group.

Darcy Gehl aimed his message at their spiritual connection. "May his memory live on."

Johnny's former girlfriend offered her own plea directly to him: "Hope they find your body soon so that they can grieve for you properly," she wrote. "You will be missed."

His mother had the simplest of messages: "Johnny, wherever you are, I love you."

THE INTRIGUE WAS IRRESISTIBLE. From her Greenview home next door, Lynda Warren noticed a stream of vehicles slowing down as they neared the property on the corner with the detached garage. Cars rounded the corner and parked nearby. They were the morbidly curious. The gawkers. The rubberneckers.

The odd person would even get out to take a look at the police tape around the garage, maybe take a picture. "The more it was in the news, the more people would drive by," she recalled. "I got so sick of it, half the time I didn't even want to see what was going on."

The kill room had become a drive-by shrine.

ANSTEY'S STRATEGY TO GET media attention had worked far too successfully. Police command was mortified that international news agencies were now swooping in on the town. The head of homicide never liked seeing criminal files be so exposed before a trial. He was furious. He blasted Anstey for days about his little press conference. But Anstey fought back. He had received clearance from the Crown's office to do it. In essence, Anstey had gone over his head.

Their office rift deepened.

Clark was at his desk, soaking in the world's disbelief at their career case, when the police switchboard put through a call from the public to his office line. "I think I know the guy you're looking for." It had been a day and a half since Anstey's press conference. Clark grabbed a pen as the caller described someone he used to work with. "His name is Gilles Tetreault."

TWITCHELL AWOKE TO THE sound of a metal latch clicking in the early morning. His cell door swung open and light streamed in, spilling on to his clammy face. A gruff-looking prison guard with tattoos snaking up both arms was standing over him. "Come on, let's go."

He had spent his first night at the Edmonton Remand Centre, a notorious tower known for its poor conditions and overcrowded cells. It was designed nearly three decades earlier for around 350 inmates awaiting trial, but on some days 800 people could be crammed inside. An underground tunnel connected the tower to police headquarters, and the courthouse across the street. Twitchell had been on the fourth floor, but the guard told him they had to move him to the sixth, and top floor, known as "the zoo" with its twenty-three-hour lockup and cells designated for solitary confinement.

"Why am I being moved?"

"You're probably on the front page of every newspaper," he replied.

The remand had a responsibility to protect him, and now, due to media exposure, he was the most infamous inmate in the entire country.

Twitchell was in a daze. He fumed over his treatment, his arrest with no warning, the long interrogation, and media interest. He hated how the police had found Traci and turned her against him. He thought back to the detective who was at the centre of all of this, the man who put him behind bars and had driven him around for hours demanding he give up the body.

Twitchell began to hate Bill Clark and everything he stood for.

The guard continued on a brief tour of his new unit cast from cinder blocks. Twitchell would likely be housed here for two years, the average time it took to disclose an entire murder file to both the prosecution and defence, prepare the case, book court time, and hold a preliminary hearing and then a public trial. The police had gathered more than seven thousand pages of evidence, which filled twenty-one thick binders.

The guard led him down the hallway and ran through a list of prison rules, like he had recited it a hundred times before. He showed him the showers, the laundry, the common areas. The guard then turned to ask Twitchell if he was aware of the risk of being "shit bombed."

Twitchell drew a blank.

The guard smirked. He'd have to explain prison life to the rookie later.

FRIENDS OF TWITCH

Mike Young didn't believe it. Couldn't believe it. Scott Cooke wasn't convinced. Neither was Jason Fritz. They lashed back at the unsavoury media coverage. Twitchell was a lot of things to his film crew and his larger group of friends, but they had never feared him as a potential killer.

The media coverage infuriated Mike. Journalists wouldn't leave him alone, having discovered his connection to the accused through Facebook and Twitchell's company website before it was shut down. Mike thought his number was unlisted, but calls from local newspapers soon became calls from American TV programs. He'd check his Facebook profile and find it was overloaded with messages from even more reporters. Mike had known Twitchell for four years. When he looked back at all their time together, he just knew deep inside that the police and the media had to be wrong. Obsessed with *Dexter*? Mike thought his friend was no more interested in the show than the typical fan. He didn't understand how detectives could charge Twitchell with murder if they were only announcing a prop mask and the movie script as evidence. He couldn't take it anymore. Mike logged in to his Facebook page, clicked on the messages section, and started typing out his feelings:

> *Mark is a very non-violent person, with no temper to speak of and an aversion to conflict, yelling, or physical violence. . . . There has never been a hint, a glimpse, even the slightest possibility, that Mark has it in him to even throw a punch, let alone kill a human being. . . .*
>
> *This is an unfortunate coincidence of a man going missing in an area where a movie was being shot. I firmly believe that's the end of the association. Mark Twitchell is a good man who has been caught up in an unfortunate series of coincidences, the most unfortunate of which is that the baseless police speculation makes for a really good news story. When he is acquitted, I hope the media sees fit to run his acquittal on the front page, just as big as they're running the stories now.*

Mike read it over and hit send. The recipient was a reporter with *Metro*, a free commuter newspaper in town. He copied and pasted the same message to a reporter at the city tabloid, the *Edmonton Sun*. He felt like he was doing his part by defending his good friend in public.

A day later, however, his strategy would change.

It was the evening of November 4, 2008. The first African American had just won the U.S. presidential election, but Twitchell's friends were far more concerned with the dramatic change in their own lives. Everyone had come together for a secret gathering at Jason's house. It had begun online, first as a private Facebook group where people could share thoughts about the arrest, but had now become a one-time meeting of Twitchell's closest friends. It was called the "Friends of Twitch" assembly.

Sitting in Jason's living room, his friends talked, discussed, debated, vented. And a decision was made: there would be a pact, a vow of silence among them.

"I'm going to go with the group consensus and not say any more," Mike wrote on the "Friends of Twitch" Facebook page afterwards. "While it helps Mark to have people speaking up in his defence, it drags out the media coverage longer, which hurts him." He had heard back from Twitchell's sister too. Susan told him the family wasn't going to say a word to the press either.

The pact stayed strong. "Friends of Twitch" became a private sounding board on Facebook for Twitchell's film crew and close friends to complain about run-ins with journalists and unwelcome phone calls and emails. But two key people remained notably absent from this group and their views. The first was David Puff, the director of photography Twitchell had used for his movie projects. He wasn't close with Twitchell's film crew, but seeing excerpts of Mike's letter in the press still made him cringe. He would need a few more facts before he ever played that game himself, and as far as he knew, the cops weren't revealing their full hand just yet.

The second had been slowly distancing himself from their efforts. He knew a lot more about the case against Twitchell, but he didn't dare share the details. How could he? How could Joss tell anyone that the missing man's car had not only been parked in his driveway, but he had helped Twitchell move it there?

—

MIKE WAS THE FIRST to visit Twitchell in remand. A week after his friend's arrest, Mike walked into the main floor of the concrete tower and strolled up to a man sitting behind a sheet of glass and beneath a sign that stated "Visitor Inquiries." A little book sat on the white stone countertop. Mike signed and printed his name. He handed over his ID and the guard gave him a little gold key. He pointed behind him. A bank of square, taxi-cab-yellow lockers stood near fake plants hanging down from the ceiling by brown yarn. Mike emptied out his pockets, locked his belongings inside one of the lockers, and walked through a metal detector before taking a seat in the waiting room.

It was a soulless place of disease and distressed families. The room had floor-to-ceiling windows facing directly at downtown police headquarters, as if to remind visitors how their loved ones had got there. The bathroom was disgusting. The maroon tile circling a floor drain had been eaten away by urine and foot traffic. The exposed concrete underneath was flaked and moist. Mike had nothing to do while he waited. There were no magazines, no television. Everyone sat there on ottomans, staring at one another.

A guard shouted up to central command to open door 1016A. The electronic locks clunked. Mike rose to walk through the thick metal door and down a concrete corridor until he reached his assigned phone booth, which was no wider than a chair. He sat in a squeaky plastic bucket seat facing one inch of Plexiglas. In front of him were a black phone receiver and a small stainless-steel counter. The glass was scratched and carved with several decades worth of names and graffiti.

He could hear inmates being led to their booths, the sounds of clanging metal and creaking hinges. Guards shouted and doors slammed shut.

Mark Twitchell appeared. He was wearing navy blue overalls with a black collar. He looked tired. Twitchell collapsed into his seat and punched in his prison access code. He picked up the receiver and his eyes met those of his dear friend through the glass.

They talked for thirty minutes.

Twitchell complained about being in twenty-three-hour lock down with nothing to do. He was bored. There was no Internet access. No one to talk with. Seeing Mike again was a huge relief. Mike was relieved too. And he couldn't wait to share his experience with the rest of the group. "He sends his best and is again very sorry at how this has affected everyone's lives," Mike wrote on the "Friends of Twitch" Facebook group page. "He's in for the long haul in there until the trial starts, but he's refusing to plead to a lesser charge and will defend his innocence to the last."

Scott was next to visit. He cracked jokes with Twitchell, they made movie references, complained about the media coverage. The last topic made Twitchell furious. He told Scott the cops were using "dirty tactics" and were lying to his family and friends to discredit him. What Twitchell was saying bothered his friend a great deal. On his way out, Scott dropped forty dollars in a remand account for him to spend at the prison canteen. "I'm really starting to doubt the police can make this stick," he wrote.

Jason visited two days later and was happy to see his old roommate was in good spirits. "He's already getting the movie ideas in his head," Jason wrote. "So if this goes well for him, he might just get his big film. . . . He said he's sorry this crap has happened and appreciates what we're trying to do."

When all three asked him about the police allegations, however, Twitchell was pointedly silent. He explained to them in his usual eloquence that he couldn't discuss the case since it was now before the courts. His lawyer had told him repeatedly to keep quiet. Twitchell kept referring to a "missing piece of the puzzle" that would soon reveal all. But he would not elaborate.

His friends trusted him. They knew him as an honest man, a committed husband, and a loving father. In their eyes, he was a man to look up to and admire, considering all he'd done for them.

Mike was upset at the thought of dirty cops and liars twisting words to suit their needs. The police had even been telling some of Twitchell's friends that *Day Players* was a big scam. He thought it unbelievable. "The cops are full of shit," Mike announced after a meeting with Twitchell's lawyer. "Their 'mountain of evidence' so far has been six pages. Of theories."

Twitchell gave Mike his online passwords so he could shut down his Myspace and Facebook profiles. The media wouldn't be able to get access to them anymore. And Twitchell asked him for help. He needed someone on the outside who could control his affairs, a partner, a man who would manage everything for him.

He needed a power of attorney.

Mike agreed to do it. He became the sole controller of Xpress Entertainment and Twitchell's personal finances. Mike looked forward to taking a look inside those bank accounts and showing the cops just how stupid their allegations really were. "I'll be going through his paperwork and his bank accounts shortly, so we'll know for sure."

He was so confident about what he would find, he concluded his message with a smiley face.

JESS DID NOT VISIT her husband in remand or let him see their daughter. Twitchell's friends couldn't understand it, but then again, they had no idea.

She was swift in executing a plan to remove herself from anything to do with her husband as smoothly as possible. She hired two lawyers to defend her rights. The first was her shield against the police. Detectives were no longer allowed to talk with her; everything had to go through her lawyer. The second dealt with far more personal matters. Jess must have been devastated and confused by what had happened, but she was seeking no direct explanation from her husband.

She filed for divorce in mid-November and cited October 20, 2008, as the last day of their marriage – the day their house was seized and Twitchell had finally confessed to his infidelity and constant lying. She demanded full custody of Chloe and wanted a restraining order against him. A legal aid was ushered off to remand to serve Twitchell the papers in person. He used one of the couple's wedding photos as a means of identifying him.

And just like that, their marriage was over.

As the dust settled from her legal filings, a letter was sent to remand addressed to Mark Twitchell. When he opened it, he saw the contents were deeply personal. Jess had poured her emotions out on paper and it came as such a shock that Twitchell refused to speak of it with anyone he knew.

Her brother had his own strong opinions. And he used far less tact than Jess when he launched a legal battle against Twitchell to get his money back from his failed film investment. "I believe he is capable of anything," he declared.

DEATH BY *DEXTER*?

Mark Twitchell's name was spreading across the world by media and social-networking sites. But under the hills of Hollywood, one of the driving forces behind the television show *Dexter* was still blissfully unaware of what horror had been transpiring farther north.

Melissa Rosenberg, in her forties with strawberry-blond hair, sat down for a series of pre-planned interviews in Beverly Hills to promote *Twilight,* her movie adaptation of Stephanie Meyer's novel about vampires and high school lust. It was opening the following week with a Los Angeles red carpet premiere. But one Canadian reporter working for a national news wire service had come armed with a few questions about her past work on *Dexter.* The journalist explained that an avid fan of the show had been charged with a murder and accused of re-enacting elements of Dexter Morgan's modus operandi. In short, he appeared to have been "inspired" by the television program. Rosenberg blinked and became visibly upset.

"Oh Jesus!" she erupted. "This is a tragic and horrible thing to hear."

It was a "worst fears" scenario for Rosenberg, who had already worked on *Dexter* for more than forty episodes as a producer and writer. She said the production team had never wanted to "glorify" Dexter and his killings in the series. "And we've been very careful not to. Every time you think you're identifying with Dexter and rooting for him, for us it's about turning that back on you and saying, 'You may think that he's doing good, but he's a monster. He's killing people because he's a monster.'"

The reporter asked if the show's creators had been worried about criticism when the show was launched.

"The executive producers were expecting it," she said. "They were ready for it. They thought we were going to get slams."

But to her surprise, it didn't happen.

Until now.

GOING PUBLIC: Det. Mark Anstey announced the arrest of Mark Twitchell outside Edmonton's downtown police headquarters (above). Holding a photograph of the suspect's hockey mask, Anstey hoped the surviving victim would see it on the news and finally come forward. Detectives had already found plenty of evidence, like this Post-It note (right).

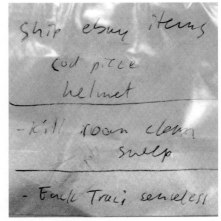

WEAPON: Twitchell's "kill knife" was found in his car, with bloodstains on the handle and blade. It was purchased at a military surplus store.

THE FILM STUDIO: As seen from the back door, Twitchell's rented garage appeared to be clean before police had a chance to examine it closely.

PROPS: Items found in the garage had links to both Twitchell's *House of Cards* movie production and the attack on Gilles Tetreault, including a BB gun (left), handcuffs (below left), and a retractable stun gun baton (below).

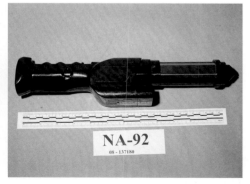

THE KILL ROOM: Twitchell bought an oil drum as a set piece, while his friends made this metal chair and six-legged table, not realizing their real purpose, to be revealed later.

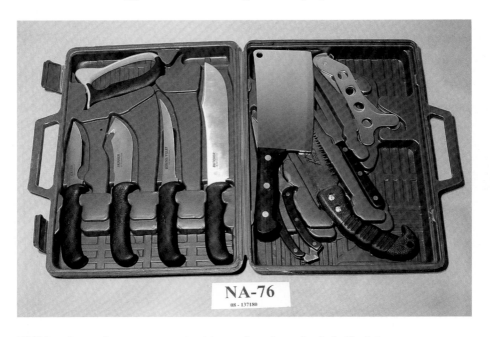

TOOLS: A hunter's game processing kit was found on a back shelf of the property. Bloodstains were found on every knife inside.

BEHIND THE LENS: Twitchell took this self-portrait with camera gear at his former college during preparations for his *Star Wars* fan film. The photograph was published widely in the media and drew comparisons to a publicity shot for *Dexter*, with his strange expression, cold stare, and similar pose, though any similarity is coincidental as it was taken years before the first episode aired.

GEEK TO DREAMER: Twitchell's appearance changed noticeably during his high-school years, from Grade 10 (left) to Grade 12 (far right). Teased for his looks, he had surgery to pin his ears back and started wearing contacts by graduation.

REALITY: Mark Twitchell and his ex-wife, Jess, on their wedding day, January 13, 2007. His sister served as his best man at a small ceremony in the Hotel Macdonald. Mark and Jess's daughter, Chloe, was born just over a year later.

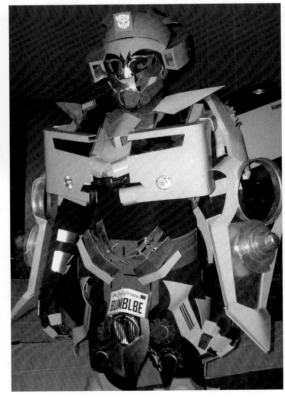

FANTASY: Twitchell loved wearing self-made, screen-accurate reproductions of movie costumes. In 2005 (above), he attended a *Star Wars* premiere as Jedi knight Kit Fisto. In 2007, he won Edmonton's Halloween Howler costume competition as Bumblebee from *Transformers* (right).

CAREER CASE: Det. Bill Clark answered questions from the media outside Edmonton's courthouse following the verdict in Twitchell's first-degree murder trial. Det. Dale Johnson (left) and Det. Brad Mandrusiak (right) had watched the court proceedings closely as their case made the international news.

SURVIVOR: Gilles Tetreault testified at length of his struggle with a masked man in Twitchell's garage.

FRIEND: Mike Young testified about his friendship with Twitchell, and their shared passion for making movies.

MUSE: Twitchell drew this portrait of actor Michael C. Hall, who plays Dexter Morgan on the television show *Dexter*, while awaiting trial, but insisted he didn't "hero-worship" the character.

SKETCHES: His prison artwork was varied, including sketches of actress Natalie Portman (left) and characters from the movie *Avatar* (right). But only Dexter adorned the wall of Twitchell's cell.

TORMENT: Surrounded by loved ones, Johnny's mother, Elfriede Altinger, held back tears on the steps of Edmonton's courthouse near the end of Twitchell's murder trial. "There will never be closure," she said of her son's death. "But it goes on to the next step, to start to heal, if that's possible."

JOY: The last known photograph of Johnny Altinger (above) was taken while driving to West Edmonton Mall in August 2008. Johnny's family remembered his gentle spirit, as captured in one of their favourite photographs of him (right).

It was the kind of honest response that journalists loved but made spin doctors cringe. At the time, no one realized how important Rosenberg's comments were: it was the last time anyone from the television show ever spoke publicly about Mark Twitchell. Every interview request, no matter who was asking, was denied for years.

The media attempted to contact *Dexter*'s creator, author Jeff Lindsay, but he didn't answer requests either and had others screen his calls. Eventually, ABC's *20/20* persuaded him to speak about the Twitchell case, but then Lindsay abruptly cancelled. The program reported that he had called fifteen minutes before the scheduled interview and explained that "he couldn't talk about *Dexter* and he couldn't tell us why."

Fans of the show wanted to know more about Mark Twitchell and what links detectives had made between his case and the motives and method of the fictional Dexter Morgan. "How could this be a Dexter-style murder if the victim was innocent?" a fan asked on an online message board. But the police weren't willing to release that information just yet, especially how Twitchell had created a plastic-wrapped kill room with a metal table, just like Dexter in the television show.

A few fans clicked through news articles featuring photos of Twitchell dressed as Bumblebee, Wolverine, and in various other Halloween outfits. "Say what you will about this evil bastard," one wrote. "But those costumes are pretty decent."

AFTER A FEW WEEKS of panic, *Star Wars* fans had calmed enough to change their approach. A few decided it was much better to distance themselves from Twitchell rather than to cower in the dark. "Frankly, us worrying about how it reflects on us is pretty myopic; it reflects far worse on Edmonton, for instance," wrote one fan, who retracted his earlier messages of alarm.

Insults then took over the online dialogue. "He always struck me as being a little nuts," the conversation continued. "Had a real sense of entitlement when he posted."

INTO THE DEPTHS

DETECTIVE ANSTEY ROCKED ON his feet, staring into the beams of television camera lights in the front lobby of police headquarters. Two weeks had passed since his first press conference. Anstey needed the public's help again, and he had just the thing to attract media attention. He had called in the cameras and newspapers to say he wanted witnesses to come forward. Had anyone seen Twitchell's Pontiac Grand Am on the road between October 14 and October 19? It would've been fairly noticeable because the licence plate was DRKJEDI.

"We're interested in speaking with anybody who may have seen that vehicle, say in a farm area or in any secluded area, and it might have been acting suspiciously," he announced to the gaggle of media encircling him.

Questions erupted. One reporter cut above the shouting with an obvious one: "Are you looking for a body?"

"We believe there is some evidence that he may have tried to get rid of some evidence . . . and that could include the body, yes."

"Is this a whole body," a scribe with a pen and notepad clarified, "or a body that's cut in pieces?"

"I'm not going to –" Anstey stopped himself. "I can't say for sure."

He hustled up to the third floor to homicide. Damn it, he thought. His boss was going to be on him again about that one. Anstey was still keeping S. K. Confessions and all the blood evidence a secret, but he knew the head of homicide would still think he was saying too much, even though he hadn't mentioned the key phrase about the police search: the sewer.

Anstey expected another verbal tussle with his superior was on the horizon. His boss had already been yelling at him about his investigative summary, a police document that the primary investigator writes to explain all the evidence and the progression of the case from beginning to end. He usually demanded such summaries on certain schedules and written in a certain way, but detectives felt their boss was beginning to micro-manage this particular file, and Anstey didn't play by those rules. For one, he liked to use Post-It notes. The team bugged Anstey about it, joking how he was just like Twitchell for leaving sticky notes everywhere, but for their boss, it was a serious issue. "Sticky notes can go missing," he used to tell Anstey. "Just write everything directly in your notes."

Despite the butting heads within the homicide unit, the case had progressed. The first victim, Gilles Tetreault, had been interviewed by Clark. The entire team was amazed at how closely his survival story mirrored Twitchell's version in S. K. Confessions. He had also luckily printed off photos of "Sheena" and her driving directions prior to his date. The details within Twitchell's document were slowly being proven true, one witness at a time.

But to the surprise of the investigators, the real-life victim was not married. While S. K. Confessions clearly stated that the killer was hunting single men, detectives had remained open to the possibility that the victim hadn't called the police in order to keep an attempted affair a secret. Gilles didn't report the attack, however, simply because he was embarrassed. He also didn't realize his experience had been a prelude to a suspected brutal murder seven days later.

A woman in Ohio had also called police a few days after hearing of the murder charge on the news. Renee Waring confessed to having participated in some very strange conversations with Mark Twitchell. She thought her Facebook record of thousands of words written by him as Dexter Morgan was going to be incredibly valuable to the case. Detectives agreed. And they were grateful that, just like Gilles, she had come forward despite the potential embarrassment since Twitchell's correspondence with her seemed to detail his step-by-step plan and changing methods for committing the perfect murder.

Anstey had backed down on his search for a possible snuff film. With the diary in hand and Twitchell's convincing denial, it seemed to be less of a priority. And tech crimes had found seventeen hours of video footage stored on Twitchell's home computer, laptop, and external hard drives. It could take weeks to squeeze in time for viewing every last second of it. But unbeknownst to Anstey, the public would actually see some of Twitchell's video before his own detectives.

MIKE FOUGHT FOR DAYS to stop it, but he was powerless, even while acting as Twitchell's power of attorney. National broadcaster Global TV had obtained footage from the *House of Cards* shoot and planned to air it on a new current events program called *16x9: The Bigger Picture*. Mike tried to claim their broadcast would be a copyright infringement of their work, but his argument crumbled under a "fair dealing" defence that allowed such material to be used for news reporting purposes. Twitchell's film crew was mortified. "If that footage airs, everyone at that garage is exposed," a worried Scott pointed out online. Some of them considered the possibility that a crooked cop could have leaked the footage, but the source was far closer than they realized.

Television editor Spencer Copeland had rented his digital camera to Twitchell, but the filmmaker had never paid him upon its return. Spencer was out a few hundred dollars. He was being hounded by the media for footage of the movie that had inspired a real-life murder. He only had a few minutes of video that Twitchell had left stored on the camera, including the special effects shot of the torso stabbing and the last scenes filmed. News anchors regularly stopped by the post-production company where he worked, hoping to charm him into releasing the footage. As the weeks passed, Spencer became so sick of the media asking for the video that he decided to give it away to the next person who walked in the door. Five minutes later, someone from Global TV arrived. He handed the camera over for no money, signed an exclusivity agreement to not give the footage to anyone else, and wiped the camera hard drive clean upon its return. "I wanted it away from me," he recalled. "It seemed to bring so much grief. It was stressing me out so I was happy when it was gone." Global had an exclusive due to pure luck and without spending a dime.

Tense and nervous, most of Twitchell's film crew watched the Global TV program when it aired on the evening of Sunday, November 30. To their relief, none of the broadcast footage revealed any of their faces. "We heard Dave's voice, saw part of my arm and torso, but no faces," Scott wrote.

The program played up the *Dexter* connection, stating that "eerily, Twitchell even looks like the character." Some members of his crew thought

Twitchell had a very slight resemblance to Michael C. Hall, the actor who played the fictional serial killer. Twitchell had taken a self-portrait during his prep work for his *Star Wars* film that was framed in a similar fashion to *Dexter*'s main promotional pose: the wry grin, cold stare, a maroon dress shirt. Dexter had reddish hair, as Twitchell did as a child, and both had a deep voice, a tomboy sister, a wife and young family. But those were all passing similarities. The comparison in the program made the film crew angry.

The six-and-a-half-minute segment then ended on the possibility that the entire case could be an elaborate hoax. "It's possible for him to have done something like that," one of Twitchell's old college buddies told the program, "to have flipped it, to basically have used the media as a tool."

Twitchell's friends looked at the calendar and started counting the days to December 10, the day Johnny's email stated he'd be back from Costa Rica.

They hoped and they prayed.

———————

THE AIR OUTSIDE HUNG heavy with frost as Acting Detective Dale Johnson peered down a sewer grate and took a long look below. He adjusted his glasses. He could see the murky water at the bottom, hear his breath echo into the depths of the city's underbelly. But he couldn't see a body. He had already checked every manhole and sewer grate surrounding Twitchell's St. Albert home and the Greenview garage film set. Now he was outside the home of Mark Twitchell's parents and he had brought along reinforcements.

A huge city drainage truck was parked nearby. Public works employees carried pick axes and camera equipment. Every manhole in front of the house and along the entire length of the street was popped open. The crew snaked a camera scope inside the sewer and drove it up and down the pipes, searching all the storm drains. It took an entire day. The crew returned the next morning to search the back alley. The camera traced the old and cracked network of metal and concrete pipes beneath the aging north-side neighbourhood.

Nothing could be found.

Snowflakes were falling and the ground was starting to freeze.

Then another promising lead. Constable Michael Roszko from the tech crimes unit had found another page of the diary on Twitchell's laptop:

> *I chose the eastern suburb of the city to dump my waste. It would be practically a ghost town with most of its residents either having commuted to work in the city or otherwise occupied and away from their homes. The housing in this part of my world was also older, done back in the sixties and seventies when neighbourhoods were not so congested so there were back alleys to be had. . . . I found exactly what I was looking for: a manhole cover placed off to the side behind a power pole.*

The team shared a collective thought: Sherwood Park. It was a community east of the city and a known criminal dumping site, where, in recent years, the bodies of prostitutes had been found. Johnson drove off to the public works department and studied their sewer maps for any location that could resemble the description in the diary.

And he found one. It was a near-perfect match. When he drove to the site and took a look for himself, he knew they had found it. The manhole was located off to the side and beside a power pole in the eastern suburb, just as Twitchell had written. Johnson called in the drainage trucks. He stood nearby, waiting. The crew took their time but returned with bad news.

"Are you kidding me?" he said in frustration. "No, this *has* to be it."

Two workers descended into the sewer and searched again. Same result. Johnson couldn't believe the body wasn't there.

The sewer search was rapidly expanded. The rest of Sherwood Park was examined, then the team moved northeast to the city of Fort Saskatchewan, to the surrounding villages of Ardrossan, Lamont, Gibbons, farther southeast to the town of Beaumont and the growing city of Leduc.

All negative.

Anstey's plea to the public to find witnesses who had seen Twitchell's car with its DRKJEDI licence plate proved fruitless too. While the car had been spotted plenty of times, none of the sightings had led to any potential sewer sites.

A thought occurred that Twitchell could have flipped the directions in the diary and had meant to say "western" suburb. Johnson searched the western bedroom communities of Spruce Grove and Stony Plain, the tiny town of Onoway. St. Albert was searched again.

Nothing.

The diary was read over once more. Maybe Twitchell was calling Edmonton an eastern suburb of St. Albert? The eastern half of the city was searched extensively. Everything east of 75th Street was included in a wide swath of searching, a section stretching north and south more than forty blocks. But the team was also open to considering tiny villages or towns. The forensics team was called in to help. Constable Gary Short and Sergeant Randy Topp drove as far away as Bawlf, a village two hours southeast of the city.

Sites were found that closely matched Twitchell's description. Sewer grates were popped open. Drainage trucks were called in with vacuum pumps. But they found nothing.

It was now early December and winter's claws were digging deep into the Alberta soil. Temperatures plunged to double digits below zero. The storm sewers were freezing up and the search had to be called off.

The team was frustrated. They believed somewhere in that web of pipes and drains was the body of an innocent man, his skeleton slowly becoming wrapped in a thick blanket of ice. And they were powerless to stop it from happening.

———————

THE 10TH DAY OF December passed by with little fanfare. Johnny's personal Facebook profile remained inactive. On "Find Johnny Altinger" there was silence as well.

Everyone who had been in denial about Johnny's fate had their last desperate hope taken away as 2008 neared its end. There had never been a Costa Rica vacation, and it was clear Johnny was never coming back.

AN ENDING

THE SPRING MELT ARRIVED as Anstey made a decision about his future: he was done with homicide. The endless hours, the death and blood, the battles with his boss, which had escalated to shouting matches. He just knew it was time.

Anstey had been dedicated to solving this last case of his career. He didn't want to take a chance that Twitchell could get off on a technicality or be provided the luxury of some kind of defence. He believed the man guilty and a danger to society. He wanted him behind bars for the rest of his life. To do that, Anstey had to prove Johnny was dead. The sewer search had failed, so he focused on eliminating the possibility that Johnny was still alive. Anstey checked hospitals, the morgue, the medical examiner's office for unidentified remains; crisis units were called to rule out mental health issues. The team had flagged Johnny's bank accounts, credit cards, mortgage payments, bills. They contacted Johnny's doctor, his dentist, a pharmacist for ongoing prescriptions. His name was flagged with every airline, with immigration in the Caribbean, and across America. The missing persons unit rechecked everything on a three-month rotation.

But there was no sign of him anywhere. Johnny had fallen off the grid.

Anstey figured about 90 per cent of the file was complete when he handed in his resignation in March 2009. The remaining work dealt primarily with finding Johnny's body, a task he feared may never be completed.

On his last day, he packed up his belongings and cleared out his desk, shaking hands with his colleagues, saying goodbye to Clark. He was leaving on a high, at least. A career case. Anstey turned in his handgun, his badge, number 1098, and was given a retired member's badge in return. He picked up a cardboard box full of his personal things and took the elevator out of headquarters. "I'm retired," his out-of-office work email message stated. "Yahoo."

THE REMAND

TWITCHELL SETTLED IN TO prison life at the Edmonton Remand Centre. After being shipped around from floor to floor, he finally resided in Room 11 on cell block 3D, a floor designed for long-term inmates. He wasn't too distressed by his incarceration, although he grew increasingly impatient with the people with whom he had to associate. "I have nothing in common with dope dealers, robbers and crack heads," he wrote later, describing the place as a "low-brow sensory deprivation tank." He felt he had to make the best of it, however, and find a way to thrive among what he considered to be a pile of garbage.

As inmate 236702, he spent most of his time in his cell, scribbling in his notepad, creating stories, and avoiding contact with the other inmates around him. The cell was tiny, with two hard plastic bed bunks stacked on one side and a metal desk screwed into the tower's cement blocks. One fluorescent bulb provided enough light to read under its harsh greenish glow. Natural light streamed in through long and narrow window slits no wider than a person's wrist. One window slit was horizontal, the other vertical. The view looked out into the Brownlee Building next door, where Crown prosecutors were working to prepare the court case against him. The cell block had three television sets in a common room, but one was frequently broken. He rarely got to see what he wanted anyway; he liked tennis while everyone else wanted to watch hockey.

The remand interior walls were painted white, but Twitchell had thought of a way to decorate. Using toothpaste, he tacked up a *Dexter* poster, featuring actor Michael C. Hall posed with a half-smile and giving a probing stare. He told inmates the poster was just a conversation piece. "I don't hero-worship him," he insisted. He kept his cell clean and demanded roommates with a shared obsession for cleanliness.

Twitchell became a model prisoner. He would often gloat that he was the only man in remand to never have been in a fight on the inside. He would use his charm to win favours rather than his fists. And he worked hard at finding ways to make the place more refreshing. Above all, he wanted to read. His mother helped as much as she could. Between his parents' regular visits – they came at least once a month, while Susan visited less frequently – his mother would research topics on the Internet for her son, find titles that would stimulate the mind, and pass on the book suggestions. Sometimes Twitchell would have to write an essay to prison management to explain why he wanted a certain book imported into the remand library. After a prolonged battle, he was granted access to several of his requested texts.

He tried to maintain a busy routine to keep himself occupied. He had always been a night owl, but he would jolt himself awake in remand so he wouldn't miss breakfast. He would then crawl back into bed and rest his eyes for several hours. The late morning would be burned away by writing. He began reading philosophy. But soon he spread his interests to topics as varied as quantum mechanics and Egyptian history. He would sit back and read his imported books well into the afternoon. He would also grab a copy of both city newspapers and scoff at the media coverage of his case, believing it was biased and too sensational. At night, he would listen to the radio until drifting to sleep around 2:00 a.m. He tried to keep to an exercise regime by occasionally filling garbage bags with water and stuffing them in pillowcases as makeshift free weights. He was slowly losing his fast-food belly. He began to hate the meal plan, which was on a three-week rotation heavy in mashed potatoes and enriched pasta. And despite his efforts to stay active, the days started to drag, the evenings became longer, the lack of activities became quite draining.

Life was a bore.

One day, the monotony was broken up when Twitchell strolled into the remand interview rooms. "Talk about the last person I expected to see!" he blurted, taken aback. Staring at him through the prison glass was a tiny woman with long black hair – the girl who had sat near him in high school and been handed his two-hundred-page *Star Wars* report. It had been a long time. They had never been really close friends. Back in school, they had often talked, but they lost touch, as people do. She was now married, had her own children, her own life. She had been told that

Twitchell's face had been broadcast across the national news. The situation confused her, so she booked a personal visit. "I was positive he had been falsely accused," she would recall later.

Twitchell had a big grin on his face as he sat down and began talking excitedly with his old high-school classmate. She asked how he was doing, they discussed his dissolving marriage, movies, life on the outside.

As she continued contact with him, she saw how his spirits rose with every passing week. They started writing each other letters. She quickly became one of his two prison pen pals. While she was fine with this level of contact, she was also insistent that it remain her big secret.

Twitchell's second unexpected visitor was an artist and filmmaker who had been travelling through Africa during his arrest. While he used the stage name William Strong and, later, Chapel Perilous, Twitchell would remember the Calgary-based artist and actor as Stakk Wezzer, a *Star Wars* character he had portrayed on the set of his fan film.

William had spent a great deal of time in southern Ethiopia and grew horrified at the sight of children with machine guns. He was experiencing a world totally removed from what he knew. "I felt an incredible sense of isolation," he recalled. "Every day I felt like I was in a cage." The encounter likely gave him post-traumatic stress disorder, he said. But a side benefit of the ordeal was that he developed a great deal of empathy for others. Such a perspective, he said, was his sole reason for contacting Twitchell upon his return to Canada. He wrote him a letter believing he could relate to the feeling of being an artist trapped in an unfamiliar environment.

Their relationship flourished. Through regular letters, the two film-makers would talk philosophy, writing, and the creative process. It was a window into a unique mind. William never asked Twitchell about the criminal case against him and Twitchell never volunteered information. "I'm not here to judge him," said William. "Whether he's innocent or guilty or whatever the situation is, he's still just a person."

Having two pen pals to write to on a regular basis was a thrill for Twitchell. It fulfilled his need for attention and gave him a sense of purpose, knowing that people actually cared about him. Twitchell began calling them his two "best friends." But both of them classified their relationship in quite a different way, though they had trouble defining what it was, what it meant.

Twitchell would write pages and pages to himself, his pen pals, and others, often surprising the recipients with the length and level of detail. His various letters and writings in prison provided him a forum to vent his frustrations at how the world had got it wrong. In some of his writings, he expressed deep regret, but was it bona fide? He resorted to defining the disappearance and presumed murder of Johnny Altinger as "the fiasco that was October 10, 2008." While many of his dates were correct, details embedded within his writings tended to take on an alternate form of reality. In one entry, composed in late January 2011, he wrote:

> Why would a normal, healthy, well-adjusted, hard-working producer facing a huge pay cheque, a glorious start in his chosen field and a happy young family he's head of just up and kill a perfect stranger? So far the weak attempts at conjecture on this matter are blatantly insulting to any moderately intelligent person.

In other entries he told pure lies, declaring that he was the one who had filed for divorce, not Jess. "Breaking up our blissful family trio was destroying my heart."

His writing continued to be both a source of entertainment and release. It was his only solace within the prison. He put pen to paper and scribbled wildly for days on end. Sometimes he had to be stirred from his cell so as to not miss supper. In his own words, it was like he was "possessed." Within two months of his arrest, he had crafted a thousand-page autobiography. He handed the heavy stack of double-sided paper to his lawyer, believing it would be of some use to his criminal defence.

He wrote of his imprisonment as if he was the king of remand, and on this point, he was telling the truth. In a cell block with more than a dozen killers, he basked in his notoriety and used it to instill fear in others. Prisoners would often talk about Twitchell behind his back, but when he entered the room, their gossip hushed. Guards soon noticed Twitchell was being treated differently within the criminal community. "There was almost a reverence toward him, a creepy level of respect," one correctional officer recalled. "Nobody knew just quite how to take him." Long-timers joined in, playing on Twitchell's high profile when the third floor became a temporary overflow unit for new arrivals. Rookie inmates were warned their lives would be in danger if they were assigned the empty bunk in Twitchell's cell. And the scare tactics worked. At least three men demanded to be moved after spending a single night with Twitchell, saying they were deeply terrified of the man. Twitchell wrote with glee how this alarming new criminal persona had been developing behind bars:

> *Other dangerous inmates who actually have violent histories proceed with caution. Even after people get to know me and how I am, they are wary. But then, I stand out anyway.*
>
> *I walk purposefully with my head high and my shoulders back. I do everything, make every movement, with specific purpose and no wasted movement. I do not speak unless I have something of substance to say. In a place where almost everyone shuffles their feet or swaggers with some comical posturing, roams around aimlessly and yammers on just to hear the sound of their own voice, I'm unique. The stigma has combined with my normal manner to create an air of respect.*

Twitchell eventually found one roommate suitable to his needs. The man had similar interests and for six months they considered themselves the "wordsmiths" of remand. The pair would play Scrabble for hours each day or work on story ideas together. The man was soon sentenced and sent to prison and Twitchell was forced to return to a life of solitude, disdain for most of his fellow inmates, and long hours of introspective writing.

He became a target for a "shit bomb" only once. A new arrival not accustomed to the established routine emptied a Cheetos bag and filled it with water, his own urine and feces, twirled the end shut, and stuck it under Twitchell's cell door. He stomped hard. But instead of spraying all over Twitchell, it backfired and shot out the other end of the bag. All Twitchell could do was mock the man's failure as he returned to his bed to continue his writing.

In his prison letters, Twitchell started describing his life story as if it was a dramatic narrative, filled with cliffhangers and even dialogue, a novelization of real events. For weeks, he wrote a running dialogue between himself, God, and Satan. "Only I used the pseudonyms Alpha and Memnoch," he explained. "It evolved into this deep, rich and engaging discussion. . . . I'm quite proud of how it turned out." Sometimes he'd run ideas off himself and made-up people. In one case, it was a conversation with a "composite we'll name Aaron for the sake of simplicity. I notice when I write philosophy it works best in dialogues." And he compared his situation often to Hollywood movies, especially *The Shawshank Redemption,* about a wrongfully convicted man who, like Twitchell, had expanded the prison library. "Nobody could guess the truth in a case like this," he wrote in one cliffhanger passage. "What brought us here is unlike anything that's ever been seen before."

DEVELOPING A BUSINESS PLAN took over Twitchell's schedule as he schemed of ways to keep busy. He imagined drawing celebrity sketches in prison and selling them for "absurdly high price tags." He'd mail the pencil drawings to his mother, who would scan them into her computer and then email them to his pen pal, William Strong, to sell later online. Twitchell went to work. He drew sketches of actress Natalie Portman, a shot from the movie *Avatar,* a close-up of singer Fergie. He found a magazine advertisement that featured a woman morphed into a flower, so he drew that too. And he couldn't resist drawing *Dexter*'s Michael C. Hall. It was a portrait he insisted was made "out of pure spite," but he was still thrilled with the realism he had captured.

The image he created *was* striking. What was most amazing about the portrait was how perfectly Twitchell had captured the likeness of the actor. In fact, when the sketch was overlapped with the publicity still from *Dexter* that was the inspiration for the drawing, the pencil lines appeared to match the photo's contours: the dimensions of the actor's face, the distance between the ears, the eyes, his nose – Twitchell's pencil lines almost appeared to be a perfect replica of the photograph.

Many of his other drawings also looked to be nearly identical to the source images he had pulled from newspapers and magazines.

It was extraordinary.

TWITCHELL CONTINUED TO READ the papers diligently as his incarceration approached a year. He would have seen Bill Clark's name pop up in city newspaper articles over the months as the detective commented on other homicide cases he was working on. The thought of Clark and seeing his name in print made Twitchell tighten his hands into white-knuckled fists. He loathed the detective, describing him in his writings as an "over-zealous pig of a man" and a "cliché." He had no respect for the officer. "I find Bill Clark to be a self-righteous, know-it-all weasel with no actual personality of his own," Twitchell concluded.

As Twitchell read the papers, he found it interesting that there was never any announcement that the police had recovered Johnny's remains. Twitchell didn't realize that the hunt would soon be leading right back to him. Despite his protests, his hatred of Clark and the search for Johnny Altinger's body were soon going to collide.

NOT GETTING IT

DETECTIVES BILL CLARK AND Brad Mandrusiak sat waiting, talking shop, in a stuffy interview room on the main floor of remand. Clark had a rolled-up copy of the newspaper and it didn't take long until their guest had arrived. Twitchell walked in wearing his blue inmate overalls, and after one look at Clark he scowled and rolled his eyes. "You gotta be kidding me, right?"

Clark stood up from the desk to address him. "No, not at all. We're here to talk."

"About what?" He was mad. "*Seriously.*"

"We wanted to show you this newspaper article about your preliminary hearing being surpassed, which is basically unheard-of."

"I don't know anything about it. I'm not interested, guys."

Twitchell stormed out of the room.

Clark shot a look at Mandrusiak. He had been the officer to arrest Twitchell and read him his rights – appropriately so because Mandrusiak was one of the few detectives with a law degree.

They both followed.

It was early September 2009, and a few weeks had passed since a judge denied Twitchell's bail and a court order cancelled his preliminary hearing – the procedure usually held to determine if there is enough evidence to proceed to a criminal trial. Justice Michelle Crighton, who heard the bail application, had concerns about public safety and undermining the public's confidence in the justice system if Twitchell was released. While the evidence was circumstantial, the judge ruled it also strongly supported the prosecution's theory that Twitchell engaged in a "macabre hobby" of luring strangers to his kill room. It was too great a risk to let him leave custody until his trial with such an "overwhelming inference" connecting him to Johnny's disappearance. A rare direct indictment, forcing Twitchell straight to trial, was issued shortly after the bail decision. The move would also prevent American media from sitting in and broadcasting evidence from the hearing on U.S. airwaves out of the domain of the Canadian courts. While Canadian media would have been forced to obey a publication ban if a preliminary hearing had gone ahead, the Americans could have flouted the law.

All of this was happening behind the scenes. Both the prosecution and defence had been worried the massive media interest in Twitchell's case would prevent him from receiving a fair trial. When the prosecution decided there was enough evidence to also proceed with an attempted murder charge for the attack against Gilles Tetreault, it did so without notifying the public – and the move wasn't noticed by the media until the direct indictment was issued. Everything about the case was being handled by both sides of the courtroom as quietly as possible. Prosecutors and Twitchell's defence team spent months placing publication bans and sealing orders on most of the evidence, and all these pre-trial motions and legal movements. By the time their work was done, the media could legally report that Mark Twitchell was charged with first-degree murder, attempted murder, and little else. His name quickly disappeared from newsprint and the American media all flew home, waiting for a future trial. Even film director Errol Morris had changed his mind about featuring the Twitchell case on *Tabloid* and instead turned his planned documentary project into a feature-length film on an American criminal.

And now, with the cops at his heels, Twitchell had retreated to a holding tank behind the bank of interview rooms. He had nowhere to go. The two detectives closed in on him as he sat on a metal bench in the tank.

Clark tried a more diplomatic approach this time. "Mark, we're not trying to give you a hard time, buddy." He put his hand to his chest. "You know why we're here. We're trying to find the body."

But Twitchell wasn't going to play. "You just don't get it. You *just* don't get it," he fumed, his voice rising. "It's been this long. All of the hype has had a chance to wear down a bit. And you still haven't put it together, have you? You still haven't got it!" He aimed a curled finger at Clark. "You're wrong about this."

Clark gave him a doubting glance. "So you're saying you didn't do it?"

"Yeah."

"Yet the judge denied you bail. *You* heard the judge."

"I knew that bail was going to be denied." Twitchell brushed it aside. "I wasn't about to give away everything."

Clark stood there, stunned, as Mandrusiak jumped in. "Mark, just listen for a second. The judge is a neutral arbitrator. She's the first person that's heard the evidence, and heard the majority of the evidence. She's neutral. She's not partisan on the part of the police or anything of that nature and you heard what her decision was. We're just here to –"

But Twitchell cut him off. "I don't blame you, okay? I understand that my case is very unique. This is a very unusual situation, and given what you guys have, I can understand how you've arrived at the conclusions that you have. Okay? I'm not going to blame you for that." He straightened his back and blinked. "But you're wrong."

"It doesn't make any sense to me," said Mandrusiak.

But Twitchell was sick of the cops and in no mood to explain. "All you guys have ever said to me has been a lie or deception of some kind."

Clark stepped in again. "What have we lied to you about, Mark? You saw me go over that PowerPoint. We knew that you weren't what we call an emotional offender. We gave you the facts."

Twitchell put his hand on his hip and began speaking rapidly. "Oh, listen to you flip flop. One minute I'm a normal, healthy, religious person, the next minute I'm a sociopath. Maybe you should make your mind up. You're even dumber than you look, Bill."

"That was just part of the deception used in the interview," Clark replied. "I agree with you there. But let's go to the PowerPoint, Mark, go to the PowerPoint, where I showed you all the evidence. And now that DNA's come back and matched up that guy's blood in your car . . . I mean, those are no-brainers. Even the judge said that."

"You guys don't know what you're talking about."

"Actually, I do. The only thing we don't have is the body, so we thought we'd give you another chance on how you'd want to be remembered."

Mandrusiak gave Twitchell a moment to take it all in, then continued on from Clark's prodding. "Let's face it. There's been serious changes in circumstance here. Your bail was denied. It was denied in a very strong fashion. There's been a direct indictment that's been issued. So these are all things that I thought would weigh on somebody as bright as yourself, and so we came back. We just came back to see if you had a change of heart. . . . We're not here to berate you or anything like that, Mark. That's not what we're all about."

Clark chimed in. "What's done is done, Mark. It's how you want to be remembered. We can at least get you outta here for a day, go for lunch, you can show us where the body is."

But Twitchell stuck to his story. "It's the things you choose to ignore. It's absolutely *hilarious*." He laughed. "Well, it's going to come out in court. That's all I can tell you."

"What have we ignored?" inquired Mandrusiak.

Twitchell laughed even louder, but he didn't answer the question. "I have no reason to believe anything you say, so just take off." His laugh faded to a snicker.

Clark returned to his first tactic and pulled out his copy of the *Edmonton Journal*. "Do you wanna read the newspaper article? Right here. It says –"

"Nah, not interested."

Clark opened it and began reading out loud: "'Yet in a rare move the Attorney General's Office has signed off on a direct indictment of the case of Mark Twitchell.' That's unheard-of! I've never seen that before in thirty years of police work where we didn't go to a prelim and the reason why is that the evidence is simply *overwhelming*. That's why you're still in jail."

Twitchell smiled. "You've been so sold on this idea, you just made it happen for yourselves."

Clark had enough. "You know what, Mark? If you didn't do this, and had evidence, I would gladly investigate that for you. Right now. That's our job. We're not here to put innocent people in jail."

Mandrusiak agreed, telling Twitchell he would be happy to chase up any new leads he could provide. He tried to talk some sense into him. "Most people that we interview, Mark, if they are truly innocent, they tell us right outta the gate. We go off, we investigate their alibi, and we clear them! It's as simple as that."

Twitchell didn't respond.

The two cops shook their heads in dismay, trying for another ten minutes to get Twitchell to talk about the location of the body, but he just brushed them off like he was dusting his shoulders. "I know the truth," Twitchell finally piped up, "and it adds up a helluva lot more than this bullshit that you're spinning."

"How are you going to explain things then?" Clark asked. "How are you going to explain the DNA evidence?"

"I'm not going to hand this to you on a silver platter," said Twitchell. He sighed. "Unbelievable."

The three of them stood there in silence. Their allotted time was almost up. The cops told Twitchell one more time that if he wanted to give up the body they could come back with a judge's order allowing them to talk properly and they could organize for the media to be there, if he wanted them. But Twitchell just stared at the ceiling.

Minutes passed.

When the guard came in to take Twitchell to his cell, both detectives raised their voices to deliver parting words to their suspect.

"I'm not trying to give you a hard time," Clark said. "I just want the answers."

Mandrusiak waited until Twitchell was walking out of the holding tank before he raised his own voice. "Give it some serious thought, Mark. Some serious thought."

The clang of metal bars brought an end to their effort.

They walked back to headquarters.

Along the way, Clark went over the failed meeting in his head. He remembered seeing something during their exchanges that had caught him off guard. But when he mentioned it to Mandrusiak on the walk back to the office, he said he had seen it too.

When they had first started talking about Johnny's remains, Clark happened to look down and notice a bulge in Twitchell's pants. At first he thought it was just how Twitchell's clothes were bunched up, but then it got bigger. It was obviously an erection. The guy was aroused by this?

Clark spent a day researching criminal behaviour to find out what it could mean. But after a bit of reading on the subject, he thought it best not to ask.

In the end, he really didn't want to know.

A TEASE, A TASTE

BACK IN THE COMFORT of his remand cell block, Twitchell brushed off his police interrogations and struck up conversations he could control. Only those who humoured his interests would become close to him. And his favourite conversationalist turned out to be not among inmates but correctional officers.

She liked to call him "Twitchy." In return, Twitchell became intrigued with the woman in uniform and they developed a rapport. She'd tease him about *Dexter*'s Michael C. Hall and he loved it. When the actor was diagnosed with cancer she stopped by his cell and poked her head in. "Hey, I heard you've got cancer. How ya feeling?" Twitchell found the comment delightful. When news spread of the actor's changed health a few months later, she couldn't resist teasing Twitchell again. "You're in remission? Yay for you!" For the remand guard, it was nothing more than a little game to break up the work routine, but Twitchell soon treated the woman as a friend. "We always find something to discuss," he wrote of their affinity. "She's a firecracker."

The experienced guard, however, knew exactly who she was dealing with. Twitchell loved to talk, but she knew it was mostly about himself. And he liked to subtly manipulate those around him to gain access to all the details he craved, including her full name and most of her backstory, gleaned from other guards and inmates. "He's incredible at grooming people and appealing to your ego," she explained. "He's very savvy. But it's all for his gain. He wants to see how he can use that information or engage you in more dialogue. It's all about him."

Twitchell despised only one officer in remand: a guard who was frequently mean to him and showed no interest in his outlandish conversations. In contrast, Twitchell would sometimes disclose tidbits of his life to his favourite guard. She once convinced him to reveal the results of an IQ test he had taken – 142, or in a genius category, he claimed – which prompted her to ask even more personal questions.

Standing near another correctional officer in the cell block, she decided her rapport with Twitchell had reached such a stage that she could finally ask the question on many minds. "I'm going to ask you something," she told Twitchell, "and it's probably going to piss you off."

"Yes, ask away," he replied.

"Did you eat him?"

Twitchell's eyebrows shot up. "What?"

"Well, you can't blame me for asking," she chuckled.

Her armed partner worried they would have to pepper-spray an enraged Twitchell or subdue him to stop a prison riot.

"Did you eat him?" she probed further. "Did you nibble on him? Did you *have* a snack?"

Twitchell turned expressionless. "I can't believe you asked me that."

"Well, if the situation was reversed," she clarified, "you *absolutely* would take this opportunity to ask."

Her comment made him chuckle. Twitchell wasn't bothered by the question per se, just surprised at the gall she had to ask it. "Why does this fascinate you so much?"

She told him he was one of a kind. Throughout her entire career as a correctional officer, she was likely never to meet an inmate quite like him again.

Twitchell nodded and smiled at her explanation. He then walked back to his cell and didn't answer her question.

As the months rolled by, he never did.

PERSPECTIVES

DOUBT HAD EMERGED. IT crept slowly, its tentacles tugging at the minds of Twitchell's friends. Jason in particular became more dubious as Twitchell's incarceration stretched on. He desperately wanted to believe his friend and former roommate was innocent, but he also feared there was far more to the story. Either his friend was a liar and a killer or the police were liars who detained innocent people for two years. He didn't know which was worse.

Their conversations remained jovial when he did take time to visit Twitchell in remand. But one meeting before the trial changed everything. Jason had stared a bit longer through the prison glass this time, watching Twitchell's eyes as he talked. And something clicked; something was different, unsettling. "He gave me this look and I just suddenly went, 'Jesus!'" he recalled later. "There was just something in the expression, something there I had never seen before. It was just a creepy look." Jason didn't go back.

Rebecca found her suspicions were also being raised as time passed. A few members of Twitchell's film crew wanted to discuss the case, which made her uncomfortable. "I was thinking if he didn't do it, then it had to be one of these other guys who had access to the garage," she said later. "There was no way I was going to meet up with any of them."

Twitchell's sister, Susan, had visited him a few times during his incarceration, but by the time the trial neared she had stopped and only Twitchell's parents remained in regular contact. They usually booked an appointment to see their son once a month, depositing cash in his remand account to buy better food at the prison canteen, more pens, more notebooks.

The approaching trial made Johnny's closest friends incredibly nervous. They feared the police didn't have enough to secure a conviction, considering there was an information blackout. The continuing sealing orders and publication bans prevented all of the evidence from being made public until the trial began. One of his friends' greatest concerns was the inability to find Johnny's remains. Without a body, could the case collapse? How could it be a proven that Twitchell committed a murder with no human remains? "Admit to your crime and start to serve your time like a man," one of Johnny's Vancouver friends begged online.

Even if Twitchell could have heard the message, he wouldn't have listened. He had something going on behind the scenes. He had a plan he had been sitting on for years, hinting at it repeatedly with detectives and his friends. He believed he was still holding the cards.

When the trial began, he was going to offer a paradigm shift he was certain would change everything. "They are convinced they see a train," Twitchell wrote of the prosecution shortly before his trial. "From their perspective, they can clearly identify the tracks, the wheels, the grill and even the window with an engineer in it. But back up a little and soon we see that the reality is not a train at all but a painting of a train, sitting on an easel in the middle of a studio."

While many friends had abandoned Twitchell, such cryptic cloak-and-dagger assertions encouraged a select few to remain loyal. Mike did not waver in his support through the years from arrest to trial. In one of his only media statements issued after his letter in defence of Twitchell was published, Mike still publicly defended his friend. "The evidence will speak for itself, and I hope and believe that it will find Mark innocent," he stated. Scott stayed committed to his beliefs as well. "I don't believe Mark did it," he told a friend over the phone. "He's going to be proven innocent. You just wait and see what happens at the trial. Just wait."

Scott repeated such strong opinions online. In one of his last posts on "Friends of Twitch," he wrote how he had received a court summons in the mail and he was going to testify in a few days. "Make no mistake," he told the group. "I'm still on his side."

It was the kind of talk that made Twitchell very pleased.

CRUELTY EXPOSED

THE FOG HAD ROLLED in. As the sun crested the horizon, Twitchell slid his feet out from his prison bed and peered out the tiny rectangular window. Outside, a thick blanket of grey and white drifted low among downtown office towers and skimmed the top of the six-storey courthouse. The building stood across the street and one block south from Twitchell's cell. One wing of the courthouse heard provincial matters and had a main-floor counter where drivers paid speeding tickets; the taller wing housed the Court of Queen's Bench, which was reserved for the most serious of crimes. The square-shaped building looked like an upside-down pyramid with the top floor much wider than the bottom. Its concrete walls tended to glow white in the summer heat, but on an overcast day like today they turned a shade darker, to a soft light brown. Twitchell had worked his way to trial from the provincial side, starting in a massive docket court. He then was transferred to the Queen's Bench – Alberta's Superior Court – and moved slowly up the tower, floor by floor. By the time a trial began, most facing a murder charge would end up on the fourth floor. The fifth was reserved for appeals; the top floor held the offices of the chief justice.

Twitchell rubbed his face, pausing for a moment at the view, but his thoughts were interrupted by mumbling sounds from within the room. Sleeping in the other bunk was a new roommate, some homeless dumpster diver who had been talking to himself and snoring all night. A pile of stale food sat near his bed. Twitchell sighed. He wasn't used to waking up so early, and the lack of sleep from this nuisance didn't help. He started getting ready anyway just as morning radio programs were blasting previews of his case. Between weather and traffic updates, announcers were making wisecracks, calling him the "small-time filmmaker with big-movie dreams" who would soon have the "lead role" in a riveting courtroom drama. He would stand trial for the murder of Johnny Altinger in a matter of hours, more than two and a half years since his Halloween arrest.

It was March 16, 2011. The fog retreated into smaller patches within the river valley as journalists began their trek to the building. Melting piles of late-winter snow crunched under boots and shoes, mixing with chocolate-brown mud and road salt. Reporters joined a growing crowd that jammed the security gates at all three entrances. Everyone had to remove their belts and jackets, empty their pockets, and dump everything into grey plastic bins. Their belongings were sent through an X-ray machine. Guards then swung metal detectors around each person in the search for weapons.

The first reporters to arrive spotted Twitchell's name in the docket list displayed on a flat-panel monitor and took the elevator to the fourth floor to gather in a central foyer with black leather chairs. Room 417 was a quick stroll down the hallway, where clerks were busy preparing the chosen courtroom. Producers from American television programs *48 Hours Mystery* and *Dateline NBC* had already arrived. National broadcasters, wire agencies, and newspapers had called in their prairie correspondents to cover the trial. The *Edmonton Journal* assigned two journalists, as did the *Edmonton Sun*. Three CBC reporters were in attendance, joined later by a producer with the national network's investigative program, *the fifth estate*. Every local television station was there. Photographers and camera operators huddled around each entrance on the off chance someone who knew Twitchell would show up or make a statement. Deadmonton history was being made under the gaze of the awaiting media, ready to broadcast the story around the world.

But at the moment, Twitchell looked no different than any other inmate. He was crammed within a pack of a dozen other prisoners, lined up in rows of two. Guards led the group through a lengthy underground tunnel connecting remand to the courthouse. Twitchell's right wrist was handcuffed to another inmate's as they shuffled into the basement of the court. The only televisions down here were within "the bubble," where guards could monitor security camera screens from behind thick glass, watching closely as inmates were escorted individually from the holding tanks up to their respective courtrooms.

On the fourth floor, Twitchell's defence lawyer, Charles Davison, strolled out of the elevator in the customary black robes worn in Canada's superior-level courts, tugging a cart of boxes and binders behind him. Throughout his legal career, the salt-and-pepper-haired barrister had secured case victories for many accused killers. And in preparing for this murder trial, he had spent months trying to have S. K. Confessions excluded from evidence, but the court had dismissed his pleas and decided that the writings could be read by the jury. This morning, Davison would try another approach. He was also planning a surprise for later in the day, while his competition had a few of its own.

The court held a voir dire a mere three hours before the jury would be called in. Such hearings, a virtual trial within a trial, are common practice in criminal proceedings, but not on opening day. A publication ban would also be placed over the entire voir dire, meaning nobody would know what was discussed, or even that it had occurred, until after a verdict. Twitchell was led in by one guard, emerging from the interior corridors. He took a seat at the defence counsel table and looked up at Davison just as the judge appeared and the courtroom was called to order. Everyone rose to their feet and bowed.

Justice Terry Clackson walked in at a brisk pace, smiling as he took a seat perched high above the room. The jury waited in a backroom, unaware of what was transpiring in the court. Davison stood up, pushed his glasses up his nose, and launched into his eleventh-hour argument.

The writings within S. K. Confessions were "not entirely true." That was the defence's position. And the forty-two-page document contained statements that were far too prejudicial to Twitchell's right to a fair trial to ever be heard by the jury. Davison suggested some of the worst sections could be removed and still not seriously undermine the prosecution's case. He wanted the document edited with certain sections deleted or censored. A key concern was the sordid details of the dismemberment, which were so lurid and horrid, he said, that it would inflame the jury's passions. "What's on those pages is simply so graphic . . . that it could even bring on physical reactions."

Twitchell blushed. Shifting his weight in his chair, he focused intently on a notepad on the desk in front of him. As his lawyer spoke, he rubbed his temples and started scribbling.

The prosecution's argument was that S. K. Confessions was a diary and a confession – to everything. It provided insight into Twitchell's state of mind and his consistent levelheadedness in planning, executing, and cleaning up after the murder. The fact that he could dismember a human body with such a lack of emotion – to write about it methodically, clinically – was evidence in and of itself. The case was unavoidably gory, violent, sickening.

The judge listened carefully but reserved his judgment to a later date. The issue of the diary's contents would remain unresolved before the trial officially began later that afternoon.

TEN MINUTES BEFORE THE trial's scheduled start time, Detective Bill Clark emerged from the elevator, having taken the short walk to the courthouse from police headquarters. He pulled on the brass handles to the courtroom's creaky wooden doors and surveyed the crowd. Room 417 was already half full with fifty people as a stream of onlookers came in through the other entrance. Twitchell wasn't there yet. He was being held in the holding cell in an adjacent room.

Clark exchanged a glance with Lawrence Van Dyke, one of the two prosecutors, seated at their counsel table.

"Ready to deliver the opening?" Van Dyke quipped.

Clark rolled his eyes, chuckled, and slapped him on the back. He leaned in and whispered in his ear. Behind them, the crowd had grown to seventy. Few watching would have known that Clark was a detective, that this murder trial was his biggest homicide file to date, or that Twitchell hated him so deeply. Clark spoke with Van Dyke for only a minute to wish the team good luck. He would have to testify in a few weeks so he couldn't stay in the courtroom once the jury was let in. Clark stuck his hands in his pockets and strolled out the door with a smile on his face.

In the front row, a court sketch artist had pulled out a large sheet of paper and was madly scribbling. Behind her, a row of law students was crammed together, whispering about their weekend parties. Journalists took up the entire back row of the court, pens and notebooks clasped in their hands. Police officers sat nearby, close to a few curious lawyers who had a spare couple of minutes from their own cases. Twitchell's remaining friends and his film crew, as well as those who knew Johnny, would be called to testify and were barred from observing the trial until they had given their evidence. But an elderly friend of Johnny's mother sat in the centre of the courtroom, to be joined later by the rest of his out-of-town family. Twitchell had no support. His parents and sister never appeared, even though they were allowed to attend. He was all alone.

Davison pulled up into the courtroom again, lifted his robe tight on the sides, and sat down. In a minute he would be entering Twitchell's plea. Two plastic cups half-filled with water sat on the desk in front of him. He pulled out a pen, leaned back, and scanned through his notes.

Across the court, Van Dyke was deep in a conversation with co-prosecutor Avril Inglis, their whispers drifting like a soft hiss over the murmur of the growing crowd. Together, they would be the tag team for the Crown, having been assigned the file hours after Twitchell's arrest. The sketch artist began to draw an outline of Van Dyke and Inglis: his short army-style haircut and square jaw, her long black hair and glasses. They were both tall and in their late thirties. As two rising stars within the Department of Justice, they had studied each page, every photograph, every video. Some seventy-two people had been included in their final witness list. They had been preparing for months.

The door to the holding cell suddenly thumped open. A hush spread, but the crowd roared to life once again. It was just one of the sheriffs entering the room. The remaining few seats in the public gallery were taken just as the trial clerk arrived from the judge's chambers, signalling that the start of the trial was finally moments away.

A sheriff pulled on the door and vanished behind it, heading to the holding cell to retrieve Twitchell. The room rolled to silence. All eyes fixated on the door as if it was a theatre curtain about to rise on the performance of a lifetime. Everyone was eager to get their first glimpse of the man profiled in the world's media. After more than two years behind bars, he was now notorious. How would he walk in to the room?

The door handle clicked. The crowd grew very still. An old man in the middle row whispered as he elbowed the man beside him: "Here he comes!"

But the star of this show was in no mood for an audience.

The door flew open, nearly hitting the bar, a brass banister separating the public gallery from the front of the court. In three quick strides Twitchell glided to a leather office chair beside Davison and settled in behind the desk. He never looked back. The public would stare at the back of his head for the rest of the day.

Seconds later Justice Terry Clackson walked in, took his seat, and called in the jury. One by one the jurors entered the court in silence and swore an oath. The jury had been chosen two days earlier during a seven-hour selection process. The six men and six women who would decide Twitchell's fate were a diverse group: two government executives, two retirees, a sales clerk, salesman, banker, engineer, teacher, librarian, nursing aid, and chef. Only one juror wasn't Caucasian. Four of them had never even heard of Twitchell's case before. They would be paid fifty dollars a day for their service. Only one juror affirmed. The rest took their oath on the Bible.

The trial clerk was tasked with reading Twitchell's formal arraignment and entering his plea. Twitchell was asked to rise and respond to the criminal charge.

He rose and stood tall. Folding his hands in front of him, he took in a deep breath and exhaled. Davison stood beside him. It would soon be time to reveal his big surprise.

The clerk began reading off the indictment sheet.

"Mark Andrew Twitchell," she stated, her voice echoing off the back wooden wall. "You stand charged that on or about the 10th day of October 2008 at or near Edmonton, Alberta, did unlawfully cause the death of Johnny Altinger, thereby committing first-degree murder, contrary to Section 235 Sub One of the Criminal Code of Canada." She continued reading off the paper. "How say to this charge? Do you plead guilty or not guilty?"

Twitchell did not hesitate. "Not guilty," he said flatly.

Davison raised his finger. "Now my Lord –" he interjected, coughing. "Having said that . . ." He explained that the law would allow Twitchell to enter a guilty plea to another offence arising from the same incident, despite pleading not guilty to the murder charge. "I have his instructions this afternoon to enter a guilty plea to an offence under Section 182 of the Criminal Code, in particular the offence of improperly interfering with a dead human body. Is that correct, Mr. Twitchell?"

"Yes."

The court's spectators were stunned. No one had anticipated this.

Van Dyke shot up from his chair. "Sir! The Crown is not consenting to that alternate plea being entered. We'll be proceeding on the charge of first-degree murder, sir." He sat down.

"All right. Thank you. Thank you," said Justice Clackson.

The trial clerk appeared confused. She looked up from her desk at the judge. "So do I enter the not guilty or the – ?"

"You enter a plea of not guilty to the charge," he replied, cutting her off.

The crowd started whispering. *What is happening?*

"Ladies and gentlemen, that development was a little unusual," Justice Clackson explained, looking at the jury. "And I'll have more to say about what that means for you as this trial proceeds. But for now, all you need to remember is that Mr. Twitchell is charged with murder and has pled not guilty."

It was just what Davison had wanted. The tactic worked beautifully. He caught the prosecution totally by surprise and it planted a seed of doubt in the jury's mind. All twelve jurors would remember that attempted guilty plea while every piece of damning evidence was presented. Nobody knew precisely what this plea meant just yet, which would mean a lot to the defence. It would cast doubt on the intent behind all the forensic evidence that the jury would be bombarded with over the coming three to four weeks. And the surprise came just as Van Dyke was about to give his opening statement, like a spoiled appetizer served right before the main course.

When he finally did rise, Van Dyke tried to brush off this unexpected incident and present the Crown as a friend of the jury, not an enemy of the accused. After all, Twitchell looked like anyone's son in his clean, crisp white polo shirt, khaki pants, and neatly trimmed hair. Van Dyke had to show this case wasn't a vendetta against Twitchell but a conclusion based on a mountain of evidence. Van Dyke cleared his throat, rested his hands on the podium on his desk not far from the jury, and turned to his left to greet them.

"My name is Lawrence Van Dyke and my colleague's name is Avril Inglis, and together we have the privilege of representing the Crown and the prosecution of this case," he said slowly as he read off his notes. He looked up, smiling, making eye contact with each juror.

He thanked them for taking the opportunity to become a juror, spinning it like they were empowered to make this decision rather than compelled by court order. He focused on Twitchell's right to a fair trial and stressed that each of them should keep an open mind. And with that proviso, he launched into describing a road map that Twitchell had left behind, a bloody trail that the Crown believed had exposed his deepest, most sinister desires.

"His plan was quite simply and shockingly to gain the experience of killing another human being," Van Dyke said bluntly. "He not only formed this plan but methodically deliberated on how to best accomplish this goal."

The prosecutor delivered the thirty-minute address like a story, one as colourful and peppered with clichés as any of Twitchell's own movie scripts. Van Dyke used phrases such as "fateful evening" and described the moment of the attack as when Twitchell's "murderous trap was sprung." It was quoted in the newspapers for days.

Twitchell ignored Van Dyke, turning his attention back to the notepad on the desk in front of him. He had little patience for the prosecution and rolled his eyes when Van Dyke brought up S. K. Confessions and described it as a diary. Instead of listening to the Crown, Twitchell focused on a mental exercise, one that would occupy a lot of his time for the remainder of the trial.

It started first with a little scribble. To anyone in the courtroom it would appear as if he was doodling, but he wasn't. He was writing a speech.

Back in remand, Twitchell had taught himself to write in a foreign language. He had used it to help design an inmate's tattoo and later for his own prison journal, keeping its contents a secret. The language he was using was easy to learn: each letter of the alphabet was replaced with a symbol like a square, triangle, or intricate design. It was as simple as memorizing each symbol and writing it down in place of the letters making up each word. The language was called Aurebesh. Not many people knew about the language due to its origins – it was only spoken by aliens on a distant planet in the *Star Wars* universe.

As he sat in the courtroom, where his future lay in the hands of twelve of his peers, Twitchell began writing in Aurebesh like some fictional alien in a fictional universe. It was the only way he could distract himself from the harsh reality of the court case. He wrote dialogue from the Hollywood blockbuster *Troy*, detailing a scene where two kings line up their armies but decide to let their brewing war be decided with a one-on-one battle between their two greatest warriors. One side calls in Achilles, who slays his far larger opponent in one swift blow.

This odd behaviour caught the attention of the public gallery, and at least one juror stared at him frequently. His lawyer had worked hard to gain the court's approval to allow Twitchell to wear civilian clothes instead of inmate blue coveralls and to sit up at the defence table like a professional instead of in the prisoner's box. But rather than listening intently with a blank expression, Twitchell was off in his own little world, writing page after page of indecipherable text.

As Twitchell continued writing, Van Dyke neared the end of his opening address. He had saved his best material for last. It was a conclusion the defence was anticipating, but no one sitting in the public gallery had ever thought to expect.

"You will hear evidence that over one and a half years after Johnny Altinger's disappearance," Van Dyke said, pausing for effect, "the police had a further meeting with Mr. Twitchell at the Edmonton Remand Centre." He let another moment pass. "And as a result of information provided in that meeting, the police were able to locate some of Johnny Altinger's skeletal remains."

It was a shocking revelation. Every journalist in the courtroom began scribbling furiously in their notepads, trying to write down every word. How did the police keep this secret?

But Van Dyke didn't give it much time to sink in. He went straight to summing up the evidence. "We, as the Crown, are confident that you will find that Mark Twitchell was responsible for planning and deliberating upon, and ultimately carrying out, the intentional execution of Johnny Altinger and is therefore guilty of first-degree murder."

He thanked the jury for their attention and patience.

"Order in court," the jury officer called out.

Everyone clamoured to their feet for the morning break.

TEN MONTHS EARLIER, ON June 3, 2010, two homicide detectives were told to meet Twitchell and his new lawyer. Charles Davison had recently taken over the case after Twitchell had parted ways with his first legal counsel. Twitchell had asked for the meeting, but only under three conditions: no questions, no media, and no Bill Clark. He was adamant the police detective he had grown to hate could not be involved and that no media release or tipoff to the press could occur in this case. The meeting had to remain secret or there was no deal. Police command agreed and Detective Mandrusiak took Clark's place since he had dealt with Twitchell from arrest to remand visits. He brought along Detective Kerr, who had taken over as the primary investigator when Anstey retired.

It was shortly after 6:00 p.m. and raining on the horizon when the two men walked through the remand building's main doors and headed straight to the bank of inmate interview rooms. Through the scratched glass they could see Twitchell sitting at a table with Davison hunched beside him.

The meeting was as short as it gets, but Twitchell had wanted one even shorter.

As both detectives entered, Twitchell shot up and tried to shove something in Mandrusiak's hands, as if anxious to rid himself of a terrible burden. Mandrusiak told him he would have to go over a few legalities before they could officially begin the meeting.

The detectives took their seats across from Twitchell, read him his rights once again, reminded him that he could seek legal advice – even now from another lawyer – and then they gave the go-ahead to begin the meeting.

But Twitchell just stared at the two of them.

After a moment, he pulled out a single piece of paper. It was folded in half. Twitchell slapped it on the table and slowly pushed it toward the detectives.

The rustle of the paper was the only sound in the interview room.

Mandrusiak saw the word "Google" printed on the top corner.

And that was all.

Mandrusiak slipped the paper inside his file folder, thanked Davison and Twitchell for their time, and the two detectives stood and walked out the door.

They got as far as the elevator at headquarters before they gave in to the urge to see what they had. It was a printout from Google Maps, taking up the majority of the sheet. Below the map of northern Edmonton were a few words scrawled in blue ink: "Location of John Altinger's remains."

Twitchell had signed and dated the sheet of paper and provided a three-sentence description of the exact location. On the map, he had drawn in an alley north of downtown and marked a sewer grate site with a red circle.

Mandrusiak rushed to the photocopier and made numerous copies. Then it was out the door and into the car for a mad drive with Kerr, following the directions closely to a parking spot near the mouth of the highlighted alley. The two men hustled on foot down the middle of the street to a sewer grate and a manhole near the fifth power pole from the road. Nearby was an aging fence with white peeling paint.

The sun was low and they were losing their light. Mandrusiak grabbed a flashlight and dropped to his belly to take a peek into the sewer. At the bottom of the manhole the flashlight beam illuminated two mounds floating in stagnant water. It was too late in the day to go down there now. Kerr called in the forensics team while a patrol car was parked to watch the location overnight.

Everyone returned the next day. It was Friday.

Police tape sealed off both ends of the alley and a portable white tent was pitched over the sewer grate. Police officers crowded around a team of medical examiners. Dennis Caufield, a medical investigator, had slipped on rubber boots, coveralls, and a safety harness. Waiting with a bucket in hand, he was going to rappel into the depths of the sewer.

He made several trips, but the initial descent was the most disturbing: he found a human torso. Subsequent trips into the sewer recovered a pelvis bone, a knee cap, an intact tooth, two teeth fragments, and buckets of mud, gravel, wood, metal, plastic, and smaller bones. The sewer held about half a decomposing skeleton. The limbs and the skull were missing, possibly flushed farther down the sewer during a spring thaw or heavy rainstorm. Many of the found bones showed signs of cutting, breaking, and sawing as clear evidence of deliberate dismemberment. A DNA test confirmed it was Johnny – or what was left of him.

The grim discovery officially ended the police investigation. While it was a relief to finally bring closure to a grieving family, detectives were still left frustrated and annoyed. Johnny's body had been discarded three blocks from Twitchell's parents' house. Searching a radius just a few houses wider would have located the dumping site years earlier and without his help.

But as part of the deal with Twitchell, the police, the prosecution, and the defence kept the recovery of Johnny's remains a secret. Detectives were fortunate no nosy neighbour had seen what they were up to that summer day in the back alley. While Johnny's immediate family was told, they too kept it secret. Even Johnny's closest friends weren't told.

Twitchell began his murder trial having given up the most incriminating evidence. No one really knew why he did it. The jury would hear he wanted to give the Altinger family some closure and that the timing coincided with the switch to his new defence team. Detectives such as Mandrusiak believed their relentless pressure had likely pushed Twitchell in that direction as well. But the implication of giving up the body, and Twitchell's attempted guilty plea, was clear: he may have dumped Johnny's body in the sewer, but he would be disputing that it was a pre-meditated murder. This would frame how the evidence would be heard during the entire trial.

It was the best his lawyer could do, considering the real-life killing blueprint that Twitchell had left behind in S. K. Confessions. On top of that, there were layers of forensic evidence haunting Twitchell's criminal case like a telltale heart: the body that just wouldn't go away and a trail of blood dripping from the suburban kill room into Twitchell's unravelling, chaotic life.

A TRIAL OF TERROR

THE TWITCHELL TRIAL ATTRACTED new and diverse spectators each day until lineups started forming outside the courtroom an hour before the doors were even opened. A curious couple – a man with a skull tattoo and piercings, a woman with pink hair – watched for several days, as did a young teacher with big-rimmed glasses who was on spring break. They had no connection to Twitchell or Johnny but, like so many others, were mesmerized by the case. Four sheriffs were stationed inside on the busiest days to keep order over this burgeoning crowd of onlookers.

Prosecutors Van Dyke and Inglis brought more than 110 exhibits to court and settled on calling forty-six witnesses to testify. Their case started with the police forensics team and ended with a statement declaring Dexter Morgan to be a fictional serial killer who relies on his "dark passenger" as both an alter ego and his desire to kill. The defence agreed on this final point.

A great deal of testimony over the four-week trial descended into the grotesque. Explanations arose about decomposed mushy and waxy tissue, sliced rib bones, and cracked teeth. Outside the courtroom, city residents complained of the "absolutely disgusting" media coverage as testimony dipped into such disturbing detail. "Is this just another example of extremely dark entertainment for the masses?" a reader queried in a letter to the editor.

There were moments of misery and torment, especially when Twitchell's former wife took the stand on the fourth day of the court case. Jess wore black and had dyed her hair red. She entered the courtroom with confidence but was quickly reduced to tears. Over two hours, she revealed her entire history with the man on trial: their private discussions and marital difficulties, his costumes and failed career. "We were living pretty separate lives," she sighed. "He was selling scripts and had a bunch of projects in development, but he wasn't making any money." Inglis showed Jess several photos and asked her to identify them. "That's a photo of our house in St. Albert." Jess began to cry, staring at the picture of her former home.

Another photograph appeared on the computer screen beside her. She completely broke down. It was a photo of the game processing kit, each knife cleaned, sharp and shiny. Jess covered her mouth in a gasp and wailed. She grabbed a tissue and wiped away her tears. She had never seen such things before, but she knew what it meant. In her grief, she was allowed to leave. Twitchell had rarely taken his eyes off his ex-wife throughout her entire testimony, but she left in a hurry, having barely acknowledged that he was even there.

Departing the courthouse, Jess lifted a big parka hood over her head to shield herself from the probing lenses of television cameras. But her attempt to preserve her privacy proved to be a futile endeavour. The *Edmonton Journal* had already uncovered her wedding day pictures, retrieving them from a forgotten corner of a personal photo website. Her pictures were reposted that afternoon on the newspaper's website, then went viral on the Internet and appeared on the six o'clock news. Under her white veil, her blue eyes stared out in a lasting gaze at thousands of viewers, Twitchell standing tall in a black suit, nestled in beside her. The photo dominated the front pages of all the morning newspapers.

Twitchell's friends and film crew were infuriated by the media circus. They were being forced by subpoena into an unwanted procession as the start of the trial's second week focused intently on their lives. Upon giving his evidence on the making of *House of Cards,* Scott Cooke thundered out of the building with Jay Howatson by his side, both chased by an eager media pack. "You guys have no respect, you know that?" Scott growled over his shoulder. Twitchell's director of photography, David Puff, was quick to clarify that he was *not* a friend of the accused killer. But Mike Young made a specific point of calling Twitchell his friend, even though he refused to discuss that friendship with the media following his testimony, sticking his hands in his pockets as reporters tried to hand him their business cards. Actor Chris Heward, once strapped to a metal chair for Twitchell's low-budget thriller, stared down the filmmaker as he testified, telling the jury of his experience on set. And Joss Hnatiuk, now long removed from contact with the rest of the crew, took the stand a day later to share his story of moving the red Mazda 3 to his parents' driveway and being foolish enough to believe Twitchell had bought the vehicle for only forty dollars.

As the weeks passed, this procession of witnesses became more solemn. Traci Higgins gave her account of a love affair with Twitchell; Renee Warring spoke of exchanging dark fantasies. Johnny's friends shared all: the confusion, determination, and panic at his unexpected disappearance turning into shock and, finally, to anguish.

And then, a tale of survival.

Gilles Tetreault was called into the courtroom near the end of the prosecution's case. He was still rail thin but dressed sharply in a navy-blue dress shirt and gold tie. The gallery had filled to capacity earlier than usual on word of his coming testimony.

He began slowly, telling of his arrival at the garage to meet his date and being forced to the floor with duct tape over his eyes. "A lot of things were going through my head," he testified. "When they say your life flashes before your eyes, that's what it was."

The jury listened intently, riveted by his story. Gilles explained his split-second decision to fight back, grab the gun, and his complete surprise in discovering it was a fake. "I tell my friends it was the best feeling I ever felt in my life," he chuckled, "because I wasn't afraid of the gun anymore."

Gilles spoke with confidence, recalling every detail of the attack. "I was fighting for my life." He repeated the statement a number of times. And after an hour, he left, having given his evidence, the impact of his testimony becoming quite clear from the reaction in the room. Both the public gallery and the jury appeared to be completely astonished by what they had just heard: how lucky he had been for the stun gun baton to have failed, for him to have reached for that fake firearm, to have crawled to freedom, to have somehow survived.

TWITCHELL HAD BEEN LARGELY isolated from this emotional upheaval until the prosecution's focus returned to his interactions with police. Halfway through the trial, Detective Bill Clark entered the courtroom to finally give his evidence. He would present a video recording of his first overnight police interview with Twitchell, the night the homicide unit took over the case.

Clark took a seat behind Twitchell as the lights were dimmed in the court. The video was played on a projector screen in front of Twitchell, who found himself sandwiched between Clark in the past and Clark in the present. It was his life on the big screen and he was reliving his own destruction, every flaw exposed along with the lies that would inevitably bring him down.

Twitchell kept his head lowered, pretending to be absorbed in his notes. It didn't help. He was beginning to feel like Clark's questions were coming at him once again in an endless, repetitive inquiry, breaking through the hardened exterior Twitchell had built up in preparation for his trial. *What happened to John, Mark? What happened to John?* The question echoed in his head and brought back memories of police and blood spatter.

His eyes became glassy. Twitchell reached for a tissue and blew his nose, one nostril at a time. He rocked backwards, closed his eyes, and pointed his chin at the ceiling as hot tears streamed down his face. As the video interrogation escalated into intense questioning, he began hyperventilating.

Van Dyke glanced over in the darkness and saw Twitchell's chest heave. He leaned into Davison's ear and whispered. Van Dyke rose and asked the judge for a break.

The video was stopped. Twitchell, now a slobbering mess, scurried to his cell, wiping his face.

Van Dyke and Clark were stunned by the reaction. It was the first emotion, other than anger, that the detective had pulled out of Twitchell in more than thirty months on the file.

The twenty-minute break did little to calm Twitchell. When a guard led him back into the courtroom, his face was puffy and red, his eyes still watery. He sat down for a moment at the defence table just as the judge walked back in. The jury was still out of the room.

Twitchell's lip began quivering. He was anxious and noticeably shivering.

Suddenly, he spun around to face Clark, who had his head down at the time. "I have to do this," Twitchell blabbered through more tears. "I'm sorry for lying –"

But Clark cut him off quickly, raising up his hand like a stop sign. "You shouldn't talk," he stated, turning away from him.

Twitchell was still reaching his hands out toward Clark, palms up, when his defence lawyer realized what was going on behind him. Davison spun Twitchell's chair back around and scolded him through gritted teeth.

Clark hadn't seen an accused do that in a hundred trials. Twitchell could have derailed the trial right then if the jury had been in the room, but they had yet to be called back in from the break. Justice Clackson recognized the impact the detective's presence was having, so he directed Clark to move away from Twitchell for the duration of the video.

Twitchell fared no better, his despair crashing upon him in a series of waves. By the time the video concluded at the end of the day, he had collapsed across the table, his arms sprawled out, his head down, his cheeks pressed against his notes.

As he was led back to remand, the guards became increasingly concerned for his well-being. He was put on suicide watch the moment he was returned to cells. He would spend the weekend wearing the "oven mitt" – the one-piece suicide-proof gown inmates call "babydolls" – in the mental health ward. He would be kept awake by the wails and screams of disturbed minds. He would have everything sharp and pointy taken away, including all his pens and pencils. There would be no journal entries in Aurebesh tonight.

THE MIND OF THE SUSPECT

IT WAS A DECISION that would change their lives. Justice Clackson eventually ruled that, with a little editing, the vast majority of S. K. Confessions could be presented in court. All twelve jurors would examine each passage of cold and calculated immorality. Under his orders, only the most inflammatory passages would be removed, meaning the jury never heard some of the most explicit descriptions of dismemberment – not that the passages deemed to be admissible weren't graphic too. It would take more than two hours for the edited version of the incriminating journal to be read into the record.

The document weaved together Twitchell's personal life and sordid details of spilled blood. No detail was left unsaid. What was especially unsettling was the written perspective on acts of violence. "It's not me who chooses the victims, but fate," Twitchell wrote. "Oh sure, I choose the victim to match my own criteria in the interest of remaining free and at large, but for the most part I am merely following my nature which was devised by the grand design of the universe."

The document, which included an elaborate description of the entire modus operandi, viewed killing as fun, as some sort of sadistic career choice: "Starting a kill on a Friday works on so many levels. For one thing, most people are not hard and fast expected to be anywhere on the weekend, which gives me three days to clean up and tie up the loose ends."

Constable Michael Roszko from the police tech crimes unit was called upon to read aloud from the document he had recovered from Twitchell's laptop. He read slowly as the jury followed along with their own printed copies. Twitchell's defence lawyer had asked him to read the text with as little inflection as possible. And so he read aloud from the various pages, which explained how a garage had been chosen as a kill room, a street hockey mask and green hoodie purchased to hide his features, and disposable coveralls obtained. The officer continued:

I bought a hunter's game processing kit, which, if you think about it, is ideal for this scenario. Why not use a whole set of tools designed to take apart large mammals in the forest on the fly? It reduces the spatter caused by power tools, takes the noise level way down too and there's also just something more gratifying about sawing through tendons and bone with your bare hands than using something else that takes the fun out of the work.

My kill knife was different though. I wanted the weapon used for the deed itself to be simple, elegant, and beautiful in its own way, so I dropped by a military surplus store and picked up a well-crafted hunting knife with an eight-inch blade.

The jury listened closely and critically as the narrative detailed the failed attack on Gilles Tetreault and reached the point of Twitchell's final encounter with Johnny Altinger in the garage. S. K. Confessions described how Twitchell tightened his hands around a metal pipe as Johnny returned to the property for a third time, expecting to finally meet his date.

Crouched, poised, I had a whole new plan. No mask needed this time. Just pretending to be poking around at the back of the set and then, WHAM! I would slam him unconscious and his survival would be a bonus, but not necessary.

He played into it perfectly. He reappeared from the garage door and I soon followed.

"I guess I'm just a glutton for punishment," he shrugged.

"You have no idea."

The room filled with the echo of the pipe crashing into the back of his skull as I could feel my predator self take over. That one single motion was the end all, be all. I had committed now and there was no going back. The jig was up and it was kill or get arrested for aggravated assault with a deadly weapon, maybe even attempted murder.

I won't go to jail for an almost. But the son of a bitch didn't drop like the sack of potatoes I was expecting. Are you serious? I asked myself. I continued thwacking him over the head repeatedly but it only seemed to fuel his adrenaline too.

He began screaming at the top of his lungs. "Police! Police! Police!" and I just about shat my pants. My fury doubled and I blasted him so hard blood spattered everywhere, but primarily on me. He hit the floor, but was still conscious.

Just like they all do, he offered money immediately. I always find this a little degrading for both my victim and myself. Like I couldn't just kill them and take it anyway. No, please Mr. Victim, give me some petty cash from your wallet and run along to the cops only to lead them back here. Ridiculous.

I paused for a minute. "You promise?" I said.

"Yes, just please stop hitting me. Oh, my skull," was his reply. And then in the instant he had to think about it, I wailed on him again. Despite receiving several mortal blows to the head, the shock and adrenaline of the situation gave him the fire to fight back a little.

"I've had enough of this," he said as he feebly and dizzily tried to grab the pipe away from me. My anger resurged, I wrestled it from him, and that was the last straw for me. I pulled my hunting knife from its sheath and watching the shock on his face as he saw the blade, I thrust it into his gut. His reaction was pure Hollywood. The lurch forward with the grunt was dead on TV movie of the week.

I didn't even notice the garage door was still part open. Wasn't I supposed to close that? Will I never learn?

No one came. No one rustled, not even from across the alley. My little notices that I sent out to the neighbours about shooting thrillers here did their job and no one paid attention, assuming it was a scene or something. Oh, it was a scene alright.

He moaned and groaned. I plunged the knife deep into his neck. Days after the event I would reflect on this and wish I had tricked him by offering to call an ambulance if he just gave me his debit PIN code before I sliced open his jugular. Maybe I'll save that for the next victim since they never seem to just fall the fuck asleep like they're supposed to.

I let him bleed out right there on the floor, away from the plastic sheeting specifically put up to avoid that sort of thing. But hey, I had bigger problems. I had no real idea if a jogger, a dog walker, an unconvinced *neighbour or some other random individual had actually called the cops, just as a precaution.*

I was standing there covered in blood. It was all over my face, my hoodie, my coat and my jeans. I was holding the murder weapon in my hand, standing over what would be in moments, a corpse, and not nearly enough time to make it go away.

I got my things ready and I did the only thing I could do. I waited. I waited for a sign on what to do next. I waited for the fast approach of sirens as a cue to leave and come up with a damn good story for later. I waited and I was rewarded with silence. Sweet, sweet silence. I got lucky. No one freaked out, no one reacted, no one inadvertently witnessed it and no one called the boys in blue. I was home free.

I assessed my situation and went to town on my improvised solution. I had a dead guy that needed processing, so that's what I did. I processed him.

A juror covered his mouth.

Most seemed to be descending into a deep trance as Twitchell's words were read into the record and entering their minds. They tried to remain stoic as Constable Roszko continued, reading aloud passages that came with even more disturbing detail as Johnny's body was hoisted on the table and the hunter's game kit opened for use:

I decided the best course would be to go from the feet up. First things first, I pulled out his wallet and keys and placed them on my computer table. Then I used the scissors to cut his pants apart and pull them away. . . . I poked and prodded the joints to find the path of least resistance. I began cutting the legs off at the knees, all in one piece. I didn't even bother to take his shoes or socks off. The knife went through flesh like it was nothing. I was surprised at how utterly non-resilient human tissue can be. Even the tendons and ligaments separated cleanly.

There was almost no blood. Not surprising since the grand majority of it was pooled on the floor, thankfully soaked up primarily by his jacket, which had come off during our struggle.

I put the severed leg in the trash and moved on to the thigh, which was essentially the same routine, only thicker, more fatty. . . . I took the arms off at the elbow joint and used the scissors to cut off fingertips for added confusion in identifying the body. This man was very common with no special internal additions to speak of.

Severing the head was also a simple matter, and going through the vertebrae in the back of the neck didn't take much at all by going through connective tissue.

The torso was surprisingly heavy all by itself and I cut that in two across the diaphragm. Human intestines just look like one long roll of uncooked sausage as opposed to the gruesome mileage of stringy nastiness they appear to be on film. I was surprised. Funny sounds and pressure releases took place on my table as the torso sank.

The jury listened with furrowed brows as S. K. Confessions revealed Twitchell's own written feelings about such horrendous acts:

Dismembering a human body was a relatively unexciting event. But I had my ways of making it more fun. I sang to myself as I worked, talked to myself, reflected on the new tools I would get to make the next one easier. . . . Once in a while I would take a break, check my email, answer a few phone calls, check the status of my eBay page and have a bag of chips.

A woman sitting in the public gallery scowled in disgust.

It reminded me of emptying a pumpkin for Halloween. Somehow every single event in life would have a whole new level of perspective to it. Carving a pumpkin and spilling its guts would now carry a double meaning. So would slicing up a steak, carving up Thanksgiving turkey or laying plastic down to prepare for painting the family room.

This experience changed my sense of place in the world forever. I felt stronger, somehow above other people. I felt like the proud owner of a very dark secret that no one would ever be in on. Things that I said

to people would carry double entendres like they hadn't before. "Oh, honey, work was murder today" would be more literal. . . .
    I felt good about this.

Some in the public gallery were brought to tears as the constable continued reading, a muted repulsion drifting through the courtroom with every spoken passage. Twitchell had written with amusement of dismembering his victim. S. K. Confessions told of severed body parts being thrown into garbage bags, the plastic walls of the kill room torn down and trashed. And Twitchell wrote of his surprise in seeing pools of blood seeping under his plastic sheeting, soaking into his table, and down on to the floor.

He cleaned the garage vigorously. Two bottles of ammonia were used, Twitchell explaining in the document how he believed the liquid would destroy DNA and fingerprints. He then changed out of his bloody clothes and drove home to his family, leaving the bagged-up remains behind in his darkened property, undisturbed for the long weekend.

Twitchell then tried to incinerate the body parts in an oil drum he had taken to his parents' backyard, but the poor results saw him abandon the plan quite quickly. He met an ex-girlfriend for a night of sex, then returned to the garage in the morning. He wasn't satisfied with his first attempt at dismembering his victim, so he made another effort to cut up the body parts into even smaller pieces.

As the saga of Johnny's second dismemberment was read out, a multi-page description of stomach-turning detail far more graphic than the first, his mother's friend began to openly weep. She sat in the second row of the court, tucking her chin into her chest as the tears streamed under her glasses. It was clear from the words being read aloud in court that this further dismemberment was no longer just an act of disposal, but fuelled by a morbid curiosity. Twitchell wrote of working so thoroughly that he had to stop several times to sharpen his knives. Every body part was dissected and examined, skin and muscle shaved down to the bone. And the document described the experience as if he was a child playing with a new toy, his warm hands sinking into the cold torso, picking it apart and exploring in delight at the visual, tactile prize. He knew these vile acts separated himself from those around him, reducing a man to the tiniest of pieces and tossing them into garbage bags, once again to be loaded into his car:

> *It's an interesting feeling driving around town with what used to be a human body bagged up in your trunk. No one has any idea. They are stopped at a light right next to a serial killer with what could very well be one of their friends, now sacks of meat parts in a hidden compartment. It made me wonder, in all my ten years of driving around, had I ever unknowingly passed a vehicle or sat parked at a red light next to someone just like I would be one day? It blew my mind.*

The jury kept reading along as the officer approached the final passages he had retrieved from Twitchell's laptop. The document explained how Twitchell had hoped to use the city's river to dispose of the remains. But his failure to locate a suitably secluded spot over several days eventually led him to decide on discarding Johnny's body parts down a storm sewer grave:

> *With each bag I sliced the tops off and turned them upside down, letting the pieces fall into the sewer, hearing the splashing sounds as they touched down. I crumpled the bags up, put them back in the trunk and then closed it. I got back in the car, fired her up and took off. My total time there could not have been longer than three minutes max.*
>
> *I drove back to the kill room to finish destroying evidence. Once there, I packed my trunk remnants into a garbage bag and put everything else in there that needed to burn . . . I had five full hefty bags full of garbage that actually would burn, this I knew for a fact. Plastic sheeting, cloth backdrops and paper towels. It may not have been good for the environment, but one less person creating pollution for whatever forty-some odd more years he would have walked the Earth more than evens that out.*

A sombre change had come over the courtroom. These passages brought with them silence, a state of complete incomprehension.

Even when breaks were called, those sitting in the public gallery shuffled out of the courtroom as though they were departing a funeral. The lively chatter of the previous days was gone. No whispered conversations. Each life had forever been altered by the startling convictions of the darkest mind.

RABBIT HOLES

Twitchell was exhausted but tried to walk tall, chest out, in a confident pace toward the holding cell concealed just off the courtroom. A guard followed behind him and to his right as he hugged the wall. He had been unable to fall asleep until at least 2:00 a.m. and no amount of caffeine could lift his sluggish feet. He was moving slowly, plodding along in a dazed stupor.

It was Wednesday, April 6. Today was supposed to be Twitchell's turn to finally fight back after two and a half years in remand. His lawyer was scheduled to open their defence case within minutes. Twitchell had impatiently sat through the entirety of the Crown's case and now – either due to nerves, anxiety, or otherwise – he was suffering from a lack of sleep. It wasn't going the way he had planned.

He viewed his forthcoming defence as a sustained attack on S. K. Confessions, a document even he had grown to hate. Now he wanted to make it vanish; he wanted to wipe the slate clean. Twitchell compared his strategy to bursting a giant bubble of misinformation. "The world is completely fooled," he wrote. "Right now they think and believe only what I initially designed for them to think and believe."

It had been two weeks since his breakdown in court, and a psychiatrist had cleared him to leave the mental health unit. He was feeling fine, bolstered by lengthy preparations with his lawyer. Over cups of jailhouse mocha – hot chocolate mix, coffee whitener, three sugars, and instant coffee – Twitchell had spent the past weekend digging into the far corners of his mind, recalling every tiny detail, anything that could be used to help in his case. A legal decision had been finalized: he would be taking the stand in his own defence. He was the only person who could refute that incriminating diary.

Davison had spent hours with him to prepare for his court appearance. He warned Twitchell repeatedly to reply to questions on the stand with very specific answers, to always tell the truth, and to certainly drop his wry sense of humour. The final point resonated with Twitchell. He had been hoping his testimony could begin on April Fool's Day as a way to hint at his "inner prankster," but the timing was off by five days. But he did understand the courtroom was no place for a comedy routine. "Although I often do have a morbid, inappropriate sense of humour at times, many times done for the sheer shock value, even I have my limits," he explained later. "Cracking one-liners while I'm testifying at my own murder trial is too over-the-top – even for me."

Between his restless nights and bouts of studying to prepare for his defence, however, Twitchell did find time to compile a fantasy cast for a future Hollywood movie about his life and trial. He decided Jim Carrey would be a great fit for the role of his own lawyer – "His last crack at drama" – or perhaps Hugh Laurie, who could use the role to shake off the typecasting from the TV series *House*. The prosecution would be played by Casper Van Dean, a chiselled James Dean lookalike who had starred in *Starship Troopers,* and Natalie Dormer, a British actress best-known as Lady Anne Boleyn in Showtime's *The Tudors*. The judge would be given a tough guy image with Robert De Niro presiding over the courtroom battle. Twitchell couldn't decide between his top three picks to play himself: Ryan Phillippe, Matt Damon, or Guy Pearce. Even on trial, he couldn't help drifting into fantasy.

Davison clearly had his work cut out for him in bringing Twitchell back on task. His client had a burning desire to go on the attack the second he was confronted with the evidence against him. As they prepared for court, Twitchell likened Davison to a disciplined piano teacher, slapping his hands whenever he ventured into territory that was pointless or out of bounds for his upcoming testimony. He appreciated Davison's thoroughness and expertise.

Twitchell debated how realistic his chances were of winning his murder trial as he sat in the holding cell awaiting the start of court. Other inmates in the basement tank frequently asked Twitchell this very question at the beginning and end of each day. After all, he had attracted a certain notoriety in prison. Everyone knew of him as "the movie killer" and recognized his face from television and in the newspapers. Twitchell was expecting these kinds of inquiries. When asked, he would always reply that the extent of the prosecution's evidence against him was no surprise, but he wouldn't have waited years for a criminal trial if he didn't honestly believe he had a fighting chance.

He still believed that as he waited for court to begin. Twitchell felt his defence was so strong at times that the jury would be overcome with a beautiful epiphany. He imagined jurors having a change of heart and deciding the possible life sentence he was facing should be reduced to a lesser charge, perhaps even going so far as to set him free for time already served.

Minutes later, Davison tried to "set the context" of the trial during his opening address to the jury. He compared this criminal trial to watching an artist paint a picture. "What you think he's going to draw or she's going to paint at the beginning isn't quite what the finished project turns out to be." There would be a new perspective put on this entire case, he said, and the defence was relying on only one piece of evidence to make its point. Today, Davison would call his first and final witness: Mark Andrew Twitchell.

Wearing his white polo shirt, now yellowing from being worn nearly every day of the three-week-old trial, Twitchell took an affirmation instead of swearing an oath to God. He wasn't much of a believer. People sometimes thought he was an atheist since he often described the Bible as a "bizarre book," but when asked directly he explained he was of two minds on the religion issue. "I have chosen my own purpose in life and it's very empowering to do so. I'll worry about the ethereal plane when I get there."

He began his testimony haltingly, stumbling over his words. Standing a few steps up from the floor beside Justice Clackson, peering over the tops of the heads of observers seated in the packed gallery, he appeared nervous. Today, he was the main attraction. Guards once again were having to turn away people at the door.

Davison stood in the centre of the court at the main podium, asking Twitchell basic questions about his filmmaking career until he had settled in and was more comfortable, ready to tell his side of the story. He would remain standing throughout his testimony.

Twitchell turned to face the jury. He began speaking slowly, projecting his voice. Oddly, he referred to himself as "we" several times until he was warned to stop. He knew this was the critical moment that would decide his fate and freedom. But even now, in his tiredness, Twitchell didn't know how best to explain himself.

He liked comparing himself to Dr. Frankenstein, but he didn't dare broach this subject in front of the jury. Just like the infamous doctor, he had considered the possibility that he, too, had created a monster that had gotten out of hand. The difference was Twitchell honestly believed his own monstrous creation had surpassed even the worst nightmares of Frankenstein. His creation had resulted in his arrest, a murder charge, the end of his future as a filmmaker, and it had sucked countless innocent people into its massive jaws.

Twitchell's monster was called MAPLE.

It was an acronym, he explained: Multi-Angle Psychosis Layering Entertainment.

The prosecution and the detectives watching him in court shared a collective look of surprise. It was the first anyone had heard of it.

Davison gave Twitchell plenty of time to elaborate. On the witness stand, his client soon became animated and looked confident, moving full-on into a mini sales pitch.

Twitchell described in excitement how early on in the development of *House of Cards* it had become clear the project had the potential to go beyond being just a simple short film. There was promise of so much more. He had envisioned a feature film, a novel, and an online marketing campaign working together to sell the same product through his new concept, MAPLE. The point was to keep the audience believing fiction was reality long after they had seen the film or read the novel. Twitchell brought up *Alice in Wonderland* and how he loved the idea of keeping everyone "down the rabbit hole" or in a fantasy world for as long as possible.

The movie, he said, would follow the story of a man's progression into becoming a serial killer. The man would use a suburban garage as a kill room. This horror film would detail how there are dangerous people everywhere: at the bank, the bakery, perhaps even in the movie theatre. The novel, to be released shortly after the movie, would be a first-person account written from the perspective of the producer who made the film. But the book would also reveal that the producer is actually a serial killer who had made the film to hide the evidence of his real-life slayings. The novel would include plenty of detail from the producer's own life, Twitchell explained, to fool readers into believing the novel was the true story of a serial killer, blurring the line between fiction and reality so thoroughly that there would be controversy and debate over what was real and what was fake. Is the producer really a serial killer? Is the movie a true account of a murderer's method? Is the book a confession or a work of fiction?

The jewel in MAPLE's crown would be a final ploy to use the Internet to spread the story virally, so it would become an online urban legend. Twitchell imagined his audience would immediately search online for any evidence of fakery, and such online buzz could go a long way in keeping the mystery alive. A plan developed. Twitchell wanted to locate "recruits" to support the MAPLE concept by luring them off dating websites, just like in the plot of the movie and novel. When these recruits arrived, he would pitch them the idea of supporting the MAPLE concept by having them "pretend" to be survivors of real-life attacks when the movie and novel were released. But Twitchell testified he changed his mind at the last minute and decided to scare the arriving recruits into thinking they were actually under attack. These so-called victims would be so terrified, he said, they would flood online message boards, the film's website, and social-networking sites such as Facebook with comments. "I was there. I *saw* the room," they'd say. Their belief that they had survived a real attack would support the reality/fiction structure of MAPLE even more and keep the audience guessing. Twitchell testified that he had come up with this concept following the *House of Cards* wrap party. After dinner, he had stayed up late, his Internal Creative Genius striking him again.

Twitchell testified that his interest in such horror-themed material led him to borrow ideas from multiple sources, including writers Stephen King, Thomas Harris, and Jeff Lindsay. But he explained away his Dexter Morgan profile on Facebook as just a way to interact with fans of the show. His message on October 14, 2008, that he had "crossed the line on Friday . . . and I liked it" was a reference to falling in love with Traci at the movies all over again, not killing someone.

His testimony was a virtual admission to all of the evidence against him, but he contended that essentially everyone had been fooled by what it meant: the homicide cops who arrested him, the Crown prosecutors who pursued him, and now the court for denying his bail and pressing forward with a first-degree murder charge. All of them had been pulled down the rabbit hole, he said. It was all fantasy. Twitchell was the puppetmaster, but his puppet had turned on him and implicated him in a real-life murder when it was all a work of fiction. Those murder weapons? All movie props. The table and chair? Props too. The garage? A movie set. And S. K. Confessions? That was the first draft of the novel portion of MAPLE. Of course the writings are brash and insensitive. And for good reason: it is the fictionalized diary of an evil serial killer! The reason why it had so many elements of Twitchell's own life within it was all due to MAPLE. The novel could only work if reality and fiction blended and merged so thoroughly that nobody could tell the difference.

The jury hung on to every word of Twitchell's explanation. But did they buy it?

One problem was how closely the testimony of Gilles Tetreault had matched the account of the first attack in S. K. Confessions, right down to the most minute detail. But Twitchell explained away the incident as a plan that went horribly awry. He testified that he had only wanted to fool Gilles into thinking he was under attack as his first MAPLE recruit. He had no intention of actually hurting him – just a plan to scare him, let him escape, and spread the word online about his own terrifying experience with a masked man in a garage once the movie and novel were released.

A second problem was obvious: Johnny's skeletal remains.

Twitchell, on the witness stand, then made a startling admission: he killed Johnny Altinger. But it wasn't what the prosecution thought, he testified. It wasn't murder. Not even close.

Davison stepped in at this point and began guiding Twitchell through his testimony point by point. He asked his client to explain what happened when Johnny arrived at the garage, having been lured there off the Internet by Twitchell pretending to be a woman named Jen.

Twitchell said he had learned from his mistakes with Gilles. So when Johnny showed up he wasn't pretending to be the masked killer anymore. He identified himself as a filmmaker. But he also wanted to draw this experience out as long as possible so he'd have more material for his novel. He started toying with Johnny, making him come back and forth, thinking Jen was just late and still on her way. When Johnny returned for the third time and said, "I guess I'm just a glutton for punishment," Twitchell testified he decided to finally spill the story about Multi-Angle Psychosis Layering Entertainment. He explained to Johnny that Jen did not exist because it was all just a hoax that he had cooked up, but that he wanted Johnny to be part of the MAPLE concept to help promote the film in the future.

Twitchell said Johnny "didn't seem too humoured by it" and appeared indignant and angry. "He was telling me, 'This is what you do? You're luring people over here and then, what, springing this on them?' I don't remember his exact words or phrasing," Twitchell told the jury. "And then at the end he just goes, 'Well, that's pathetic.' And then of course I'm gonna react so, in not the kindest way, I tell him, 'Pathetic? Hey, look who's talking?'"

"What were the words you used, the best you remember them?" Davison asked.

Twitchell licked his dry and cracking lips. He had been on the witness stand for more than two hours by this point. He grabbed the plastic water cup beside him, took a tiny sip, paused, and then exhaled. "I turned my back on him and then I told him that he should probably just crawl back to whatever little hole he crawled out of." Twitchell hesitated and rolled his hand out in the air like it was something he didn't want to say. "Because he could probably never get a woman that good-looking in his life anyway." He said he then turned away and thought Johnny was walking out the door.

"What happened next?"

"The next thing I remember was an impact in my lower back, which I assumed to be a kick, that he tried to kick me. And I turned around and I push him back. . . . And then again we come to a place where it's a matter of not being able to read each other or mixed signals because we're right there next to the wooden table with my laptop on it. And I get this idea in my head like, 'What if he retaliates and he tries to smash up the laptop?' He must have seen me looking toward it and I'm starting to make a little bit of a move to block it. The pipes are also right there too. So, to counter, or to beat me to it, he grabs one. . . . Swung it a couple times. . . . I dodge the first couple and then I put my arm up to block one. Took it right here, across my forearm on the bottom." He raised his arm and pointed to his elbow.

"It's like a stinging, so I recoil and then snap back and then *I* grab the pipe, sort of a miniature half-second tug of war, until I twist it out of his grasp. And then *I* swung. Seems to me that he saw that portion or at least reacted in some way because he flinched back and the edge of the pipe caught him on the top of the head."

"Carry on," Davison urged.

"We proceed to get into a pretty intense altercation. . . . We grab each other's arms. Trying to get an advantage over each other. It's basically just turning and side-stepping." Twitchell curled up his fists and squeezed them tight. "I'm trying to get him off of me. Of course, I'm not thinking very rationally at this so I'm using the pipe again." He raised his one hand like he was swinging the pipe up and down. "I'm trying to hit him, I'm . . ." Twitchell paused, took his gaze off of Davison for a second, and stared at the floor. "There's this physical, if I can call it an aversion to hitting people? But I'm feeling it pull back?"

Davison looked annoyed. He raised his voice. "Just focus on what *you* did or *he* did and what things that you said, okay? What did you do with the pipe?"

"I'm swinging at him, he had a grip on my arm and I was sort of grabbing at his sleeve at the same time. And it's a matter of, like, pulling and pushing on each other. And so I'm swinging the pipe trying to hit him off of me." Twitchell's voice started wavering. "I keep hitting him on the head because he's pulling on me. He's moving forward. He's a little taller than me. Maybe an inch? . . . He's swinging back at me. He swung for the body, mostly. I took a few shots to the stomach area, maybe the chest. Nothing like super hard, but it seemed like he was trying to protect himself while still fighting back."

"And what was he striking you with?"

"Would have been his left fist?" Twitchell raised up his hand.

"Okay. Carry on."

"Now we're struggling some more and I keep increasing the power each time, with each hit, with the pipe, to try to separate us. And toward the end of it he's, he just switches." Twitchell shook his head and frowned. "It's like a switch of pressure from pushing back to a sudden pull, and he pulls me in toward him and he's bent over and the pipe connects with him again, it's just a lot of mangled mess of swings." He gave Davison a look of disgust.

"Do you have any idea how many times you struck him with the pipe?"

"I don't know."

"What happened after that?"

"He finally got mad enough to rear up and grab the pipe. This time he let go of my right arm, grabbed it with both hands and twisted it out of *my* grasp." Twitchell started speeding up his words. "In that moment, that's a panic moment for me, I just back off and I try to step back as far as I can. . . . Then I realize, you know, he's standing there. He. Has. The. Pipe. And he's bleeding, a lot." Twitchell's eyes flared. "I really don't know what to do. I'm far enough away from the other pipe where I can't really make a move for that without him charging me immediately. I don't really want to provoke it any further. So I reach for . . . the knife."

Twitchell told the jury he was wearing a KA-BAR knife on his belt. He motioned to his hip and showed how he undid the button on the sheath and wrapped his fingers around the handle. "I thought that would send a clear enough message, saying we're pretty much equal, but again, there's no real rational thought in it. I'm just thinking to balance the situation out. Here I am, I'm going to go hold on to the handle of this thing. So I have a pretty tight grip on that and I'm watching John touch his head." Twitchell motioned again to his own head. "And notice the blood all over his hands." He brought his hand down to his eyes, staring at his palms like they had blood on them. "And he says something to the effect of, 'My head, my head, you fuck!' . . . He comes after me swinging." Twitchell's voice quickened. "It's just an instant knee-jerk reaction. The pipe is in the air, I just, both hands come out. One's got the knife in it. I put the other hand up to block the pipe and then . . ." He breathed in and closed his eyes. "Sickest. Feeling. Ever."

"What did you do?"

"It all happened so fast. . . . I just started to feel this wet sensation around the hand that was still holding the handle and I let go instinctively . . . and then I saw it sticking out of him."

Twitchell's face flushed as he described his panic. He testified that he froze as Johnny looked down, staggered back, and fell to the floor, blood pouring out of him in a flood of dark red.

"It's one of those things where I'm just stuck there and can't decide what to do, just frozen by inaction." Twitchell composed himself and raised his voice. "There is this war going on between . . . screaming out in my head, 'Call 9-1-1!' but at the same time, 'How bad does this look? Take a look around. Look at what this place looks like!'" He paused for a moment as he stood in the witness box, looking down and running out of words.

Then, he said it was five or ten minutes before he could move again, watching Johnny bleed out all over the floor, doing nothing to help him. "I kept saying to myself, 'Oh shit, oh shit, oh shit, oh shit,' and then a series of 'No, no, no, no.'" His voice lowered into a whimper.

Twitchell paused, lip quivering, eyes squinted. Tears flowed down his cheeks. "Sorry," he said. He shook his head and grabbed a tissue.

There wasn't a sound in the courtroom as he dabbed his tears away.

"When I could finally move," he continued, voice crackling, "I walked over to him . . . Not even a pulse. Nothing was even moving." He started to cry. "It took me a really long time to figure out what the hell I was gonna do." He began blubbering. "I just started thinking about . . . how I could have been so fucking stupid!?" He stopped to wipe away more tears. "Even all the precautions I took. You can't just think you can predict human behaviour. . . . I could have avoided that whole thing." He started mumbling. "No way to see how it was gonna unfold."

"What did you do?" Davison asked softly.

Twitchell clenched the tissue tight in his hand and composed himself. "I started just to try to buy myself some time and I figured out first before I could actually act that, uhhhhh," he groaned. "I was gonna start using my set for things it had never been designed to do. I couldn't touch 'em or move 'em until . . . I tried to set my mind to the task and the only way I could do that was to block out what I was feeling."

Twitchell likened it to putting up super-strong Plexiglas walls to separate himself from his emotions. "I tried to keep telling myself, it's not him anymore. The man's not there. It's just a shell."

Davison asked what he did next.

"I tried to lift him up. I can't remember how many attempts I made at actually standing up. I lifted him and carried him over, part dragging, part lifting to the table. And then set him on it."

"Did you get him on the table?"

"I did."

Twitchell testified that he then proceeded to dismember Johnny's body. He returned to the garage a few days later to finish the job.

Davison asked him to compare the description of the dismemberment in S. K. Confessions with what he actually did. Was the document accurate?

"In general terms, for the most part," Twitchell said, "yes."

"MONSTERS DO LIVE AMONG US"

THE ALTINGER FAMILY BOARDED a flight from the West Coast, touching down in Edmonton in time to attend Twitchell's cross-examination. Gary Altinger was fuming. He knew in his heart his brother would never hurt anyone, let alone fly into a furious rage and repeatedly charge at a man who had his hand wrapped around the handle of a deadly military blade.

Gary was the first person to enter the courtroom once the doors were unlocked. He hurried to the front row and saved a seat for his mother, Elfriede. Detectives Clark, Johnson, and Mandrusiak arrived, sitting near the back. Actor and comedian Chris Heward had shown up too, hoping to see Twitchell squirm under pressure now that Chris had testified and was allowed to sit in the public gallery. The courtroom filled to capacity a half-hour before the jury was allowed in.

Crown prosecutor Avril Inglis placed a binder full of typed questions on a podium atop her desk so she could check each one off as they were answered. Inglis had gone head to head with some of the city's toughest criminals and made a name for herself by winning a high-profile rape case. Twitchell, with no prior criminal convictions, would be a pussycat compared to some of her previous cross-examinations. As a bonus, she had no shortage of material to draw from. She planned to force Twitchell into an uncomfortable paradox: to have his own testimony believed meant also having to admit to every lie he had ever told. There were so many that by the end of her questioning his credibility would most certainly be destroyed.

"Good morning, Mr. Twitchell," she began.

Twitchell offered no greeting in return. He was about to be interrogated for nearly four hours until he was weak, tired, and out of breath. As he stood, he kept his elbows locked, hands clasped tight on the wooden edges of the witness box, and his body leaned backwards, as if bracing himself against a hurricane-force headwind. And then the storm blew in.

On the witness stand, Twitchell admitted to breaking into Johnny's condo by using his key and stealing his printer and laptop. Johnny had left himself signed into all of his personal accounts on his computer, giving Twitchell the ability to send messages as the dead man for days before he finally threw out the equipment in a random city dumpster. Johnny's friends, family, employer, and acquaintances had therefore all been lied to through these impersonated emails and MSN Messenger and Facebook messages.

These acts were not the extent of his lying. Both victims, Gilles and Johnny, had also been lied to repeatedly, whether part of a hoax or intentional luring – that much Twitchell had already admitted during his earlier testimony. But when asked by Inglis in cross-examination, he confirmed he had also lied to his friends and loved ones too. Repeatedly. Joss had been thrown unwittingly into a murder investigation because of Twitchell's dishonesty. Nearly every single police officer Twitchell had come into contact with had heard lies, even a traffic cop who caught him speeding. Traci was told lies for years, as was Jess, who thought for months Twitchell was going to work when he had no job. And later, he had lied to her about attending Friday-night therapy appointments. Finally, he had lied to Jess about being at the gym when in fact he was standing in the garage with Johnny's blood soaking into his clothes, the man's lifeless body lying before him.

Inglis focused on this last point for several minutes as she summed up a half-hour of exposing Twitchell's constant and elaborate deceptions.

"Right after Mr. Altinger died you were still able to smooth that one over with some lying to your wife, right?"

But Twitchell had some fight in him. "You have to remember, again, how those events took place and what happened in that timeline," he said with confidence. "Before I could even go anywhere near John's body, I had to emotionally separate myself from that situation in order to even handle it."

"And you did it so successfully that you were able to carry on a perfectly normal conversation with your wife that required you to come up with a snap-decision lie."

"Definitely not nearly as easy as you make it sound."

"But you were able to do exactly what I just described."

"Sounds like it." He shrugged.

In the back row, all three detectives sat with arms crossed, shooting crooked glances at him. Twitchell saw their doubting faces as he stood in the witness box and it annoyed him. In the front row, Gary Altinger was getting angry. He couldn't stand the litany of pathetic lies and the hideous things Twitchell had admitted doing to his brother.

Inglis raised her voice. "Well, you wrote it *down* that you were able to do exactly what I described, and your wife, Jess, *told us* you did exactly what I described. So does it sound like it or is that actually *it*?"

"I guess I'm just trying to reconcile what other people are perceiving versus what was going on inside of me. So if I had to, if you're asking me based on what's in the document and what Jess heard, then yes."

"That's true?"

"Right."

Inglis circled back to her main point: "Moments. After. Mr. Altinger bled to death, in your garage, in front of your eyes, you had a perfectly normal conversation with her and were able to come up with a quick lie. That's correct, isn't it?"

"Yeah." Twitchell sighed. He had admitted to a lot of damning evidence. He tried to compose himself, but it was clear he had already been made a fool. During the cross-examination, he started rocking on the balls of his feet. He furrowed his brow, started to blush, and at points he curled up his fists like an angry baby. He drained a cup of water in one big gulp.

An early morning break was his only relief.

The public gallery stood as Twitchell hurried off the witness stand. But before he could make it back to the holding cell, Gary Altinger leaned over the brass banister and hissed: "You piece of shit!" Gary was so infuriated his head was vibrating up and down as he spat the words.

Twitchell jumped back, startled. He had no idea who was yelling at him, but he assumed correctly it was Johnny's brother. He kept walking as another sheriff came over to warn Gary to tone it down or he would be tossed out of the courtroom. "I know what's going on here," the guard said. Gary nodded, sat, and tried to calm down.

The prosecution's attack on Twitchell was even more scathing upon his return to the witness stand. In response, he became rudely defiant, sticking his nose up at one point and rolling his eyes several times. He tried to justify lying to the cops by saying they had lied to him too. Inglis asked him if the cops were questioning the right man, and he had to meekly reply that in fact they were. When asked, he couldn't provide a name for anyone who knew of MAPLE's existence or provide any document to prove it was true. "I know my own concept," he said.

"So you weren't planning on using that pipe on Mr. Altinger?"

"No."

"You just talked about it, you talked about using it as a weapon, you prepared it as a weapon, and, ultimately, a *day* after buying it, when you did use it as a weapon . . ." She snapped her fingers. "That was an unfortunate turn of circumstance. Is that what you're saying?"

"I understand how bad it looks, but yes."

A trickle of chuckles drifted from the public gallery. Twitchell scowled in the direction they had come from.

Inglis intensified her line of questioning to portray him as an uncaring, ruthless killer. She didn't believe Twitchell had put his emotions behind a piece of Plexiglas, as he had testified, and suggested he was acting for the jury when he cried the day before. She used his own writings as evidence, pointing out how he had even revealed that he felt no empathy.

"The reason you had no remorse is because you did exactly what you intended to do – and that was to murder someone, and unfortunately for Mr. Altinger, it was him."

"No," he said loudly.

"It's quite obvious that you had no remorse because you enjoyed not one but two Thanksgiving Day dinners while his corpse was in your garage."

Twitchell fell silent.

Inglis continued. "Correct? You enjoyed your time with your family that weekend?"

"When you say *enjoyed*?"

"You participated just fine with your family that weekend, correct?"

Twitchell mumbled, and Inglis cut him off.

"And then you dismembered Mr. Altinger not once but *twice*?"

He stopped and in a lowered voice finally stated, "Yes."

"You tried to *burn* his body."

"Yes," he replied even quieter.

"You put his body in garage bags and hauled it around like it *was* garage."

"I certainly didn't think of it that way." His face flushed.

"That's how you conducted yourself, isn't it?" she shouted. He didn't answer. "Mr. Twitchell?"

"I physically did those things, yes."

"And then you dumped his body into a sewer."

"Yes," he whispered.

She attacked him for hours, flaying his reputation into tatters. How convenient it was that he had an armoury of weapons in that garage, she suggested. "And because of your savant inspiration for your project, you just happened to have all these tools lying around to help you dismember the body and get rid of the evidence. . . . Correct? That's what you're saying?"

Riled up, Twitchell thought in silence for a moment, placed his hand on his hip, and stared down Inglis with eyes as black as marbles. He raised his voice and snarled: "You can paint it as any kind of coincidence you want!"

THE PROSECUTION CALLED TWITCHELL'S MAPLE concept "the most elaborate lie of all." The defence countered during closing arguments by comparing Twitchell to the boy who cried wolf. "The stakes in a criminal trial like this are too high. . . . We don't have the luxury of simply turning our back and saying, 'You've lied too many times. We're going to ignore what you say now.'"

The jury, however, needed only five hours of deliberations before they reached a decision. And that included time off for lunch.

It was 5:25 p.m. on Tuesday, April 12, when word spread that the jury was back with a verdict. The Altinger family had been waiting on couches in the fourth-floor foyer. Journalists were hovering at the ready. Everyone rushed inside Room 417 when guards opened the doors.

Davison was in court three minutes later, followed by Clark, Mandrusiak, Johnson, and Kerr. Prosecutors Van Dyke and Inglis spotted the row of cops already gathered inside as they entered the room shortly afterwards. "That was quick," Van Dyke said.

Inglis dropped her books and binders on the desk and turned to Johnny's mother, Elfriede, who was waiting in the front row. She was sandwiched between her partner, Dennis, and her good friend. At the end of the row, two of Johnny's relatives joined them. Gary had already flown back to British Columbia.

"Are you okay?" Inglis asked the bereaved mother.

"Oh yeah," Elfriede said. "We've been waiting for this."

Twitchell was led in shortly and took a seat beside Davison. The judge and the trial clerk also arrived and took their places. When the jury arrived a minute later, Twitchell stood and attempted to read their faces, but no one lifted their eyes toward him as they shuffled to their seats.

"Members of the jury, have you arrived at a verdict?" the clerk called out. "If so, say so by your foreperson. Please stand."

A woman in the back row of the jury rose and met her gaze. "Yes, we have," she replied.

"What is your verdict against Mark Twitchell?"

There was no hesitation, no sign of emotion or conflicted thoughts in her response. She was direct and clear: "Guilty of first-degree murder."

Twitchell swallowed hard as loud gasps and exhales overtook the courtroom. He looked straight ahead as his face blushed to a light pink. He tried to show no emotion, but every line in his body looked like it had trembled, ever so briefly. In that moment, he seemed to have been stricken by a terrible realization, a deepening blow that had at last brought him down as he tumbled to his chair.

In the front row, Elfriede's tears flowed as she was hugged by everyone around her. The crowd wept as the room rumbled in a low hum. Inglis spun her chair around and gave Elfriede a knowing smile.

One by one, the trial clerk polled each juror to confirm they were all in agreement with the guilty verdict.

Yeah. Yes. Yes.

Elfriede looked at each juror as they stood and replied.

Yes. Yup. Yes. Yes.

She dabbed her tears with a tissue, then bobbed her head in thanks, giving each of them a bright smile.

Yes. Yes. Yes. Yes. Yes.

Looking puzzled, Twitchell adjusted in his seat as he chewed on his lip. He had expected this was coming after his disastrous cross-examination, but it was still surreal.

Justice Clackson discharged the jury, expressing regret for having put them through such an experience. "I know that this has been a very difficult case, even for those of us who have been in this business for a long time," he said. "Some of what you witnessed . . . was difficult to see, difficult to hear, and especially difficult to have it repeated time and time again." In a rare move, he offered counselling services to every one of them and praised how stoic they had appeared throughout some very lurid testimony.

Dismissed, the jury walked out of the courtroom and returned to their jobs and their own families. They would remain anonymous forever. By court order, their names would never be known publicly, and under Canadian law, their deliberations would remain secret. These six men and six women would live with this burden and experience in silence for the rest of their lives.

When the judge left a moment later, the courtroom blossomed with emotion.

Inglis walked over to Elfriede and reached out her arms. They embraced in a big hug. Van Dyke joined them and with one look at Elfriede, he was tearing up too. "I'm sorry for your loss," he choked. And he embraced her in a warm hug as well. "You did a great job," she said to both of them. "Thank you." Clark strolled up to lavish praise on both prosecutors. The detective gave Inglis a hug and Van Dyke a sturdy handshake.

The room was brimming with love, tears, and memories of Johnny, of justice served.

"It's over," Elfriede's friend said aloud to no one in particular.

Elfriede slumped back in the court bench, smiled once again, then sighed in agreement.

"It's over."

THE JURY'S DECISION MEANT the judge had no choice: Twitchell would be receiving an automatic sentence. Justice Clackson returned to the courtroom ten minutes after the verdict to go through the motions of this legal process. It was also a chance for the victims to speak up and have their own voices officially documented in court records, forcing the killer to hear and face the pain his actions have caused.

Van Dyke stood and began reading out loud a letter from Johnny's brother, Gary:

> *I have the same recurring nightmare of not being able to help John in his time of need. . . . I continue to suffer from guilt, pain and anxiety of not being able to help him 29 months ago in those horrific minutes before he was butchered. I have had to take a lot of time off from my workplace. . . . My wife, who used to be the picture of health, has been off work for almost two years now with a debilitating and chronic affliction entirely the consequence of extreme stress. Our two children, left without their Uncle John, wake in the wee hours of the morning with nightmares about monsters. It's impossible to be honest with them, living with the reality that monsters do live among us.*

Inglis read Elfriede's letter on her behalf:

> *I can't imagine the fear, desperation and pain Johnny must have endured. As a mother, I feel I can't think about it without going over the edge. I go through each day with a feeling of numbness. There is no joy in my life. It has been ripped away from me. . . . People have asked me if I wish there was still the death penalty and I must answer, 'No.' My wish is for the perpetrator of this unforgivable and horrific act to reflect on his actions and die a slow death every day of his life.*

The trial had seen countless photos entered as exhibits. They were photographs of Twitchell, of his costumes, his movie props, his bloody knives, his messy car and home. They numbered in the hundreds, perhaps more.

But what all this documentation had failed to capture was the most important photo of all: an image of the victim himself. Both Gary and Elfriede filled that gap by including snapshots of Johnny in happier times as part of their victim impact statements. These three photos were entered as the final exhibits, the bookend giving a face to the name of the victim everyone following the case had come to know.

In the three photos, Johnny looks happy and loved. In one, he has the Rocky Mountains stretched out behind him; in another he is simply smiling; the final photo shows him pointing, trying to get one of his nephews, a toddler, to look at the camera.

A typical family.

THE JUDGE TURNED HIS attention to Mark Twitchell.

Justice Clackson told him it was now his last opportunity to offer whatever he wished to say before his sentence was delivered.

But Twitchell had fallen silent. Just like back at his first police interview with Clark, there was an excruciatingly long thirteen-second pregnant pause before he would stir to make a single sound.

An air fan hummed above as the gears grinded in his head.

"You know," he began slowly, "I was actually going to address the court with some comments, but in light of everything that's been happening here, considering what's going on at the moment . . . I'll pass on that."

The judge spared Twitchell a lecture since he never considered it his role. Instead, Justice Clackson simply stated the hard facts: "You are sentenced to spend the rest of your life in prison and you are not eligible to apply for parole until you have served twenty-five years of that sentence."

For many, Twitchell's final comments seemed cowardly, a pathetic conclusion for a man who had refused to accept responsibility for his actions and who lied non-stop to everyone he knew to cover it up. Defiant until the ugly end, Twitchell, even now, offered no apology to the Altinger family, no apology to even his own family, his shattered ex-wife, or his daughter, who would now grow up with a notorious father behind bars.

Not that he'd get very far before the sheer magnitude of the situation would be rubbed in his face. Twitchell turned away from his lawyer to be led out of court by a sheriff for the last time. And standing tall beside the cell door to remand was his nemesis, Detective Bill Clark.

Clark had wanted his face to be the last Twitchell would ever see on the outside. He had taken a seat in the bench as close to the door as possible, and he had a smile of sweet satisfaction underneath his neatly trimmed moustache. It was a moment few detectives will ever experience in their careers. He had told Twitchell all those years ago that he was coming to get him. And he did. He got him.

Twitchell blew right past him.

The Altinger family saw the back of Twitchell's head as he stormed out and they couldn't resist having the last word.

"See ya!" one man said, giving Twitchell a sarcastic wave.

"Bye!" another chimed in as the cell door was about to close.

"Have fun!"

A DARK SIDE

THERE WAS A SENSE of elation as Clark, Mandrusiak, and Johnson walked together out of the courthouse with the verdict they had wanted for years. Both prosecutors were already standing outside and being interviewed by reporters, stuck in a scrum of television cameras and microphones packed together a few steps from the west doors. The three detectives watched Van Dyke and Inglis give their answers for a few minutes. Twitchell's defence lawyer snuck out undetected. The media pack then turned and surrounded the three officers, eager for a quote.

Clark was asked where he would place Twitchell on the long list of criminals he had dealt with over his thirty-year career. He did not hesitate to place him at the very top. "He's a psychopathic killer," Clark announced to the gathering. "And we've taken him off the streets of this city."

It was a blunt assessment. But there was a reason why he was so confident in airing his armchair diagnosis. For there existed *another* interesting document in the case, one so prejudicial that the jury had been prevented from hearing its contents or even knowing of its very existence. The document was made public upon the trial's conclusion. It appeared to have been written in the weeks before Johnny's murder, and just days before the filming of *House of Cards*. And Mark Andrew Twitchell – alias Dark Jedi, Logan, Twitch, Achilles of Edmonton, Tyler Durden's Hero, and Dexter Morgan – was most certainly the author. It was seven pages long and began with a description of a deeply personal struggle:

> *I go by so many names so I will leave tags out of it. I am simply me. I am different from most people. I suppose I've always been different for as long as I can remember but didn't truly understand the true depths of it until recently. Not until an inadvertent intervention by a family member woke me up to the truth – the truth that I am a psychopath.*

The document, titled "Profile of a Psychopath," focused on elements of Twitchell's life story and how he studied personality disorders to come up with a self-diagnosis of psychopathy. He fit most of the criteria, he wrote, but not all. The profile had been found on his laptop after his arrest, another echo of a document still existing on a temporary file his computer had not yet discarded. Within the document, Twitchell based his assessment on an honest reflection of his own failings throughout life:

> For example, I am a pathological liar. I've habitually lied my entire life and despite my incredibly well-adjusted and healthy family life and upbringing, it never stopped. I've always apologized but never meant it and never corrected the behaviour. I lie to my wife and to my family on a practically constant basis. Sometimes I do this to protect them, to shield them from knowing the truth about what I really am and sometimes I do it for my own gratification and there's no reason to it all. . . .
>
> My whole life I've always just done whatever the hell I wanted without any consideration for anyone else and it's never bothered me. I don't experience things like remorse or guilt. Occasionally I mentally kick myself for making an idiot move or decision but it's not the same thing. . . . My wife only has a very small picture of what goes through my head. She still thinks I have remnants of compassion or honesty when none of these things remain. I put on a show for her benefit. . . .
>
> I've always had a dark side I've had to sugar coat for the world. I've always had to pretend to be more social than I want to be and it's worked out well for me. Despite the disorder, I'm still a somewhat upbeat outgoing person. Until lately I used to think my laid back approach and total lack of fear of the unknown future was due to my disposition and outlook on life. This may still be partially true but I cannot deny a major part of it is also the fact I just don't feel what others feel. I'm not quite sure I'm capable of love.

There was a tinge of sorrow in the prose as Twitchell described his life and how he was heading toward a seemingly inevitable conclusion. He wrote of the decision to incorporate his real-life dark side into his movie script as a way of satisfying his violent fantasies, but "lawfully and without harming anyone." If he produced a violent film and someone else happened to be "inspired" by his work and committed a real-life version of his fiction, he wrote that he may "feel flattered, a little honoured." He would get the thrill from experiencing violence by acting it out but with none of the responsibility of actually committing a crime. He was worried about getting caught. His tone was often callous, writing of animals having no more value than the human race, which he held in contempt anyway, especially "trash" like killers and rapists. But despite his compromise to fulfil a fantasy with fiction, he wrote of still finding himself standing at a crossroads. He felt he had to make a decision on how he wanted the rest of his life to pan out.

Twitchell gave himself two options. Option A: "Come clean" about his lies and what he really felt deep inside. Option B: "Live out the charade" of his normal life, suppressing the real him from public view. Less than a month later, it appeared as if Twitchell tried to have it both ways: exploring his dark side in reality while still trying to convince Jess, and himself, that nothing was wrong. He knew he had a deep desire that he could not easily shake, a desire to experience every act imaginable, whatever that may be:

> *Life is far too short to not partake of every single experience you can before you kick the bucket and I want to experience it all. We only get one shot and that's why I've lived my life with a policy of total lack of inhibition. . . . I don't want to miss out on anything, not any one experience left to try before I get snuffed out forever and this tends to be the driving force behind how I engineer my life. It is what it is I suppose.*

The document offered investigators a solid theory into how and why the script for *House of Cards* became the foundation for a real-life murder. A snuff film had never been found, leading detectives to believe his motives were of a different persuasion. Detectives wondered if the document could therefore prove that Twitchell had crossed that boundary between make-believe and reality in his mind, that he had stopped fantasizing to really become the strange beast he had only imagined he could be. It was a possibility Twitchell's acquaintances were willing to accept. "He's always been lost in fantasy," his high-school friend and pen pal explained, "but this is the first time where he actualized a fantasy."

MARK TWITCHELL'S POTENTIAL NEXT moves if he hadn't been caught so quickly were a source of constant speculation – until an answer was revealed after the trial because it, too, had been written down. Such intentions had been scrubbed clean from S. K. Confessions before the jury had a chance to read it, along with any reference to "psychopath," of which there were many. With the full diary exposed upon Twitchell's conviction, however, passages that detoured deep into Twitchell's psyche were illuminated: he had chosen at least two more victims for a visit to his kill room.

One of Twitchell's old employers was supposed to be next. He hated the man in part because he had fired him. "I owed it to the world to remove him from its glorious surface and would take my chance when I was ready," Twitchell wrote, explaining that most people can't stomach going all the way with their dark urges, but he could.

His second victim was meant to be Traci's ex-boyfriend. He had chosen him as a way "to pay homage" to Dexter because he knew the man was a fan of the show too. "I thought he'd be honoured to find himself duct-taped and cling-wrapped to the kill table, stripped of all clothing, scalpel scar on his right cheek," he wrote, describing some of the hallmarks of Dexter's method.

It appeared as though Twitchell wanted to choose his future victims because they meant something to him. All were men he despised. And he had quickly outgrown the rigid code Dexter Morgan had lived by. "By the third season of that show he was taking his own liberties with it anyway," he justified.

When detectives read these passages they were certain Twitchell was serious. It was no different than when he reasoned in his movie script: "write what you know."

Clark was thrilled the investigation had stopped Twitchell in his tracks. "There's no doubt in my mind that he would have kept on killing," he theorized. "We caught him on his first one, so he's a very poor serial killer. And thankfully, he will never become a serial killer."

But to each detective's dismay, a full copy of S. K. Confessions was never found. Twitchell would not reveal to police if one still existed in some corner of cyberspace, or how many pages the detectives were missing, how many more dark revelations he had made that were forever lost in the ether of the digital world.

Twitchell, of course, saw things differently. As a way of explanation, he later described "Profile of a Psychopath" in his prison writings as a "literary social experiment," where he was trying on the psychopathic personality "like a tailored suit" for the sole purpose of making his fictional writing better. It was *not* reality. "I did all I could to set the stage for the world to believe I was a psychotic killer and now . . . they're buying it. It would be funny if it weren't so tragic."

He wrote of the criminal case against him: "What I've done is disgusting but I am not a disgusting person – I just play one from time to time. . . . You can't get a garden to flourish without getting your hands dirty, but elbow deep in blood was not what I had in mind."

And yet, in prison writings he penned after the trial, Twitchell revealed unspoken desires to kill *another* two "worthy victims," taking his future target list to a total of four. He made sure the entire passage detailing these wishes, however, was written as a hypothetical, beginning with a description of his disgust with another friend's ex-boyfriend. "I don't mind admitting this too," he explained. "If I really were capable of premeditated murder, he would have been my first target."

Twitchell also thought an in-law's former husband deserved to be killed, describing the man as "the kind of guy the *House of Cards* killer would have loved to have gotten his gleefully maniacal hands on." But Twitchell was speaking hypothetically here. Only *if* he was a murderer, he had stressed in these writings. *If.*

SENSATIONAL

ON MAY 9, 2011, a three-page form filled out in pen arrived in the mail room of the city's law courts. Mark Twitchell had come up with more reasons for why he wasn't guilty and taken the time to file this new list of grievances in a notice of appeal. "The media attention surrounding my case was so extensive, so blatant and so overly sensationalized that it is unreasonable to expect any unsequestered jury to have remained uninfluenced by it," he wrote in his application.

He argued there was "sufficient evidence" to raise reasonable doubt, noting his "advanced knowledge of computers" that, if examined properly at trial, would have proven suggestions he'd use a computer to carry out a crime were ludicrous. Twitchell was now insisting that he knew all along that S. K. Confessions was still a recoverable file, demonstrating how deleting the document on his laptop had never been an attempt at destroying crucial evidence.

Twitchell was also representing himself. The decision was not surprising because he was also blaming his lawyer, in part, for the guilty verdict. Interestingly, he now wanted his character to be put into play if a new trial were heard – a contention Davison had avoided at all costs since it would also make "Profile of a Psychopath" admissible evidence, a document he told court was "destructive of character in the most extreme way possible." Twitchell, however, didn't like how the jury had been left with the impression that he was a "lifetime liar." He believed his case could be assisted if he spoke more frankly about his life.

His biggest enemy, however, remained the prosecution: "The Crown's theory leans on too many fallacies of logic and contradictions in reasoning to make any sense. This must be corrected."

Twitchell's appeal, regardless of sufficient legal grounds raised or not, could take years to work its way through the judicial system. In the meantime, the prosecution decided to stay the attempted murder charge for the attack on Gilles Tetreault. The decision came after years of vigorously pursuing the allegations, but a disappointing court ruling forced the criminal charge to be heard separately from the murder trial. Gilles had only been allowed to testify to help prove the truthfulness of S. K. Confessions, not to prove if the attack itself was an act of attempted murder. And the guilty verdict of first-degree murder handed down in April 2011 meant Twitchell had already received Canada's maximum prison term – life with a minimum of twenty-five years. This made a second court case a moot point, especially since victims would have to relive their trauma once again on the witness stand for a best result of no additional prison time.

Twitchell will therefore be fifty-four years old before he can apply for parole for the first time in 2033. When he'll actually be released from prison is unknown. If he continues being a model prisoner, he may be shown leniency. But there is also a community expectation in such high-profile cases for the parole board to deny such freedoms multiple times. And in cases featuring the most heinous of criminals, those inmates with no remorse and a demonstrated risk to the public, parole can be denied for years – potentially forever.

Despite these possibilities, Twitchell would not be silenced. Shortly after his appeal was filed, he turned his attention to William Strong, his prison pen pal, for assistance. At Twitchell's request, his pen pal finally created a website Twitchell had dreamed about in remand that would feature excerpts from his prison writings. His celebrity sketches were also listed for sale. Such acts drew intense controversy and national outrage in the media, which was perhaps one of Twitchell's objectives. The website was pulled off the Internet within a day of being discovered by the press, the community backlash cited as one of the main reasons why.

The thing the public could not understand was why the media kept publishing anything that Twitchell did or said. "I am really hoping this is the last we hear of Mark Twitchell," read one exasperated letter to the *Edmonton Journal*. Editors themselves seemed willing to put the entire ordeal behind them, writing how the guilty verdict brought "an end to one of the darkest chapters" in city history. "The efficient work of 112 police officers investigating Altinger's disappearance stopped what might have been a series of murders," stated the *Journal*'s main editorial.

Others were left puzzled by unsolved elements in the criminal case. Twitchell had seemingly come out of nowhere, a rare self-professed psychopath whose first criminal conviction didn't arrive until the age of thirty-one. There was no warning. The crime had also been entirely random, terrifying a community that demanded explanations for such seemingly unpredictable behaviour.

For Mark Twitchell was a product of a simple life, of a family that did nothing wrong and tried their best to raise him, but he had somehow changed, become a chameleon, a man of many faces. He was a pretender and a trickster, the so-called committed husband and father who was hiding a sinister plan and a girl on the side.

But Twitchell believed this innate desire to understand people like him was pointless. In fact, he treated the continued search for clues into his background and motives to be like stumbling alone in a smoke-filled labyrinth. "It would appear that I'm unique in the world," he declared in his writings. "There is no key. No root cause. . . . There's no school bully, or impressionably gory movies, or video game violence, or Showtime television series to point the finger at. It is what it is and I am what I am."

As the years passed by, it was as close as he would ever get to making a full confession.

EPILOGUE

A RETURN

FEELING REAL

THE TWITCHELL CASE HAD a prevailing impact on both the city of Edmonton and how the media would cover future murder trials, whether they drew an international audience again or not. Before the jury was called in for the first time, Justice Clackson made it clear his starting position was one of openness. "Whatever I see, the media is entitled to see," he told the court.

But in a measured ruling issued minutes later, he granted access to all exhibits while banning the use of electronic devices. "My preference is not to risk the fairness of this trial." Essentially, he was striking a balance with transparency, seeing a potential distraction brewing in his courtroom if two dozen reporters were bashing away on their laptops or smartphones. It was a wise move. One juror proved to be easily bothered by even the slightest of whispers. At one point the juror even requested that a journalist stop writing in his notepad. His pencil was making too much noise.

But Justice Clackson also appreciated the huge public interest in the case and the media's goal of providing coverage on a timely basis. He decided to set up a secondary courtroom two floors below that would receive an audio feed from the trial. Down the hall from the courthouse library, Room 211 became a hub for city journalists filing minute-by-minute updates on blogs, Twitter feeds, and online news sites while traditional newspaper, television, and radio reporters remained upstairs. By the end of the trial, thousands of people were reading near-live coverage online. Whether city councillors, police officers, or some of Johnny's out-of-town friends – all received news of the verdict nearly simultaneously with Mark Twitchell.

Justice Clackson's ruling was a development in how court cases could be run smoothly in Alberta, despite a massive media presence. No doubt the case will be used as a benchmark by media lawyers to achieve similar levels of open access for high-profile cases down the road.

The trial's biggest impact was on those who had followed the case, especially those closest to Twitchell. It exposed his secret life and his elaborate lies, his bizarre descent into the gruesome and the wicked, and his exploitation of those around him to achieve his dark plan. Friends who had given him the benefit of the doubt saw their faith in him crumble. "I thought he had the perfect family, but he had this whole other life going on that I didn't know about," said Rebecca. "He would always talk about making it big. I never imagined it would be like this."

Twitchell's former roommate Jason Fritz felt he had lost a friend but regained faith in the justice system. "Before there was a police investigation or a global news report, before there was CNN calling our houses, it was just a bunch of guys coming together, making movies with this awesome dude," he said. "He was a charming and persuasive guy." But after the trial, everything changed. "Nothing can excuse what he did. When I heard what actually happened, I had no idea who that guy was. That's a guy I never met."

Twitchell's friends had trusted him, been led to believe it was a horrible mistake, perhaps a hoax fuelled by corrupt detectives. But even in the best-case scenario, Twitchell had openly admitted to dismembering and burning the body of a stranger before discarding his remains in a city sewer. Such admissions did not evoke a sense of compassion for Twitchell's predicament. Whether it was a planned and deliberate murder became almost secondary for some of his acquaintances; at the very least, he had committed one of the most disgraceful acts imaginable against another human being. "Thinking about it actually makes me feel uncomfortable," said one member of his film crew. "Mark knew where I lived. He was in my house. That's a strange thing looking back on it now. Imagine finding out Ted Bundy visited you regularly."

The brutality of Twitchell's misdeeds also elevated the city's already notorious crime status. Edmonton had always been a blue-collar city with blue-collar problems, but its reputation as a crime capital tended to be exaggerated by media coverage. Then the Twitchell case happened. It was the stuff of nightmares, a bizarre crime that only seemed imaginable in a Hollywood horror film. And the Twitchell case was the third serial killer investigation in the region within four years. For a city region of only a million people, it was an extraordinary figure that drew sustained interest in the press. Civic boosters could only shake their heads.

Local columnists began calling "Deadmonton" a term of "ironic endearment." In an effort to take back the nickname, Deadmonton also became the name of a city Halloween festival. A new art gallery was built, public transit was rapidly expanded. Plans were finalized for a downtown arena district and a potential new museum. The city looked toward the future with pride. Fingers crossed.

In St. Albert, Twitchell's home changed owners three times between his arrest and trial. Johnny's condo in south Edmonton was purchased by an oil worker who moved in with his girlfriend. They had no idea their home had once belonged to a man whose brutal murder had transfixed the city. Mail addressed to Johnny continued to arrive at the condo for several years.

In Edmonton, Twitchell was one of the last inmates to await a murder trial entirely within the cell blocks of downtown remand. The thirty-year-old building was scheduled for decommission. The long underground tunnels leading to the courthouse would soon be emptied and inmates transferred to a brand-new facility on the northern outskirts of town. Inmates would be housed in smaller buildings or pods. Court appearances would occur via video-link or see inmates driven in big vans that parked in the courthouse basement. It was an end to the plastic beds, double or triple bunking, and a view of the city skyline. Girlfriends would no longer leave chalk or spray-painted messages of love on the sidewalk outside. But some things never change. Shit bombs would remain a popular prison prank no matter where its concrete walls were raised.

Mark Twitchell's kill room continued to be a morbid draw well after the slaying. Neighbours such as Lynda Warren would sometimes look out their front window and see a driver slowly pass by, locate 5712 40th Avenue, and pull in to the nearest parking spot. She'd then stroll to her kitchen window and see them standing in the back alley. There'd be whispered talk and pointing. Some would just stare at where Johnny had taken his last steps, where Gilles had fought and escaped. "It just doesn't leave your mind. I think of Johnny every day," she said. "I don't even know him, but he's certainly not forgotten. We think of him more than of who did it."

The property lived on. Half of the old maroon fence was replaced. The back door to the garage was given a new lock, but the wood door remained with the holes once drilled for Twitchell's padlock still visible. The old couch was removed. For years after the murder, pencil sketches made by the blood spatter expert could be seen on the white door frame.

A new tenant was found for the garage too. He was a construction worker based out of the city. He used the garage as a storage space for his machinery and tools. He had barricaded the back door with his gear. A firm body check could not open it.

The two owners, a young married couple running a property investment company, held on to the land after the murder trial, but the house continued its revolving door of tenants. In the basement suite, a father and his young daughter were never told what had happened in the garage prior to signing a lease, though the owners had no legal obligation to do so. When they did discover the property's deep secret on their own, one of the owners became quite furious. He had previously been debating the impact such widely publicized news could have on his property value. The startled tenants, however, did not share these same concerns.

The house was listed for rent a few weeks later.

CHANGES AND CONSTANTS

DETECTIVE BILL CLARK HAD less than a day to bask in the joy of his biggest case victory. About twenty hours after the verdict, a man driving in the city's western outskirts made a discovery on the side of a dirt road. Clark was called in. At the scene, the bodies of an elderly couple had clearly been dumped among melting snowdrifts and piles of exposed earth. Dale Johnson, promoted to detective and now a permanent member of homicide, was assigned as the primary investigator. The couple had been missing for three months.

For a brief moment, the case was a media sensation. Then the killing in the city continued at an alarming rate. While none were connected, the trend triggered more stories. Clark, Johnson, and the rest of the team worked double or triple shifts. By June 2011, there were twenty-five homicides in Edmonton – one a week, or by far the highest in the nation. By comparison, three hours south in the larger city of Calgary, there were only two. The 2005 homicide record was shattered by October, prompting gripping front-page headlines such as MURDER CITY in the local tabloid. Politicians, nearly breathless at the awful statistics coming back yet again, could only call the city's skyrocketing homicide rate truly "horrifying."

It was Deadmonton, after all.

And this was Clark's city. He didn't plan on leaving the homicide unit any time soon. In fact, he was later promoted to co-head of the squad. He thrived in the pressure-cooker environment, loved grilling the bad guys, getting that confession. And by the look of it, there'd be no shortage of opportunities in the future. When the oil boomed, so did the violence. But the question remained: would either of them ever stop?

RETIRED DETECTIVE MARK ANSTEY was relieved to have left such a bull pen and found a far less stressful job in the building next door. Not far from the Crown Prosecutor's Office, Anstey became an investigator who audited the province's peace officer program. He considered it a great career move, one toward semi-retirement.

Brad Mandrusiak moved on to investigate homicide cold cases after being praised for his efforts on the case from arrest to prison interview; Brian Murphy, the first detective to hear Twitchell's forty-dollar car story, was transferred into the arson unit; Jeff Kerr was promoted one rank to staff sergeant in crime prevention programming; the head of homicide retired from the squad in mid-2011.

And then there was Paul Link, one of the city's best interrogators, who, like Clark, had failed to draw out a confession from Twitchell. Link knew he had initially got it wrong. He had been convinced of Twitchell's guilt once he saw all the evidence, but the team never forgot about his doubts in the case – and made sure it didn't slip his mind either. Shortly after the trial, with a murder conviction secured, an email arrived in Link's inbox. "Still fifty-fifty?" the sender had teased.

THE COURTS CLOSED THEIR records on the Twitchell trial with a few parting words for the detectives. It was an unusual move. The judicial system typically looked down on the police force, but the response this time was far more eloquent. "You should be very proud of a job exceptionally well done," Justice Clackson wrote in a letter to the entire team after the trial. "The time and effort expended was obvious. The result of the trial was determined by the excellent work that you did or directed to be done. I wanted to acknowledge your exceptional efforts." Such praise was a thrill for every detective. The letter found its way into personal scrapbooks.

MIKE YOUNG, WHO REMAINED Twitchell's friend and his power of attorney, emerged from the experience with his passion for the arts intact. He co-wrote several plays for the city's theatre festival, which showed he had no fear in continuing to produce works of stylized violence and dark humour. One play featured hordes of zombies roaming the countryside and attacking Captain Hook and Peter Pan. He called it "Tarantino-esque."

He continued to work in set design and construction, hoping one day to break into the film industry. It was a path forged from his days on Twitchell's movie set, but Mike appeared hesitant to give him any credit in public. During a thirty-minute recorded interview about his play with a community website, Mike described beginning his new career because someone "tapped him on the shoulder" for help. The journalist had no idea that the shoulder tapper he was referring to was none other than convicted killer Mark Twitchell.

THE FILM CREW DRIFTED apart. David Puff never worked as a director of photography with the rest of the group again. Joss Hnatiuk remained distant but was still fascinated with the movies after working as a soundman on Twitchell's projects. Mike continued his friendships with Jay Howatson and Scott Cooke. They were all upset at how their names had been forever associated with a horrible crime but most decided to stay silent. When reporters called, Scott started saying they had the wrong number before hanging up the phone and moving on with his life.

IN HOLLYWOOD, CHRIS HEWARD finally achieved his shot at fame. He landed a gig at The Laugh Factory – a performance that led to a sprinkling of bookings in comedy clubs across America. But within the celebration there was a tinge of loss. He remained confused about his surreal experience as the original movie victim, strapped to the metal chair in Twitchell's *House of Cards*. "I'm not sure what to do with it," he said. "It's not funny. You can't do anything to even *try* to make it funny."

AFTER A COURT BATTLE stretching on for fifteen months, John Pinsent finally received his film investment money back, minus legal fees. It had been a straightforward case until his lawyer realized Twitchell's brother-in-law was claiming the same funds simultaneously. A judge ruled in favour of John Pinsent's company and a cheque was written for around $35,000, or every penny Xpress Entertainment still had to its name. Joss Hnatiuk and his family never sued, and Joss was left with a $30,000 hole in his pocket, most of his life savings.

In contrast to his early attentiveness to Twitchell's affairs, Mike Young appeared to have quickly given up. He didn't file a single piece of paper during the entire investment legal battle and rushed into one court hearing more than twenty minutes late. While the judge gave him a chance to speak, the court had already ruled against him. He didn't fare much better with Twitchell's personal finances. While he notified the court that he was Twitchell's power of attorney, these same court documents reveal few other details. His friend's house was repossessed, sold, and stuck with a $21,000 debt from the property loss, growing each day with interest.

JESS AND HER BABY had the city's deepest sympathy, but she told a neighbour she was too mortified to continue calling Edmonton home. She moved away and adopted a different last name. Some of her family members weren't even sure where she ended up. Jess also kept her lawyer in place after the trial. In seeking as much privacy for Jess and her daughter as possible, her attorney wouldn't even offer the media a "no comment."

TWITCHELL'S FIRST LOVE, TRACI Higgins, continued to suffer from personal hardships. She wanted to become a dental hygienist, but her grades were too low. Yet one bright spot in her life remained constant too. Long after Twitchell's arrest, she still cuddled inside her trailer with her two little dogs, always a great comfort as unconditional companions.

THE POLICE TRIED TO shelter Gilles Tetreault from public view before, and even after, he testified at Twitchell's murder trial on the off chance the attempted murder charge was ever pursued. But gradually he began telling his story beyond an inner circle of friends and granting interviews with the press. He even shared his feelings of guilt for not calling the police earlier, and of his surprise at unexpectedly meeting Johnny's mother at the trial. "She grabbed my hand and said, 'I'm so happy that you're still with us.' And that meant so much to me," Gilles told *Dateline NBC*. "I didn't know what she'd feel toward me, but when she did that, it was wonderful. It was almost another closing moment for me."

And life moved on.

Gilles became a father with a long-time girlfriend, but the couple later drifted apart. He found himself drawn back into the world of online dating. Maybe he was playing with fire, but Gilles soon decided it was time, once again, to open another dating account on plentyoffish.com.

DEAREST DEXTER

THE CREATOR OF *DEXTER* eventually did speak publicly of the Mark Twitchell case, albeit indirectly and without acknowledging him by name. After another case of a killer infatuated with Dexter Morgan had emerged in the United States, author Jeff Lindsay finally felt a need to address the nagging concern.

Writing in *The Huffington Post,* he called accusations that he inspired criminals and murderers "stupid."

"Reading *Dexter* will not make you a killer," he wrote in his opinion piece. "If you are not already capable of killing another human being in a cold, cruel, deliberate way, no book ever written will make you capable of doing so. There are no magic words that will turn you into a psychopath."

He was adamant that both the *Dexter* books and the TV show should be seen as a form of entertainment, not voodoo. "Don't try to make it into some kind of Satanic incantation that creeps into your subconscious and transforms you into an avatar of evil," he wrote. "It just can't happen, and pretending that you think it might and I am therefore somehow guilty of conspiring to turn us all into killers is completely brainless and it makes me so angry."

Obviously, he was hypersensitive to the question. His opinion piece, however, also revealed a trace of hurt feelings woven throughout the intensity of his argument. He was treating accusations that he inspired killers to mean he was to blame, even though the two concepts were markedly different.

When asked to elaborate on his comments, however, he refused.

As the end of 2011 approached, the opinion piece remained his first and final words on the issue.

TWITCH

JUST AFTER SUNRISE, THE clouds reflecting a golden hue, Mark Twitchell emerged from his remand cell to be crammed into the steel compartment of an enormous armoured van. His wrists were shackled to a chain belt, his body seated in his own private metal chair. He was on his way to a maximum-security prison and it was another Friday: April 15, 2011. Authorities had taken less than two days to sort out where he would be transferred to serve out his life sentence. And it was a surreal moment for the remand guards. They had come to know him over the past two and a half years. Despite the fact that he was a killer, he had been oddly charming, always good for a story and a quick laugh. "It was almost like it created a pause," one guard said of Twitchell's departure. "It didn't feel like it was done, that it was really over."

The city streets blurred past. Twitchell stared out for the last time at his hometown. He was heading out of the city – and not by choice. While the Edmonton Max was a few minutes away, Johnny's friends still worked there and Corrections Canada had a mandate to restrict convicted murderers from having contact with anyone connected to their victims. Twitchell would have to be sent elsewhere.

The nearest maximum-security prison he could be sent to was an eight-hour drive straight east into the flatness of the central prairies. Constructed of red brick in the early 1900s, it also happened to have a reputation for housing the worst offenders in the nation: Saskatchewan Penitentiary. High-profile gang members and troublemakers made up the population of more than five hundred inmates. It was the dumping ground for the baddest of the bad in western Canada and for decades housed many of the country's notorious "rats and skinners" – informants and rapists. They were prisoners with no hope of rehabilitation, the vile and the evil. Inmates were killed in frequent brawls. Even gang leaders weren't safe. Yet, the selection of this location for Twitchell's life sentence seemed almost fitting, considering the circumstances. The prison lay on the outskirts of Prince Albert, which had an unintended resonance with the filmmaker's long-held view that he was the creator of an out-of-control idea. For the town was once home to Boris Karloff, an actor who played the original Frankenstein monster in the 1931 Hollywood classic. Twitchell was amused at his twist of fate.

Upon his arrival, he was locked up in solitary confinement for twenty-three hours a day until prison officials could decide what to do with him. He was allowed to shower every second day. His cell was no bigger than a small bedroom; and he had only the tiniest of windows to let in a stream of natural light. The walls were concrete blocks. His meals were slid through a slot in his metal cell door. His high-school pen pal stopped writing him while the frequency of William Strong's letters slowed. He had no television, no radio, no magazines. Just a pen, some paper, and a hard bed.

But Twitchell was already plotting his next move.

He dreamed of being granted a transfer into medium security as soon as possible. Then he'd get a computer. He'd sign private art contracts. He'd go back to school and take advanced classes. He fantasized about completing a doctorate while in prison so one day he could be called Dr. Twitchell. "It has a nice ring to it," he wrote from his cell.

The film industry remained top of mind. Twitchell wanted Mike to chair a new production company on his behalf. He thought they could finally finish *Star Wars: Secrets of the Rebellion,* a film he refused to admit was never going to be released. The two of them would make features and made-for-web film content. Twitchell thought he could develop the ideas inside prison and Mike could produce them on the outside. Using the profits from their various endeavours, he dreamed of paying back everyone that he owed money. And he would never stop writing. Stories, novels, journal entries, scripts. He would complete them all. "I can't shut my creative engine down and wouldn't want to if I could. I'm also not going to turn off my Internal Creative Genius, shunning its influence over an isolated event. That would be like never getting behind the wheel again because you crashed your car once."

Whether before, during, or after the trial, Twitchell often stressed that he wanted to fight the "absolutely ridiculous" notion that he was a murderer.

"I still can't accept what just happened as reality," he wrote. He maintained that MAPLE had become a trap from which he could not escape. And anything he did say at sentencing would have been taken as "sour grapes," he said, which is why he refused to address the court. He often stated he was one of the wrongfully convicted who would some day, against all odds, clear his name and be restored to his rightful place in society. Twitchell stated of his conviction: "They built a monster up in their minds. They wanted one and now they feel they've gotten what they wanted."

His goals remained focused on loosening the prison system's stranglehold until one day he'd be living in minimum security, counting the days until he could apply for parole. In such a setting, he pictured having near-open access for personal visits. He imagined his daughter coming to visit him. She'd be old enough to be in school.

In his mind, the future remained bright. Grand plans were forming, he still had friends, associates who would offer a helping hand, and loved ones who would never leave his side.

His reality, of course, was far less majestic, far more uninteresting to ever admit.

BEFORE HIS JOURNEY INTO the macabre, before dark fantasies of death merged into film and script, Twitchell had lived in the United States for four years, selling electronics to anyone who would buy them. To trace his movements back in time, down the long highways in his maroon Grand Am to the beginning of this voyage, led to the small-town characters of the Midwestern plains. Twitchell's first wife had called it home. Now she was a confused young woman who realized she had the first glimpse of what he would become. Throughout the spectacle of his arrest and public trial, however, she had kept her association hidden from view, like a prequel to the horror that transpired in a future far removed from her own. She was never called to testify.

Megan Casterella had the round face of a cherub, big brown eyes, and a demeanour to please. She had grown up in Colorado Springs, and one night in an Internet chat room she had become acquainted with a man in northern Canada. They began to email, then talk on the phone, send each other pictures and flowers. Twitchell was twenty-one; Megan, twenty. During one of their long-distance phone calls, he asked for her hand in marriage. It was Halloween. Megan thought the offer exciting and agreed, as long as she had a return ticket in hand. She boarded a flight to Canada a few days after Christmas and was married in Edmonton on January 4, 2001. There was a small gathering afterwards at his parents' place.

But the relationship was virtually over before their honeymoon began. Megan looked back on the situation years later by comparing Twitchell to a kid with a new puppy: fascinated for a few days but quickly losing interest. He cheated on her regularly. She caught him surfing a porn website all the time. She couldn't pry him off the Internet. With no Canadian work permit, she headed to Davenport, Iowa, to be near her sister. The newlyweds lived apart. Twitchell started up a relationship with another woman but didn't tell her he was married. He tried to divorce Megan via email. The situation eventually blew apart and Megan and Twitchell made amends, deciding to give their nuptials a second chance. He moved to America to be by her side.

Four years passed in the Midwest as they worked on their marriage. Megan went to school. The couple moved two hours away to the small town of Peoria in the deep soils of the Illinois prairie, south of Chicago. Twitchell became a top-tier salesman at American TV, Appliance and Furniture, but yet they never seemed to have much money to spare. He met local actors and *Star Wars* fans, called himself Psycho Jedi online, and it was here where he first began talking about making his own fan film for the sci-fi franchise.

Megan saw how her husband was a dreamer, always seeing the big picture but failing miserably at the little details. He made costumes but sometimes cut corners, buying props on the Internet but then passing them off as if he made them himself. And despite several years together, she never felt like she got to know him like a wife should know her husband. "He kind of had that really dark, secretive side," she said later. "He would make comments like, 'You can't handle what goes on in my mind. You can't handle it.' It makes me wonder now."

The relationship soured.

He took off one September weekend to Atlanta for Dragon Con, a huge sci-fi, fantasy, and comic book convention, and met another girl. He cheated on Megan once again and had no regrets whatsoever. She knew the moment he returned. He promised a divorce, but it never came.

Eventually, Megan took control and cited "extreme and repeated mental cruelty" in her divorce documents as grounds for their separation. Twitchell did not dispute her explanation. Together they had accumulated a $40,000 debt. She tried her best to forget about him, but it was a difficult task considering he moved only a few doors down. And he was suddenly in another relationship, living with a California girl who had moved to the Midwest to be with him. In a few months, she was gone too, another woman tossed aside and out of Twitchell's life when he lost interest. He finally packed up his car in 2005 and drove northwest across America, back to his hometown to achieve his new dream – and find a new wife.

Lingering memories of him came back to Megan. She had moved on, met a new man, but suddenly she saw her ex-husband's face on the international news. While she had quite the story to tell of her former life with him, she did not utter a word in public. It wasn't until months after Twitchell's arrest when she was finally convinced to come forward. A homicide detective from the Edmonton Police Service flew down to meet with her. And she confided some of her deepest held secrets. Upon reflection, she felt it would mean something for the investigation. The police did too.

About three days into their marriage, Megan had been sitting in a bedroom with Twitchell. It was one of those lazy days of rolling around on the bed, when the weather outside was chilly and nobody wanted to dare leave the house to face the Edmonton winter.

Twitchell had been sitting in silence when he suddenly turned to Megan and began a conversation with an outrageous hypothetical question: "Have you ever thought about killing someone?" He honestly wanted to know.

Startled, Megan realized she had met this man over the Internet and was now a five-hour flight away from her own family. She still wasn't really sure whom she had just married.

She treaded carefully.

"Sure, I guess everyone has gotten angry enough in their lifetime that you'd think about it," she said. "But I could *never* do it, if that's what you mean."

Twitchell didn't stop to consider her answer. "Well, I've thought about killing somebody," he confessed in a cold monotone. "I've actually thought about finding a homeless person and killing him. I figure nobody would really miss him or even think about it."

Megan looked at her new husband in shock.

Twitchell had an odd expression on his face, a shimmer in his eyes she couldn't understand. She couldn't quite comprehend what she was hearing. But it was almost as if Twitchell had found the very idea of it . . . enjoyable.

SHEATHS OF BEING

ON THE SHORES OF Canada's southern Pacific, waves send driftwood tumbling past long wooden piers into beaches of dark brown sand. The ocean laps in one spot at the pebbled feet of a giant white boulder as the tidal payload of dead branches is delivered. Above the water's edge, the large stone stands as a sailing beacon and symbol of town folklore, giving the surrounding community of White Rock its name. With their ordeal finally behind them, Johnny Altinger's family could look at this place with a degree of finality. In their grief, they had collected his ashes from Edmonton and returned him to this coastal city he had once called home.

Closure for his family did not come easily. Their hearts remained wounded and scarred long after Johnny's remains had been returned for a proper burial. What little comfort they did feel came from detectives who told them Johnny was a hero. Police would never have stumbled upon the garage if it wasn't for Johnny's foresight. The driving directions he passed on to his friends remained the crucial piece of evidence that unfolded the entire case. Detectives feared what could have happened if their investigation hadn't swooped in on their suspect and his property so quickly.

Johnny's mother, Elfriede, hung a plaque on a memorial wall in her son's memory. She wanted the world to remember him as a man of kindness. But there were no plans for a funeral service. Like his father, Johnny had wanted to be laid to rest with as little fuss as possible. At his core, he had remained a simple and modest man. "John was the most selfless person," said his brother, Gary. "He was always helping everybody. He was gentle. He was a good friend to anybody who ever knew him."

Fittingly, his memory lived on through the Internet and he has not been forgotten. Johnny's Facebook profile was transformed into an online headstone. Even years after his death, friends continued to post messages of love or to wish him happy birthday. His friend Marie Laugesen was relieved she had made amends with Johnny and that they had enjoyed a wonderful day of riding indoor roller coasters before his sudden passing. "I know you are not here to read this anymore, but know that you had many friends who cared deeply for you," she shared on his Facebook page. Another friend simply added: "Johnny, you will remain in my heart forever."

Having bonded with Johnny through their shared interest in spirituality, Darcy Gehl paused to remember his friend in a moment of silent reflection. He had witnessed first-hand how Johnny had likely achieved a level of nirvana most people fail to explore. It brought him comfort knowing a man facing such a tragic demise had at least developed a mindset of tranquility and acceptance. "He would have been the type of person to say, 'It was my time to go.' He had put his mind at peace by then," he explained. "He believed there was something more."

Johnny had offered clues of this profound insight long before his death. In searching for answers to the meaning of things, he had often stumbled upon others taking the same journey and commenting within online newsgroups. One searcher had shared excerpts from an ancient text that described how one must merge the "sheaths of being to realize the unity of life."

Reading the posting late one night, Johnny had considered these words and felt compelled to respond. "Well said and absolutely true," he replied. "Everything is one. Life is an illusion. Now if only we could get people to wake up and realize that."

AUTHOR'S NOTES AND SOURCES

THE TRUTH IS IMPORTANT to me – and it proved difficult to find in this case, often hiding behind layers of exaggeration and falsehoods that had merged with real life. But as a journalist, I was only interested in writing the factual account of these events so I could document the story's historical value and impact. This non-fiction narrative has therefore been drawn from extensive research, beginning during my time as a police reporter at the *Edmonton Journal* and continuing on for years afterwards as the case progressed from arrest to conviction.

Anything that appears within quotation marks or as an excerpt has been taken from a written document, court testimony, or interview and been edited for minor points of grammar and clarity. Publicly accessible archives were also of assistance, ranging from newspaper records and lawsuits to government databases maintained by Environment Canada and Statistics Canada.

No dialogue has been fabricated. Conversations have been taken directly from police evidence or court testimony, or have been recreated from the accounts of first-hand witnesses. Descriptions of mannerisms are based upon witness recollections, my direct observations, or are evident from dialogue or within video recordings and photographs.

Wherever possible, I utilized multiple sources of information for each person described in the book: my interview with them, their police interview and court testimony, and their own written words, including (but not limited to) personal blogs, online message board postings, and activity on social-networking websites. Many interviewees had kept old emails or had vivid memories of specific moments in time. There were videos and hundreds of photos taken of witnesses at key points in their lives. No names have been changed in the entire book, with two exceptions: "Rebecca," who requested anonymity, and "William Strong," who did not want his birth name published.

Nearly every chapter has been assisted by my own history. I was born in Edmonton, lived in the area for more than twenty-five years, and visited virtually every scene depicted in the book. Furthermore, I also read, listened, or watched every story in the media about the case to add colour to scenes that I may have previously missed.

Large pieces of the narrative were filled in by members of the Edmonton Police Service, who gave detailed accounts of the inner workings of a homicide investigation. Many detectives agreed to be interviewed, some on numerous occasions.

I firmly believed that Johnny Altinger deserved to be a major focus in the text. I wanted the reader to get to know him; I wanted to focus on how he lived, not only on his tragic death. I was able to recreate the last days of his life through the accounts of his friends, court records, and his own writings. I was fortunate in locating many old posts he had written on Internet newsgroups.

Lastly, I attended every day of Mark Twitchell's murder trial and took extensive notes of the proceedings. On the witness stand, he largely acknowledged his controversial document S. K. Confessions as a true account of his actions. Police had also estimated that their own investigation had proven more than 85 per cent of the writings as accurate. The forty-two-page document therefore provided a solid foundation on which to build further research around.

And there was no shortage of information available about Mark Twitchell, who was a willing participant in my research efforts. Months before the trial, he called me quite out of the blue with a genuine offer to participate in this project. "If you're going to be writing a book about me," he began, "it's probably best for both of our interests that you come straight to the source." He had heard about me through his friends and associates. But he sounded nervous as he began pitching me reasons as to why I should listen to him. "I would never ask you to just up and take my word on anything," he insisted. "Obviously anything that I would talk to you about would be checkable." He saw his participation as a chance to tell his story accurately and on a different level than media accounts of his case.

It was a rare opportunity for a journalist, but one I seized upon with extreme caution. I laid down some ground rules: if we did talk, we would remain nothing more than subject-author and there would be no conditions placed on our contact. He would have no editorial control. "I wouldn't expect otherwise," he told me. No money exchanged hands.

We remained in contact for months, and I was the only journalist to interview him before and after the trial. He mailed me more than three hundred pages of letters from prison, which gave me my first insight into his compulsion to write everything down. We spoke several times in person at the Edmonton Remand Centre and over the phone as well.

Major hiccups were obvious: how much was truth and how much was fantasy? Mark Twitchell was an admitted liar, convicted murderer, and self-professed psychopath. It was a challenge to decide what I could actually use from the wealth of material he was providing. After all, anyone in his position would use the opportunity to portray himself in the best light possible, to fudge the facts, or manipulate me with continued lies.

I therefore attempted to confirm everything he revealed. While he did embellish at times, and dodge the most serious of questions, many of his stories contained details that could be verified through court proceedings, my own research, and interviews. In those cases, I used his information. I excluded his accounts of events that could not be confirmed by a third party, of which there were many.

In the end, I had to make a judgment call on what could be trusted as fact, what was Mark Twitchell's version of events, and what should be entirely ignored. Upon reflection, I am confident that I have struck the right balance.

ACKNOWLEDGEMENTS

JOURNALISTS ARE OFTEN TOLD "no comment" throughout their careers, but never before had I faced so many slammed phones, closed doors, and unanswered emails. I am therefore grateful and indebted to the many witnesses, acquaintances, victims, and sources who eventually shed their fears or concerns and agreed to help tell this story. You've helped write history, and in return I offer you my sincerest and deepest thanks.

Special thanks must go to Darcy Henton, a fine journalist, editor, and author, who provided direction and support throughout this entire project. This book would not have been possible without his critical and guiding hand. Fellow writers Ben Gelinas and Ryan Cormier also deserve a mention, as does novelist Todd Babiak.

It would be impossible to name all of the 112 police officers involved in this case, but I must acknowledge Detective Bill Clark, Retired Detective Mark Anstey, and the rest of the Edmonton Police Service homicide unit for their assistance beyond what is clearly evident within the text.

I owe a debt of gratitude to the Edmonton media for providing extensive coverage of the case, especially CTV Edmonton. And I would be remiss if I didn't also thank my informal researchers and supporters: Jag Dhadli, Kris Berezanski, Amri Benjamin, Kate Rossiter, Gabe Wong, Gene Dub, my former colleagues at the *Edmonton Journal,* and a handful of friends and relatives.

Thank you to my editor, Anita Chong, who was a joy to work with despite our differing time zones, and my agent, Martha Magor Webb, for her enthusiasm, dedication, and efforts in seeing this book published.

And lastly, I offer my thanks to Edmonton. I admit that the city may not be a pretty sight at times, but I still love it nonetheless.

IMAGE CREDITS

Grateful acknowledgement is expressed to the following people and sources for permission to reprint these images.

viii-ix
Map of Edmonton and surrounding areas: 2011. Matt Gardner.

PHOTO INSERT

Page 1
Detective Mark Anstey: 2008. *Edmonton Journal* / Postmedia Network. Ryan Jackson.
Post-It: 2011. Steve Lillebuen. In R. v. Twitchell, Mark Andrew, Alberta Court of Queen's Bench, Edmonton, 2011, Exhibit 11.
KA-BAR knife: 2008. Constable Gary Short. In R. v. Twitchell, Mark Andrew, Alberta Court of Queen's Bench, Edmonton, 2011, Exhibit 2 (C-16).

Page 2
"The Film Studio," BB gun, handcuffs, and stun baton: 2008. Constable Gary Short. In R. v. Twitchell, Mark Andrew, Alberta Court of Queen's Bench, Edmonton, 2011, Exhibit 2 (H-20), Exhibit 2 (J-37), Exhibit 2 (J-40), Exhibit 2 (J-44).

Page 3
"The Kill Room" and "Tools": 2008. Constable Gary Short. In R. v. Twitchell, Mark Andrew, Alberta Court of Queen's Bench, Edmonton, 2011, Exhibit 2 (H-35), Exhibit 2 (J-22).

Page 4
Mark Twitchell: 2005. Self-portrait. Used with permission.
Twitchell in Grades 10, 11, and 12: 1995, 1996, 1997. Archbishop O'Leary High School Yearbooks, Edmonton.

INDEX